Body Art and Performance

Lea Vergine

Body Art
and Performance

The Body as Language

SKIRA

Graphic Concept
Marcello Francone

Editing
Emanuela Di Lallo
David Stanton
Paola Tamborini

Layout
Monica Temporiti

Cover
Gina Pane, *Io mescolo tutto*,
Galleria d'Arte Moderna, Bologna, 1976
photo: François Masson

First published in 2000
by Skira Editore S.p.A.
Palazzo Casati Stampa
via Torino 61, 20123 Milano, Italy

Printed and bound in Italy. First edition

ISBN 88-8118-689-6

Distributed in North America and Latin America by Abbeville Publishing Group, 22 Cortlandt Street, New York, NY 10007, USA.
Distributed elsewhere in the world by Thames and Hudson Ltd., 181a High Holborn, London WC1V 7QX, United Kingdom.

The first edition of this book was published in 1974 by Giampaolo Prearo Editore, Milan, with the title The Body as Language ("Body-art" and Performance)

We wish to express our gratitude to Vicky Alliata, who arranged for the sending of the materials from New York. Also thanks to the galleries Diagramma, Toselli, Modern Art Agency, Milano, L.P. 220 and to their directors Luciano Inga-Pin, Franco Toselli, Lucio Amelio, Carla Pellegrini, Franz Paludetti, for their kind collaboration; the publishers Gino Ciccognani and François Zille; and Marisa C. Giuffra, Luciano Inga-Pin and Eve Rockert for the translation of the artists' declarations.
Milan, February 1974

Contents

to my mother FINA, the sole survivor of a remarkable family, a family that in its way was involved in the topics discussed in this book

The Body as Language. Body Art and Like Stories

"There are certain tremendous moments in life when a creature comes out of his corner and looks around, and it's frightening."
Katherine Mansfield

The body is being used as an art language by an ever greater number of contemporary painters and sculptors, and even though the phenomenon touches upon artists who represent different currents and tendencies, who use widely differing art techniques, and who come from a variety of cultural and intellectual backgrounds, certain characteristics of this way of making art are nonetheless to be found in all of its manifestations. It always involves, for example, a loss of personal identity, a refusal to allow the sense of reality to invade and control the sphere of the emotions, and a romantic rebellion against dependence upon both people and things. Tenderness is always the goal aimed for and missed and therefore surrounded by frustration. And this is always accompanied by the anguish that derives from the absence of an "adult" and altruistic form of love.

At the basis of Body Art and of all of the other operations presented in this book, one can discover the unsatisfied need for a love that extends itself without limit in time—the need to be loved for what one is and for what one wants to be—the need for a kind of love that confers unlimited rights—the need for what is called *primary love*. This is what gives this art its dimension of inevitable delusion and failure. This unobtained love is what transforms itself into the aggressivity that is typical of all of these actions, events, photo-sequences and performances. It is also redirected to other versions of the self, and the self is doubled, camouflaged, and idealized. It is turned into the love of the romance of the self. This avid need for love becomes narcissism in the fetus that we continue to be, but to be loved in this way is the only power that might once again give sense to the lives of so many of us.

If the word "art" can still legitimately be used, the art of the artists presented in this book is the art of the bourgeois intellectuals who struggle constantly against the bourgeoisie and who are attempting to separate what is from what has ceased to be, in order once again to be able to use it to recreate a culture. It's the same old opposition to the capitalistic co-opt of all the forms of art production and this helps to explain why so many of the actions are full of Nietzsche, Expressionism, and Existentialism.

The individual is obsessed by the obligation to act as a function of "the other," obsessed by the obligation to exhibit himself in order to be able *to be*. The over-riding desire is to live collective *ethos* and *pathos*, to grasp the *existent* in all of its brutal physicality, to communicate something that has been previously felt but that is lived in the very moment of communication, to return to the origins without leaving the present, to lead the individual to relationship with both himself and others, to lead the individual, in short, back to his specific mode of existence (Beuys, Tom Marioni, Chiari, Zaza).

The accent is placed on *nature*, the desire to go beyond the values of current morality, organic phenomena (which are considered primary), accident, innocence, and the spontaneity to which our behavior and our customs must return in order to be able to step back away from the artificial conventions of society. All of this is an attempt to eliminate culture—which is to say the whole nexus of cultivated ways of living, the concept of encyclopedism as opposed to the concept of consciousness, the collective formation of social groups within institutions that define and condition them, crystallization as opposed to evolution.

The individual is placed at the center of a continuous process that is carried ahead with persistences and repetitions, and with the hardheadedness of insisting upon a sensational event as well as an exasperating analysis of all the possibilities of every moment of every function of every part of the body—with all the activism of incessant movement and experimentation and an enormous expense of energy. In ninety per cent of the cases, the artists we are talking about are persons full of apprehension, but they are also extremely acute observers who are interested in new forms of cognition and who go about their business with attention and vigilance (Tagliaferro, Vaccari, Bugli, Fabio Mauri, Fried, Dan Graham). Like Artaud, they want an intimate acquaintance with all of the possibilities of self-knowledge that can stem from the body and the investigation of the body. The body is stripped bare in an extreme attempt to acquire the right to a rebirth back into the world. Most of the time, the experiences we are dealing with are authentic, and they are consequently cruel and painful. *Those who are in pain will tell you that they have the right to be taken seriously.*

These artists do not "take a long look at life," and their forms of expression are not genteel. They make no *a priori* exclusions and in most of them suffering is not transformed into mysticism. This is particularly true when they are involved in the investigation of our infirmities and the monstrous organization of the real. It's a question of facing up to

death through life, rummaging around in the under and seamy sides of life, bringing to light the *secret* and the hidden. Only by experimenting a little at a time with death does one come to understand a little bit more about life—only by showing the precariousness of everything that we are accustomed to call normal (Fried, Trotta, Ruppersberg). Instead of giving us a story and a character, these artists become both story and character. They are looking for the human being who isn't castrated by the functionalism of society—the man who lives outside of the laws of profit. What's important is not to know, but to know that one knows. This is a state in which culture is no longer of any conceivable use. Once the productive forces of the unconscious have been liberated, what follows is a continuous and hysterical dramatization of the conflicts between desire and defense, license and prohibition, latent and manifest content, memory and resistance, castration and self-conservation, life impulses and death impulses, voyeurism and exhibition, impulses towards sadism and masochistic pleasure, destructive fantasy and cathartic fantasy. If we were interested in looking for analogies in psychopathology, we could find them in the intemperances of neurolability, in hysterical crises (emotional reactions that lack proportion to their external causes), in abandonment neuroses, in inhibitions with respect to adult development, in autoerotism, in obsessive manias, in aspirations to omnipotence, in oral avidity, in sadistic allusivity. If we were interested in relations to perversion, we could talk about fetishism, transvestism, voyeurism, kleptomania, paidophilia, necrophilia, sadomasochism, rupophobia, scatophagia. A search for psychotic symptoms would lead our attention to the aspects of the work connected to dissociation, melancholy, delirium, depression, and persecution manias. But this procedure would lack commitment. The use of a terminology borrowed from psychopathology is incapable of leading to an understanding of the appeal of this *reductio ad absurdum* that many of the artists now considered *avant-garde* are intent upon practicing, and practicing at their own risk.
"In the course of the last few decades," according to Ernst Kris in 1952, "the kind of knowledge that psychoanalysis has brought to bear upon artistic creation has become a part of art itself. Some of the artists of our time make habitual use of free association as a technique that leads to creative thought or even as an independent means of expression. Some of the Surrealists have given their work the task of documenting the process of creation itself, thus rendering explicit what had previously remained implicit. We speak of these circumstances since they indicate a reversal of functions. Psychoanalysis and its discoveries act as a social force upon art and the artists."

This book is based upon the work of artists who have been exclusively concerned with their own bodies for years (Acconci, Gina Pane, Ben,

Egon Schiele,
Self-Portrait, 1910
(photo: Anton
Josef Trcka)

Marcel Duchamp,
Tonsure, 1919

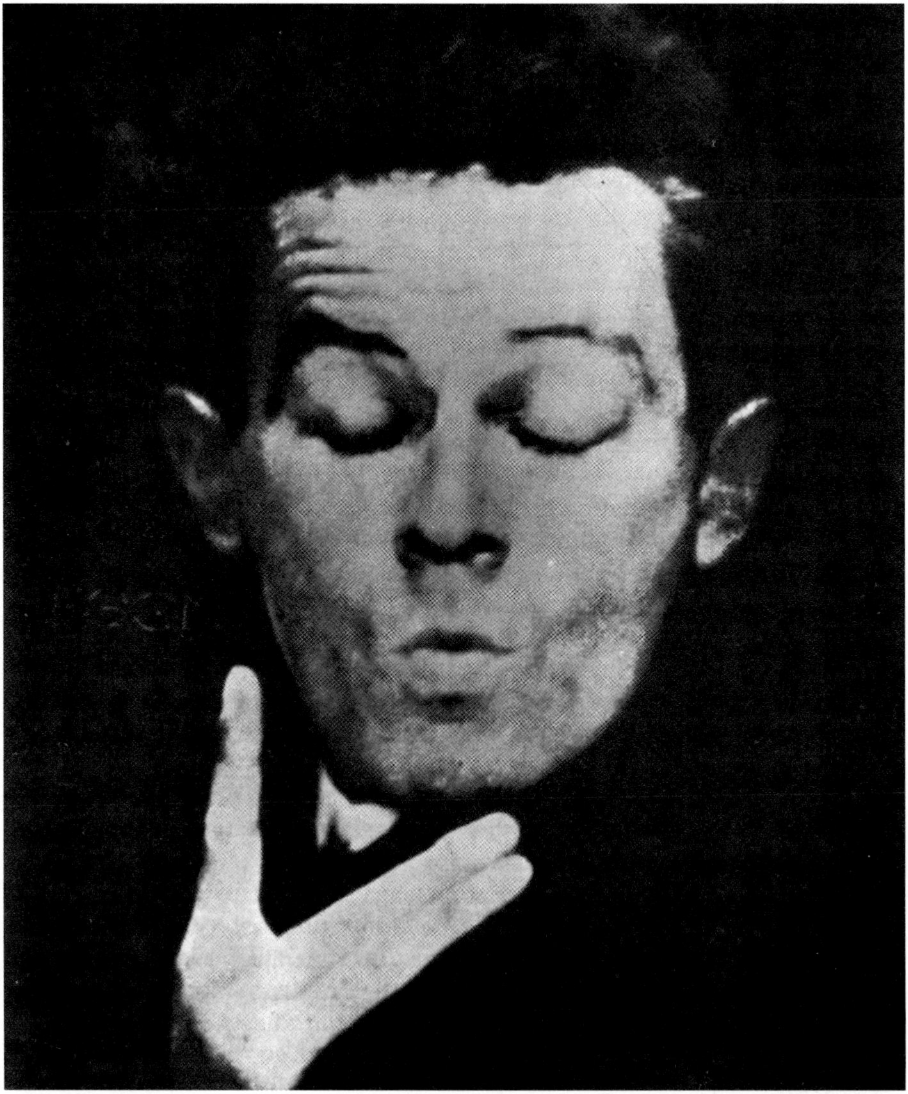

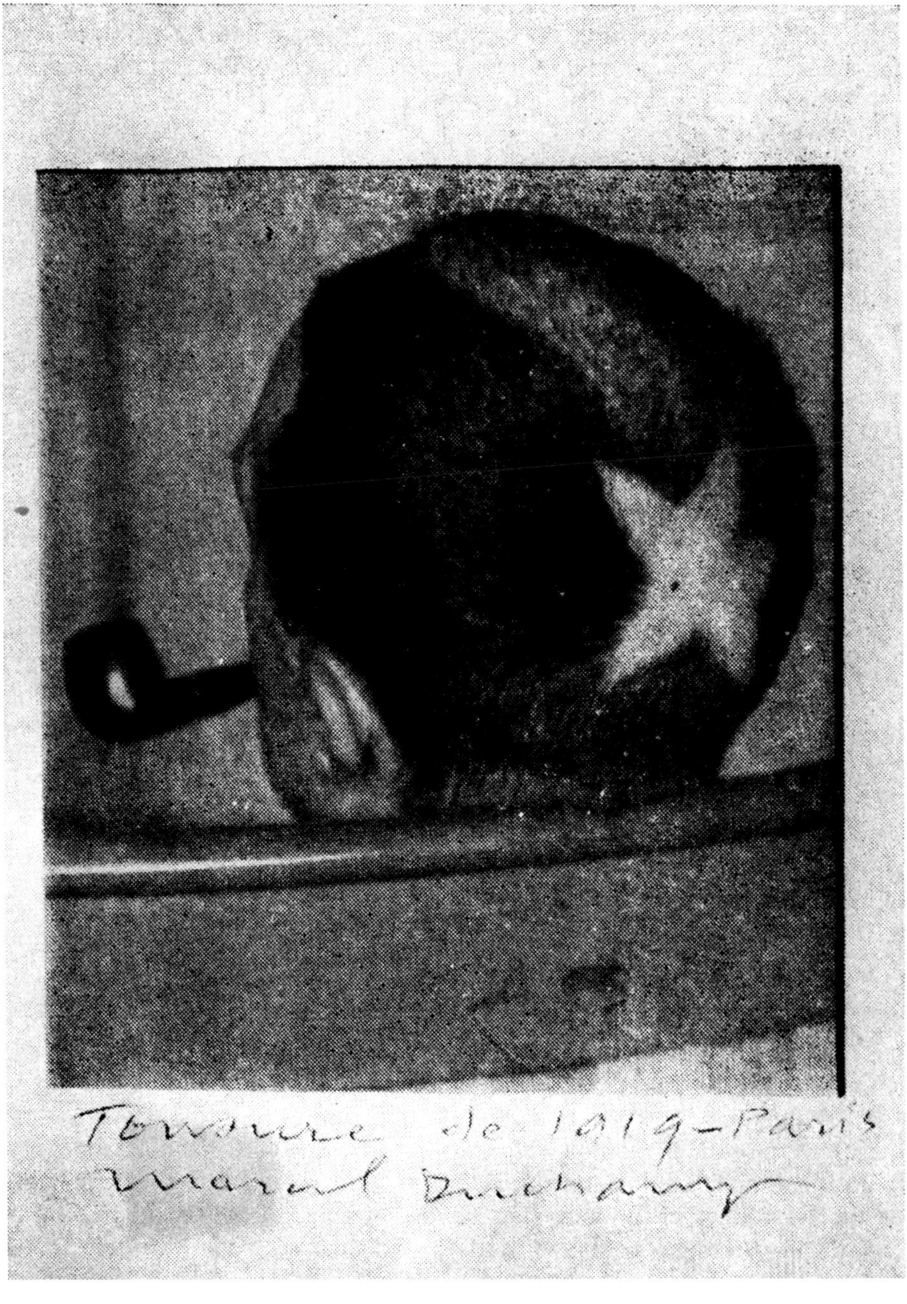
Tonsure de 1919 - Paris
Marcel Duchamp

Lüthi, Rebecca Horn, Rainer, Gilbert & George, Rinke, the Viennese group, Journiac, Ontani, Desiato) as well as upon the work of artists who have made use of their bodies sporadically or episodically, but, nonetheless, deal with something *repressed* that subsequently returns to the surface of experience with all of the narcissism that surrounds it (Job, Yayoi Kusama, Ruppersberg). I have also included mime and dance with Joan Jonas and Trisha Brown since they seem to subtract the body from the laws of gravity and project it into complex sequences in which equilibrium is constantly upset and re-established. Thus this book is also representative of nearly all of the artists who have worked with their bodies but who cannot be reduced to the label of Body Art since their primary interests are fundamentally cognitive (Beuys, Mauri, Serra, La Rocca, Berardinone, Baldessari, Mariani, Urban, Patella, Calzolari, Arnatt, Bugli, Penone).

Marcel Duchamp as Rose Sélavy, in a photograph by Man Ray. The photo has been reworked by Duchamp, who made the hands thin; the hat belonged to Germaine Everley, Picabia's lover. 1921 (Courtesy Arturo Schwarz)

The story behind all of this is a very old one, and even if one wants to limit oneself to references that fall within this century, the very least one must talk about is German Expressionism, Dadaism, Surrealism, and Artaud's Theater of Cruelty. (One should also have a glance at the photos of Egon Schiele, at Duchamp's ways of cutting and arranging his hair, and, a bit closer in time, at some of the actions of Piero Manzoni and Yves Klein. In certain respects, precedents are even to be found in the cultivated "cabaret" of Hidalgo and Marchetti of the ZAJ Group.) But the current use of the body in art is more than a revival of Expressionism. It is a critical process even though it is frequently inspired by an aestheticizing nostalgia for real relationships of which one has now become incapable. These phenomena must also be seen as so many documents of a style of living that *also* remains *outside* of art.

There is a history of manners in which the ways of making art crop up, regress, disappear, revive and diffuse themselves as a function of social situations. It's clear, of course, that judgements and definitions are full of prejudices and imprecisions, but "symptomatology is always one of the problems of art" (Gilles Deleuze) and what interests us here is the possibility of taking a look at some of the syndromes and symptoms of a phenomenon that has been slowly expanding in the course of the last ten years, and as we do so we must try to grasp some of the principles that differentiate the various phenomena.

Narcissus protests (and thus finds gratification) through the agency of himself. The feeling of the "diary" becomes (once again?) fundamental: the souvenir, the search for the impression lost and protected in memory, the reconstruction of the span of time in which certain events to be re-evoked actually took place, the association between image as stimulus and image as reaction. Tape recorders, movie cameras, photos, measurements and graphs drawn on maps are the means that are used in order to *freeze* any number of tiny private episodes. And thus the artist becomes

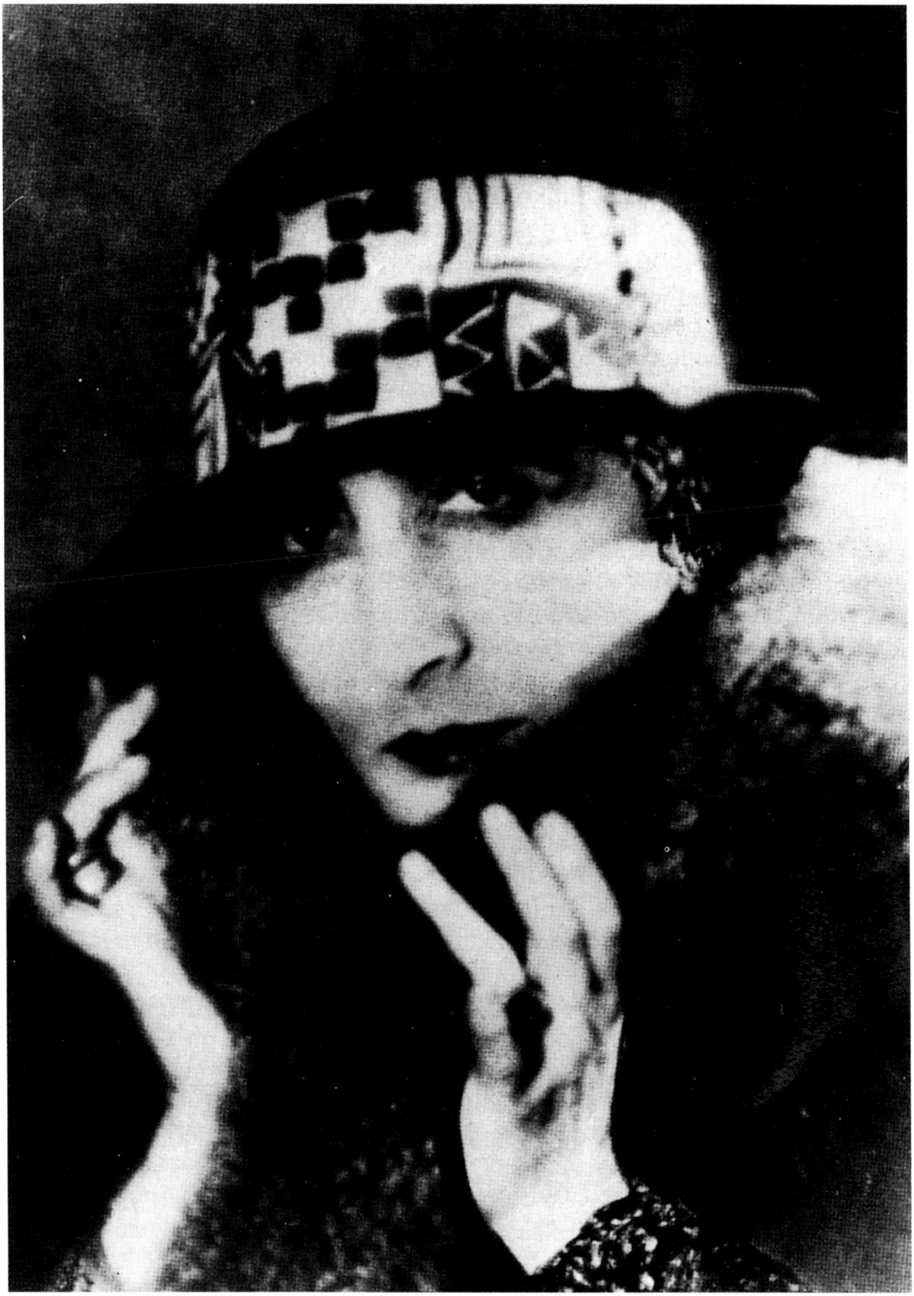

UN HOMME DANS L'ESPACE !

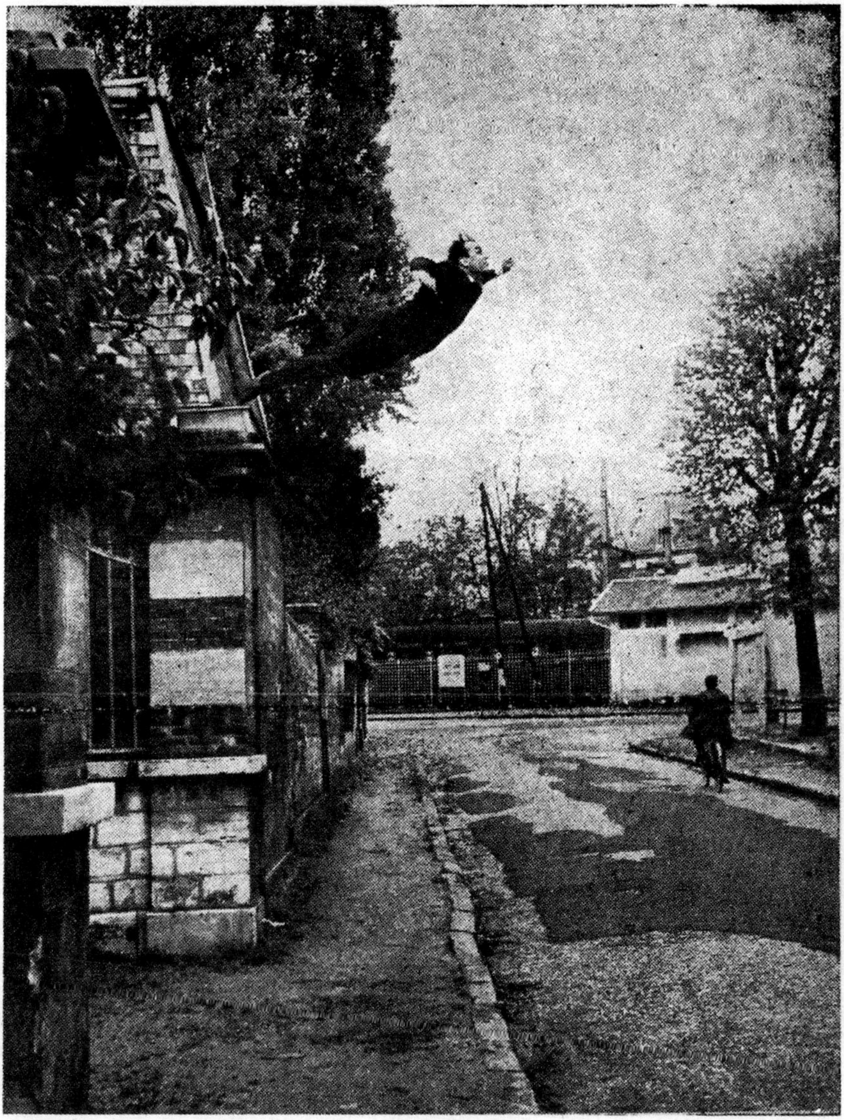

(Photo Shunk-Kender)

Le peintre de l'espace se jette dans le vide !

Yves Klein, *Le peintre de l'espace se jette dans le vide*, 1960

his object. This is to say that he *posits* himself as object since he is conscious of the process in which he is involved.

What emerges is an appeal to asceticism, a form of worldly mysticism, and a kind of negative theology. The attitude of ritualism gives further strength to a search for relationship between aesthetic activity and *regressive pleasure*. The discomfort of unrequited desire, the hazard implicit in our precarious existence, and the continuous tension that is experienced when faced with the prospects of hypotheses that may never become realizable are all understood to be *quotidian* situations that lead inevitably to a state of anguish for the *being-in-the-world*, and likewise to the pain that results from the impossibility of finding a real relationship with it. This, then, is what gives rise to the *catastrophe reaction* and the *protection delirium*. "With respect to the bodies of others as well as with respect to my own, I have no way of knowing the human body other than by living it—which means to assume responsibility for the drama that flows through me and to merge my identity into it." (Maurice Merleau-Ponty). Thus, the significant terms of this art are the things that are outside of us, our bodies, what happens *inside* of us and what happens *to* us. Objects have the task of being the proof that others are either *together* with us or not, and this is communicated to us by the physiognomy of objects. The relationship between the artist and the other is a question of being close to or distant from objects. We observe the recuperation of the love object (which is always, finally, an elaboration of the original maternal image that we have lost) and we also observe the refurbishment of this image in the external world as a kind of compensation for the charges of affective energy that have remained deluded within us.

One's own life, the proofs of one's own existence, and the entire sphere of everything "private" are used as repertory material. Anything and everything can be pressed into service: any action from any moment of any day, photographs of oneself, or x-rays, or medical test graphs, one's own voice, all of the possible relationships one can have with one's excrement or one's genitals, reconstructions of one's past or the theatrical presentation of one's dreams, the inventory of the events of family history, gymnastics, mime and acrobacy, blows and wounds. "The body is a part of every perception. It is the immediate past in so far as it still emerges in the present that flees away from it. This means that it is at one and the same time a point of view and a point of departure—a point of view and a point of departure that I *am* and that I also *go beyond* as I move off towards what I must become." (Jean-Paul Sartre). Some of the artists activate a displacement, an inversion, or a censure through anthropological citations or oneiric inventions; others bring forth paradoxical and terrifying narrations; still others give themselves over to the elaboration of their personal myths and turn their attention to infantile shocks and adolescent transfers. We end up with the individual who is nothing more than an individual. *Homo* is neither *faber*, nor *ludens*, nor *sapiens*. He is simply a man without the myth, without morality, apologue, or allegory; he is only a man full of the fear of uninterrupted banality, full of damning affections and disaffections. He lives with his acts of piety and obscenity, with his red and impure intestines, with his taste for decadence and expiation. In the same way that many small children use their excrements as a tool for affirming themselves in the eyes of the adults around them, many of the artists involved in Body Art and performances also exalt the excretory functions and the uses and abuses of all of the body's orifices. Obsessive neuroses are no longer renounced nor is coprophilia censured; everything that derives from anal eroticism is accepted and put to use. And this is not as if to say "*homo sum, humani nihil a me alienum puto.*" It is rather an alarming documentation of a pernicious autism and of a frenzied and sadistic self-satisfaction not only with respect to the artist in performance but also to the spectator—true and proper neoplasms of sadomasochistic perversion.

Piero Manzoni, *Living Sculpture*, 1961

The fear of death is also a part of our "phylogenetic heredity." And anxiety is a particular state of discomfort that arises as a response to the danger of loss. But it is also true that whenever a desire for something is repressed, the libido attached to it is transformed into anxiety and that anxiety is connected to waiting. Anxiety robs the individual of self-assuredness, and his *being with the others* takes place in a dimension of false hope. Repressed instincts are the dangers that menace the condition of civilized man. It is thus necessary to demolish the conventions of decency that support the great lie, necessary to destroy the artificial screen that separates the *public* from the *private*. Every latrine is a drawing room, every drawing room a latrine. The distinction between sublime and vulgar no longer makes sense. We are hidden beneath our opposite.

Those who manifest hostility to these operations cannot at any rate avoid being deeply impressed by what they condemn. The repulsion they feel is proof of their having been *profoundly* disturbed. To reject these forms of expression is to feel their attraction, to feel the fascination of the "show" and the *impulse to confess*. The spectator is forced to repeat psychic experiences that he has already lived through in the past, to reactivate old conflicts. The projections that he is instinctually incapable of not performing render him at one and the same time the victim and the performer of what is happening in front of his eyes. His neuroses charge the "scenes" with an *additional* meaning and *another* importance that are thus superimposed upon the events that the artists have already subjected to metamorphosis.

"You may call all of us accomplices with respect to something that damages us internally and that we experience as dramatic... I underline the fact that what I am now doing is something deadly. I live myself as something fragmented, destroyed and desecrated. Your participation in my

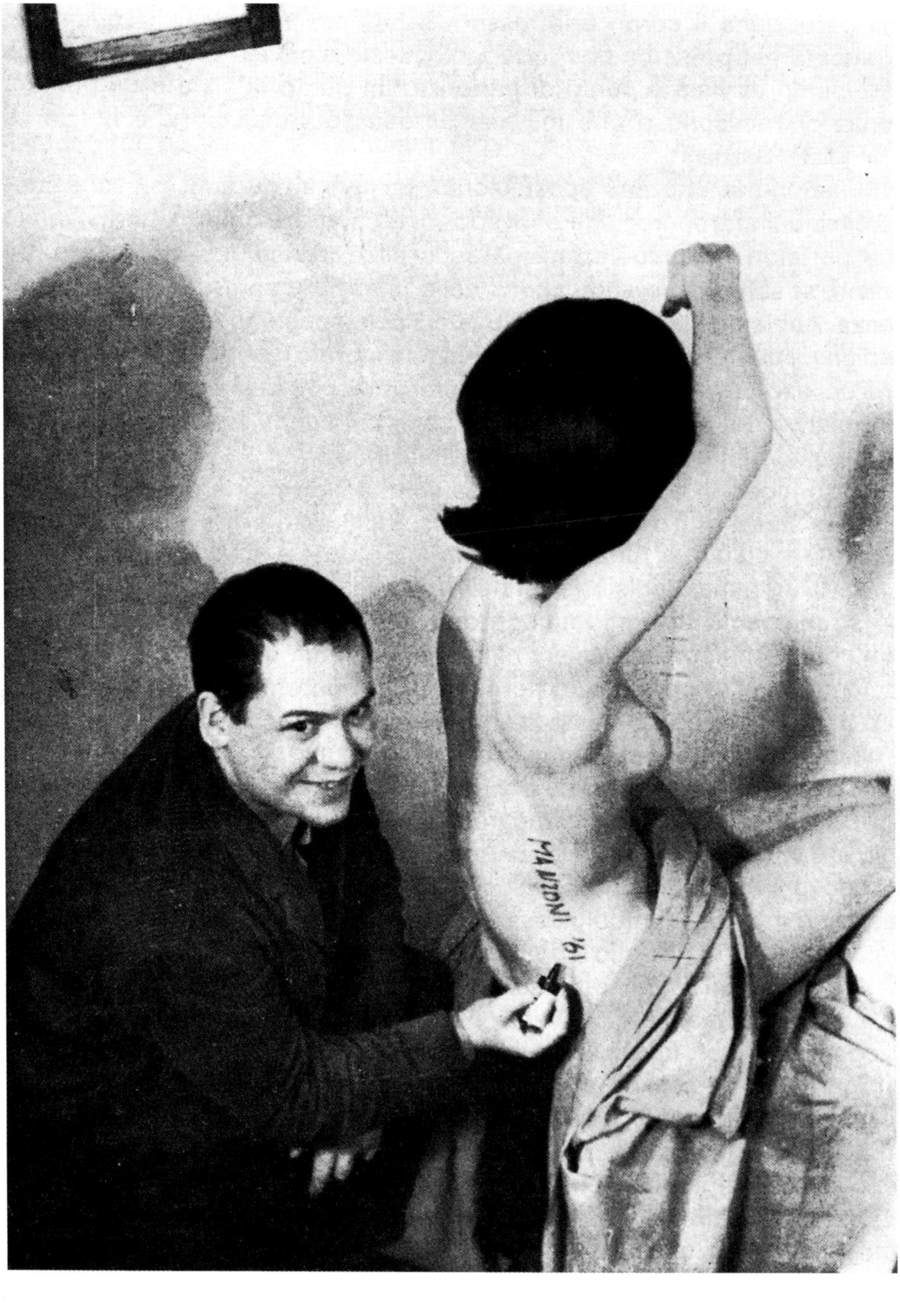
MANZONI '61

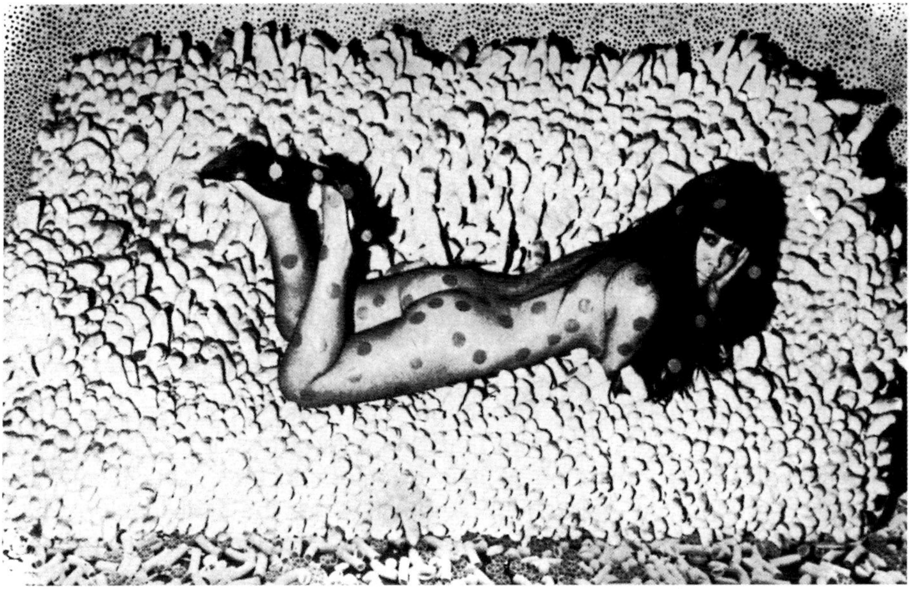

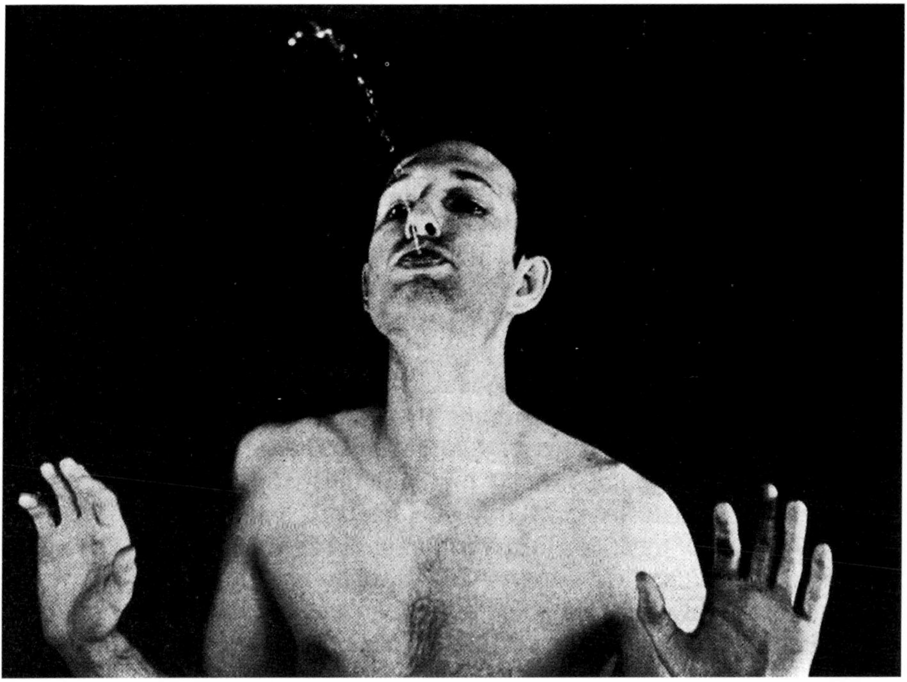

Yayoi Kusama on her *Phallic Sofa*, 1962

Bruce Nauman, *Self-Portrait as Fountain*, 1966

exhibition of this dismemberment creates the magical moment in which, in reality, I ask you to put me back together again. It is possibly your looking at me and your participation in this death that is within me that may perhaps bring me back again to life. I have the impression of the existence of this invocation, of this subtle hope which represents the need for the reconstruction of the ego. One lives the dismemberment of the ego just as one presents it." (Diego Napolitani).

As we have already seen, many of the artists we are talking about treat their own body as a love object, attribute it egocentric and egotistical functions, use it as a cult object in every quotidian event, and thus repropose the archetypal situation of the collective psychological condition: *love-hate*, and *aggression-recompensation*. (One attacks the love object but preserves it or takes custody of its remains.)
The story is reified and rendered anthropomorphic and thus the artist is able to disclaim his aggressivity and to reprove not himself, but rather something else, the object of his aggressivity and the object of his affection, i.e. his body (Gianni Pisani, Vito Acconci, Cioni Carpi, Baruchello, Pacus).
The ego is thus reassured. Everything has been covered up and denied. And reparation has surely not eliminated the impulse to start all over again. We are dealing with compulsive repetitions of acts of reparation and, according to Melanie Klein, the psychoanalyst, the success of reparation brings about the prevalence of impulses to life over the impulses to death. "Among the bodies of this nature that is reduced to *what belongs to me*, I discover my own body. It can be distinguished from all other bodies because of but a single particular: it is the only body that is not simply a body, but also *my body*. It is the only body that exists inside of abstraction and that I have chiselled into the world in which, in accordance with experience, I co-ordinate fields of sensation in various ways. It is the only body that is immediately at my service, just as its organs are at my service." (Edmund Husserl).

"We have but two alternatives left," wrote de Sade, "either the crime that will make us happy or the noose that will put an end to our unhappiness." Among those who practice forms of aggression upon both themselves and others, Otto Muehl, Rudolf Schwarzkogler, Hermann Nitsch, and Günter Brus from Vienna have chosen more than any of the others to live in a space of permanent scandal. They apply a kind of inversion of roles and identify themselves with the aggressors. This too is a defense mechanism. In front of an external danger, these artists assume the function of the aggressor; they both imitate his function and assume his symbols. The victim becomes the hangman, the tortured becomes the torturer. An eye for an eye and a tooth for a tooth. The offender is to suffer the ordeal of the same injury that he inflicted upon the offended. All of the impulses towards destruction are allowed to run free. True and proper rites of contamination are performed, meaning either a desire for infinite contamination or the power of a violence that is always to be interpreted as a means for breaking apart and decomposing the *normality* of the *persona* in which the individual is hypocritically forced to recognize himself. The analogies between obsessive ceremonials and cult practices are evident. As psychoanalysis has amply demonstrated, the obsession neuroses are the pathological equivalent of religious ritual. "Neurosis is a private religion, and religion is a universal obsessional neurosis."

Lucas Samaras, *Autopolaroid*, 1971

Much of this art also includes a ferocious misogyny, and this is especially so in those scatological actions where the ingestion of urine, feces and other products of elimination stands as a symbol for an envy of the womb and functions as a kind of exorcism of the terror of openly competing with the female genitals. This amounts to true and proper gynophobia. An interest in this kind of ritual also depends upon a diminution of the capacity to distinguish between what is real and what is unreal. These ritual actions seem absurd to anyone whose sense of reality is integral. Their horror, thus, must be sufficiently fascinating and brutal to break apart what they suffocate—in this case the intolerable tensions that exist within the self and that are therefore attributed to others. The massacres of recently past and still present wars and the wave of destruction that always announces still other tragedies to come are brought closer to a public without memory, and thus the public is denied the illusion of simply sedate madness.

Can the individual recognize himself and assume his own identity in evil? In evil as risk, as violence upon others or upon oneself; in evil as dissipation, in wounding oneself, mutilating oneself, killing oneself? The need to search out painful and humiliating situations, the mime of performing justice upon oneself, the compulsion to self-punishment that can even go to the limit of suicide, and the self-mutilation of the alienated individual are nothing more than the most absurd and terrifying examples. This need to externalize or rid oneself of something can go to the most horrendous forms of sacrifice and is the principle of a mechanism that can have no other end than death.

The situations presented almost always exhale a stink and exude panic. But "blood and death do not signify decadence; mud is no pillow." (Raymond Queneau). Thus, the Austrians present an overwhelming satire of a wearing anguish that assumes the form of a *Totenschau*. And there is also a residue of "supermanism" inherited from late Romanticism and Symbolism. One may also suspect that the emphasis on the desecratory conceals a pretence of anarchism. Moreover, the pretence of denouncing the heritage of crimes and suffering that oppresses humanity

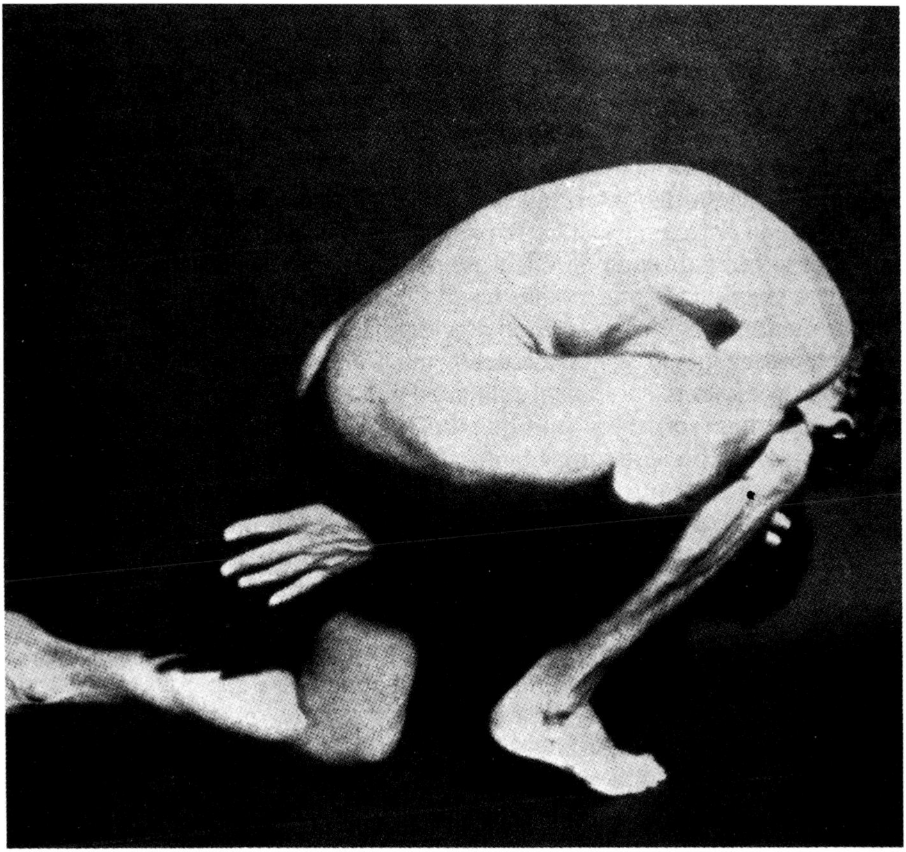

and of creating a catharsis that will permit the birth of *homo novus* may be nothing more than the most conspicuous aspect of a secret pleasure to be found in the re-enacting of the extreme forms of cynicism.

The uninhibited exhibition of their physical and psychic weaknesses is the only road that can permit many of the artists to make some sort of intervention upon their lives. Gina Pane, for example, always presents situations that are connected to antecedents or memories which are symbolically re-evoked in each of her pieces. Thus she manages to liberate herself from charges of repressed affection in a manner so clamorous as to come close to the edges of the pathological. The degree of excitation achieved finally reaches trauma. She presents situations of such great emotional discharge that you wonder if she is liberating herself from the weight of the traumatic event or trying to bring it back to life so as better to be able to hold onto it. Frequently her themes have to do with filling up some unsupportable emptiness—an emptiness that is also a kind of mourning for a lost love-object. For Gina Pane, it's a question of a love that is no longer understood as a solution that compensates existence, but rather as a kind of collision, a laceration, and a transcendence—it is love as an interpersonal and intersexual relationship, both selective and elective, love as the desire to vanquish death, love as union and reconjunction of the *self* and the other. Love, as Sartre wrote, is "the desire to place oneself outside of the entire system of values that has been created by others, the necessary condition for any and all new valorizations... I am no longer permeated with finitude, nor is my being any longer immobilized in simply *what I am*... The possession of the transcendence of the other and, in any case, as a body." The body—and especially so in Gina Pane's representations—is the cause of sensations. It is more than an instrument of action: it contributes to the life of consciousness and memory in a psycho-physical parallelism of processes that assume meaning and relief only when they are connected.

At this point, what is required of the spectator is an act of *intelligence*. If we find the work resistant or repulsive, there is obviously still some diaphragm to be broken before being able to come to complete understanding. The public is asked for an act of the will that involves an interest that is not simply aesthetic. If we so desire, we stand within the magic circle. In accordance with the ability of the artist, we can enter into the game, give ourselves without reserve, and penetrate together into a different dimension where the I of the artist becomes another, turns itself into phenomenon and spectacle, gives itself entirely to its interlocutor, and thus realizes its objective in precisely this manner of *being for the others*.

The representation of the theme of bisexuality and thus the simultaneous presence of contrasting tendencies, attitudes, affective goals and impulses is likewise frequently an attempt to keep a distance from repressed traumatic experiences that continue to make their presence felt in our lives. One holds them at bay or even exorcizes them thanks to the pleasure of reproducing the variants of the experience of conquering them. All of this becomes a means for a narration about us, which is directed at us and also at the others, who must participate in the same experience in order to enter into contact with us. As we know, there is a certain level of anatomic hermaphroditism to be found in all of us; but for most of us the dominant sex has repressed the psychic representation of the vanquished one.

"The transvestite is the man or the woman who utilizes the toilettes that are not traditionally allowed to their sex. It is not so much the questioning of the masking or concealment of a man or a woman as rather a question of a human being who transcends the limits of his own body and becomes what he desires to be and not what his society would force him to be." (One might remember de Sade's Juliet, who wants to be married twice in one day, first dressed as a woman, and then dressed as a man.) Transvestism is not a misunderstanding—it is *forbidden* in the society in which we live and the destruction of this barrier is important. Having broken the wall of silence and circumspection and having individuated an only tenuous convention that separates the confines of the roles, several of the artists (Lüthi, Castelli, Sieverding, Messager) place the accent upon the comparison and the confusion of man and woman, masculine and feminine. They invert the somatic characteristics, grotesquely accentuating appearances of bisexuality, and inventing fictitious personalities, and thus create a crisis in the crystallization of sexual roles. In any case, however, there remains the difficulty of accepting the combinations that simulate or that *are identity*. (Here the individual searches only for himself but in a guise that permits the lie.)

As was said shortly above, the desire is to create a crisis in *roles*. Urs Lüthi, for example, is truly extraordinary in bringing to the surface the most hidden vibrations of the unconscious of others. He gives himself to our gaze with extreme seductivity of dress and attitude and, thanks as well to a subtle telepathic current, he succeeds in creating a kind of emotional contamination within the spectator who thus becomes either a willing or unwilling partner and collaborator capable of closing the circuit and returning the same interchangeable perception. No one is better than Lüthi in the use of the spell of the androgyne; he sexualizes and desexualizes both himself and the others in precisely the same way and always through the means of an intent attention that strikes out directly towards the doubts and desires that have been hidden from consciousness.

Among the various forms of adaptation being dealt with, we have seen that the regressive (Vettor Pisani, Mattiacci, Nespolo) prevail upon the progressive. "A hero is a man who does what he can." (Romain Rolland). There are also some who aspire to the apathy of the Cynics and the Stoics, or rather to the virtue of a total indifference to all external stimuli. They seem to maintain an impassive acceptance of pain (but, in reality, that would be possible only for those who have no knowledge of real suffering.)

Among the most romantic exponents are two Englishmen, Gilbert and George; they emphasize the nonsense and also the values of sentiment. They create an exquisite *tableau vivant* that is enclosed within a soft reverie woven out of *intimate* actions that concede very little to the *private*. Their awareness of reality certainly implies no adaptation to reality (unless we consider their public "performances" a kind of reciprocal relationship between organism and environment); their awareness of reality is rather a question of flight, elusion and fabling. Gilbert and George do anything and everything to eliminate the difference between what constitutes their life and what constitutes their art. And their tenacity in this direction brings them close to heroism. As satirical marionettes on the border between the human and the unhuman, they pretend an ignorance of their condition as relics only to be able better to combat it. Saul Bellow wrote, "The greatest success is to survive." It's the fact of having succumbed in front of the challenge from the very outset—and this is their principal theme—that gives their work a coloration of drama. Their material could belong to a cabaret repertoire, which is to say that it could easily seem to be of fairly low status with respect to "cultivated" art, but they subject it to a treatment whose intentions belong to the strategies of the avant-garde. Their clownish sadness unifies traces of Chaplin with exquisite moments from Beckett, thus reflecting the precarious and obstinate condition of being human.

The forms of mime are quite numerous, and one of the most frequent is the distortion of "making faces" (Rainer, Masi, Nauman, Nespolo, sometimes even Samaras). The idea is to use deformation so as to be able to approach not reality, but truth. The grimace is an archaic apotropaic act that has the purpose of repelling and eliminating malefic forces or of establishing control over them. The part of the body through which to express the neurotic conversion is chosen, and thus one particular part of the body has the privilege of giving symbolic evidence of the unconscious conflict.

Parody functions as anathema and diminishes the value of content at the same time in which it modifies form. "The psychic energy saved by these operations must be considered a saving in repression—a saving that derives from a liberation of aggressivity." (Ernst Kris).

These forms of behavior serve for the development of systems of defense. The ego falsifies itself in order to avoid an experience that would otherwise be too painful, and thus it protects itself. This too is a method for achieving a certain satisfaction since the identity of the artist takes refuge in illusion, in the mask (Jonas, Vettor Pisani, etc.). It's the desperation of those who search for fulfillment outside of themselves, for those whose only object and only end is themselves. Through a series of transfers and projective identifications, the artists assimilate aspects of others. The stratagem can be successful: the personality differentiates itself by means of investments made in external subjects (Journiac, Ciam, Ontani). Introjection, incorporation, and internal conservation are also prototypes of identification; in these cases mental process is lived as a somatic operation (Terry Fox, Oppenheim).

There is also a kind of comfort (or even self-complacency) in the control of specular identification—which is to say in one's motorial coordination in a mirror (Samaras, Jonas, De Freitas, Trotta, Otth). Narcissus projects himself outside in order to be able to love what is inside of himself. The search for another self is the search for a partner, and vice versa. One is alone, and not only alone, but also separate; one dissimulates simulation (Nagasawa, Dan Graham). It's not a question of total negation of reality nor of confused romancing of reality, nor of hallucinations or delirium. Projection expels an internal menace that has been created by the pressure of an intolerable impulse; it is thus transformed into an external menace that can be more easily handled. The artists shift their problem from the subject to the object, or from the inside to the outside; qualities or feelings that they do not want to recognize as their own are projected away from the ego and situated elsewhere in other things or other people.

The consensus of the spectator is essential if the artist is to find "confirmation" in his work. The work is the artist, and his narcissism is no longer invested in an art object but allowed to explode within his own body. The relationship between the individual and the external world is continuously disturbed; every single stimulus upsets our equilibrium, but all of us have mechanisms that can re-establish it and that contribute to self-preservation.
One of the major functions of the art illusion is the protective one. As Kris puts it, "The extension of psychoanalytic awareness has opened the road to a better understanding of the notion and functioning of catharsis. We can no longer be content with the idea that repressed emotions lose their ascendancy upon psychic life once they have found an outlet. It seems more reasonable to believe that Aristotle's phenomenon of purification allows the self to re-establish a control that has been endangered by censured instinctual needs. The search for outlets serves to assure or re-establish this control and the pleasure in so doing is thus double. On the one hand it derives from a discharge of energy, and on the other from the fact that the reinforcement of control has been in fact accomplished. The maintenance of the aesthetic illusion allows us the security to which we aspire and it likewise guarantees freedom from the sense of guilt, since the fantasies to which we are giving our attention are not our own. All of this favors the growth of feelings that we would hesitate in other circumstances to allow ourselves: in other circumstances they would lead us back to our personal conflicts. We are also allowed an intensity of reaction that many individuals would be hard put to allow themselves without the protection of the aesthetic situation. We know that in many cases this reluctance is due to the pressures of education that tend under certain cultural conditions to devaluate the expression of intense emotion and to allow it to exist only if it is ordered within schemes and institutions. And art is precisely such a socially approved occasion for intense emotional reaction."

The artist's attempt to function in a *different* or *alternative* manner is an expression of the desire to eliminate the habitual position of prestige that his role comports. It is also an attempt to clear the field of interpersonal relations from the forms of alienation that art and culture continually produce and that contribute to render relationships frustrating and non-emancipatory. The objective is to eliminate aesthetic specificity and cultural deprivation. Competitivity, destructivity and the guilt feelings that accompany them are exasperated by the civilization of automation. Thus the enjoyment of something tragically total or absolute along with what might be called the nostalgia for a prenatal situation (to be found transferred into the relationship between artist and public) eliminates or distances the suspicion that the goals of this kind of communication are obscured or secretive. The public is needed to complete the event; it must be involved in a collective experience that leads it to reconsider its quotidian existence and the rules of its ordinary behavior. That is enough about the norms of passive contemplation: now the public is to serve as a sounding box. The relationship between public and artist becomes a relationship of complicity. The artist offers his hand to the spectator and the success of the operation depends upon how and how much the spectator is willing to accept it. The gesture of the artist who makes the proposition acquires significance only if his actions are met by an act of *recognition* on the part of the spectator. The artist needs to feel that the others are receptive to him, that they are willing to play the game of accepting his provocations and that they will give him back his "projections." It is indispensable that the public co-operate with him, since what he needs is to be *confirmed* in his identity. The behavior of the spectator is a gratification for the artist just as the behavior of the artist is a gratification for the spectator. When the public allows itself to be *used*, the artist has found an "other" who is willing to give him reassurance in the fantasy or utopianizing world that he is attempting to make visible, and the experiment works the other way round as well. But sometimes the situation becomes a question of "anything goes" and we end up with reciprocal deception. This is due to the fact that the spectator is a masochist desirous of being *punished*. (The function of punishment would be to eliminate feelings of guilt in order to allow the possibility for a successive moment of pleasure.) And thus we approach a kind of aesthetic terrorism which is based upon a vigorous opposition to the phenomena of elitist and consumer art.

But it is legitimate to ask a question. This manner of populating the real world with the spectres that haunt us, this conversion of neurotic and psychotic formations into surrogate cultural activities, these representations that aim less at the need of awareness than at the awareness of need... to what extent can all this create a space in which human beings will be able to meet with each other for the formulation of a comprehensive and all-inclusive form of communication? To what extent is this anti-art capable of becoming a real possibility for the transformation of the very language of art? In which way does it establish a true climate of *empathy* that allows the transmission of apperceptions so as in turn to prevent emotional participation from becoming an end in itself, thus permitting it to become an instrument for political struggle? In *The Obscene Dimension*, Peter Gorsen analyzes the ideological content of amoral rebellion and the revolutionary or pseudo-revolutionary meaning of attacks upon constituted morality, and he asks himself "if this aggressive subculture can be considered a form of alternative culture or if it doesn't in fact remain a prisoner of repressive society, nothing more than a contradiction in a sort of *repressive tolerance* that renders us all equal in a neurotic un-freedom." Two poles remain. On the one hand there are opposition (even if lived dramatically) and transgression (the totality of one's being, which is the being of a *divided* subject, is placed into question) that do not go past the state of paranoia, that do not connect the past to the future, and thus move away from authentic possibilities of communitarian significance. On the other hand there is the possibility that the flow of revolutionary schizoid impulses could cause a great deal more than a simple confusion of superficial structures.

The purpose of this essay is clear, evident and openly declared. I should like once again to underline it.
It has no intention of being a final categorization—that would in any case be dreadfully premature. It hopes, on the contrary, to be a possible path to follow; it desires to derive inferences and to offer hypotheses. Rather than judgements, it presents nothing more than notes and considerations so that the reader may more easily approach the theme of the use of the body as an art language.
I have formulated a series of ideas in order to develop possible readings for the operations that have been collected together here. Most of the artists have prepared texts to accompany their works and many of them can help to give even greater clarification to the symptomatology of the arguments that have been touched upon. The artists' declarations and notes to the works constitute the parameters in relation to which my "diagnoses" must be seen as conflicting or coincident. And in any case they seem to me to furnish a firm guide for those who desire to make use of a certain group of concepts not only in the light of the things to which they refer, but also in the light of the way in which the references are made.

Lea Vergine, 1974
Translation by Henry Martin

vito acconci

Air Time, 1973
Two intersecting areas: the "field" of the gallery and the "point" of an enclosure, off to the side.
The gallery space is a floating space: it's nearly empty, no images to focus on: the corners are resting places, listening places: "radios," white boxes containing tape loops in my voice: the sound comes from one box at a time, skips and winds across the space.
These are programs: prerecorded messages addressed by me to you, the passer-by—or storages, places to keep my voice for myself, places where I can steady myself, build myself up.
Scenarios: ways to define your position, keep you here—ways to widen the space, break through it, send you out of it. This is my voice from the past: this is in the back of my mind while I'm elsewhere, now, in the "recording studio," on the spot.
Tape excerpts: "… on the air, in the air … a field, the air is clear, you're walking in a field, you can see for miles along the hill, down the valley… you can slide down the hill, the long soft grass moves under you in your direction, aiding your slide, your slide out of this space… the plot shifts, snag in the plot, as one of them moves his leg forward, I can think of him ready to trip me, I have to sneak around in order to get to her …you can be sitting there, as she might have been,

as if creating difficulties for me, making contradictory demands on me, as she might have done..."
I'm off to the side, enclosed in a small closet space: a red light blinks on the door: recording studio: I'm "on the air": you, the passer-by, can survey me, keep an eye on me, by means of a television set outside, in the gallery space. This is a place where I can isolate myself, in order to deal with an obsession, in order to cut myself off the fantasies and interactional possibilities on tape—or a place where I can pin down an obsession that can generate the fantasies outside. I'm sitting here, looking into a mirror, not to see myself but to see myself in relation to a specific person I've been involved with for an extended time: I look at the mirror as if she's in here with me, as if I'm looking at her, as if I'm talking to her through the crowd: recreate incidents we've been through together: see myself the way she's seen me, hear myself the way she's heard me. You, the passer-by, have to be there, outside, so you can certify my position: once you've seen how I've been with her, I won't be able to deny it, I'll have to come to terms with it, I'll have to leave her—I might be able, then, to get myself off the spot, join into the fantasies, the open field, where I've already sent you.

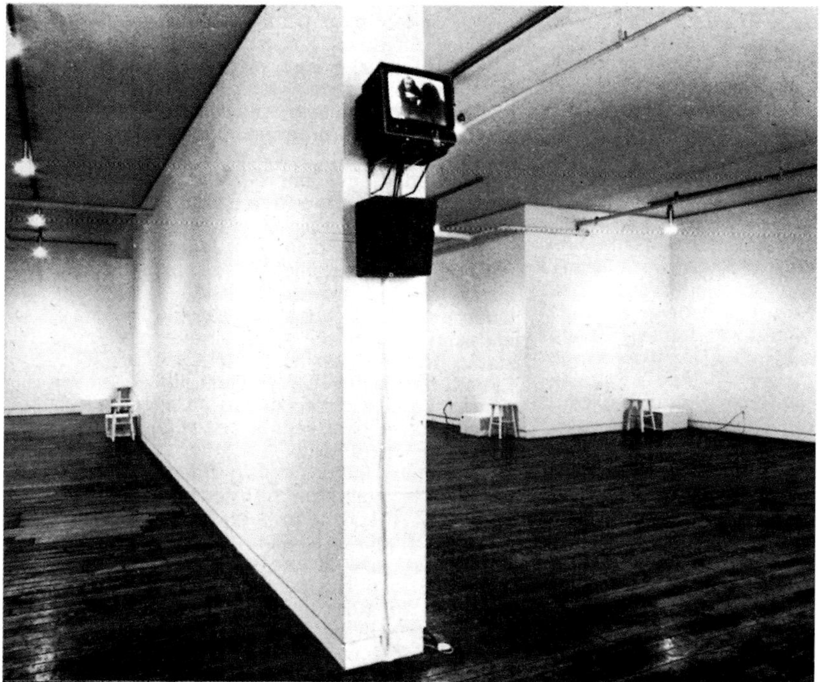

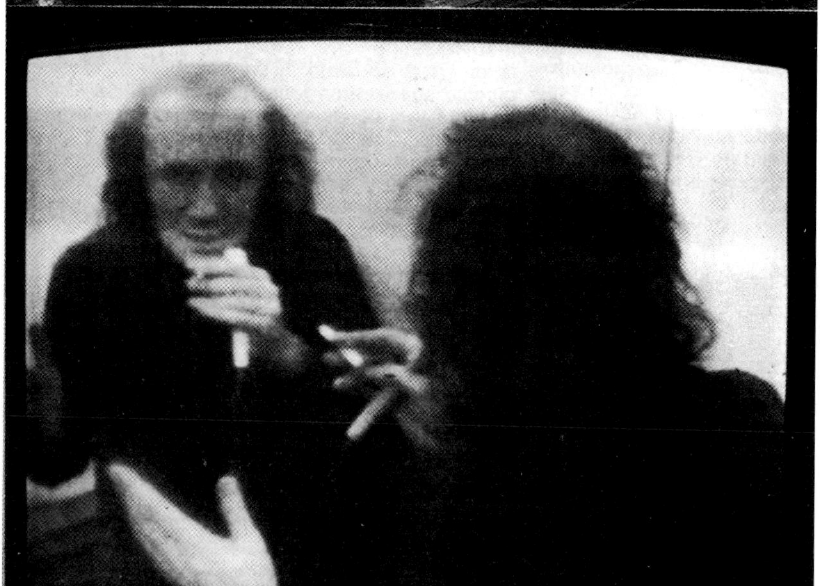

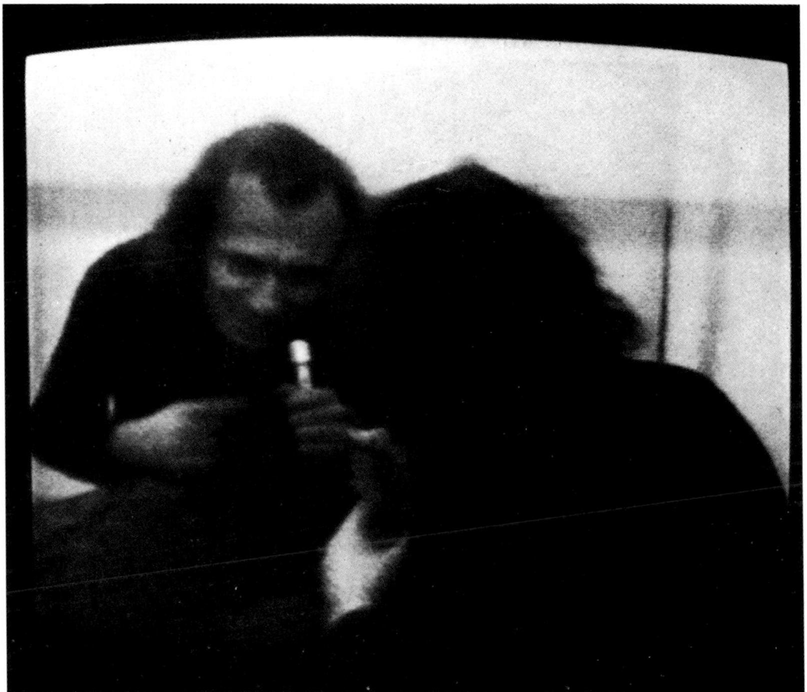

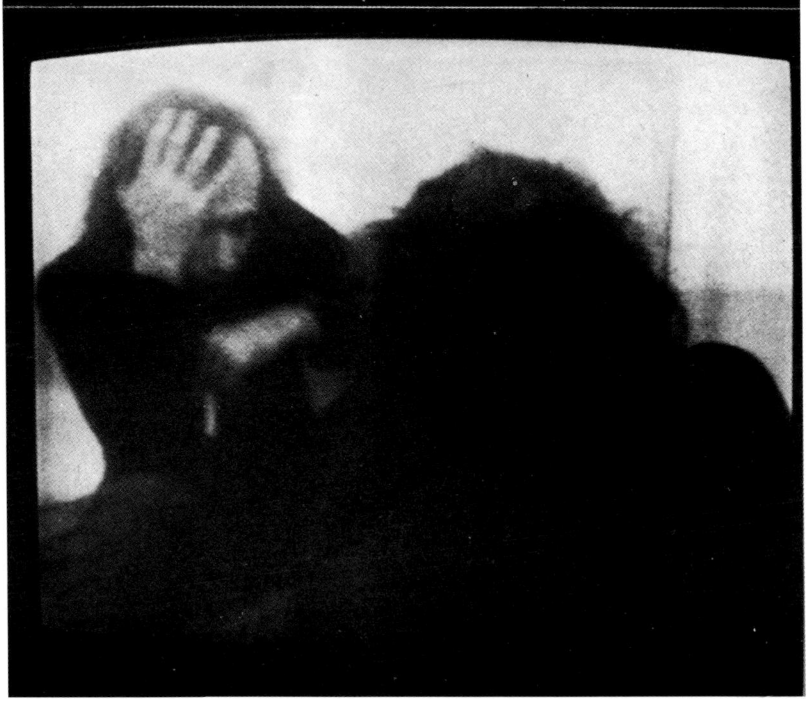

giovanni anselmo

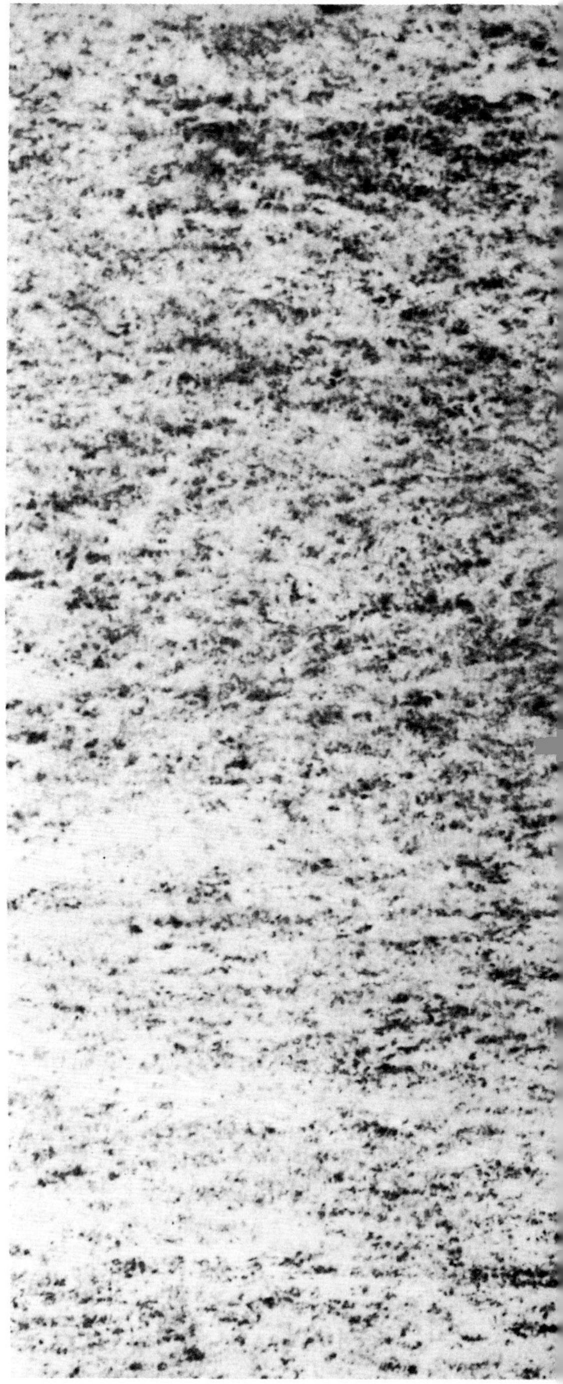

Getting into the Work, 1971
Photograph taken with a timer.

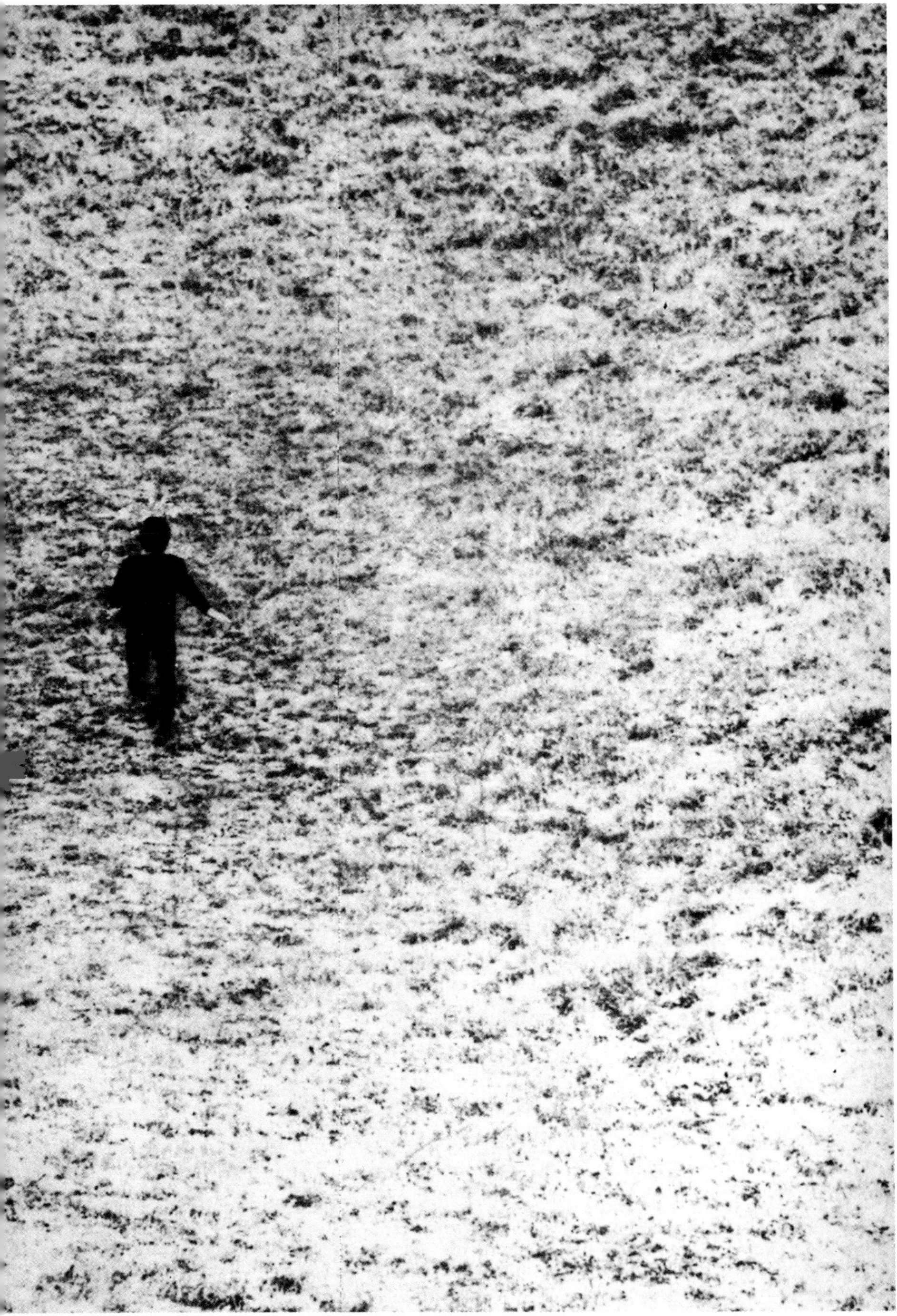

keith arnatt

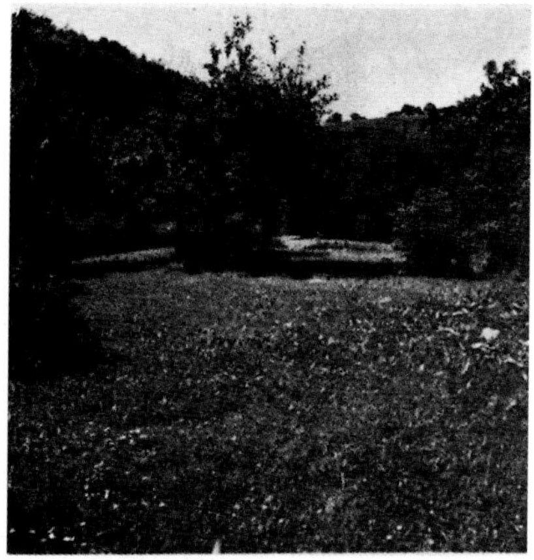

Banausic Effort, 1973
It is a record of (physical) work done in order to arrive at the artwork which is the nine photographs—it is not a record of the artwork but a record of the effort employed in making the artwork.

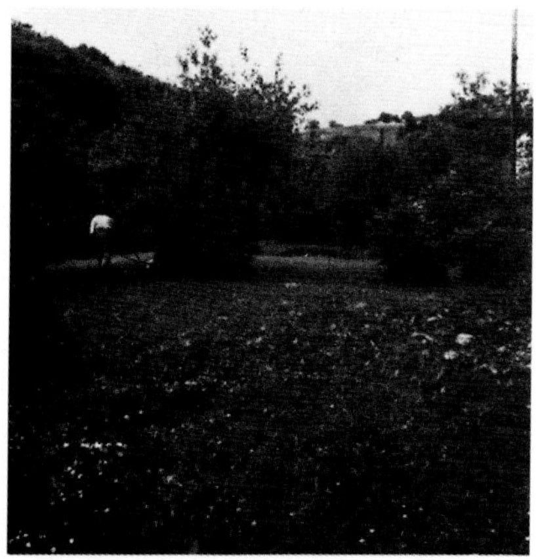

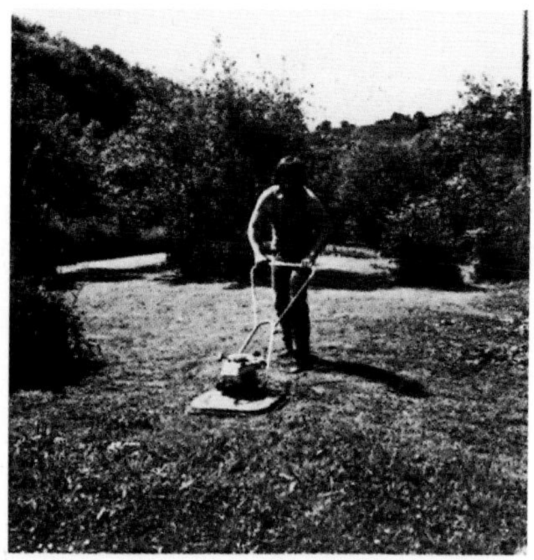

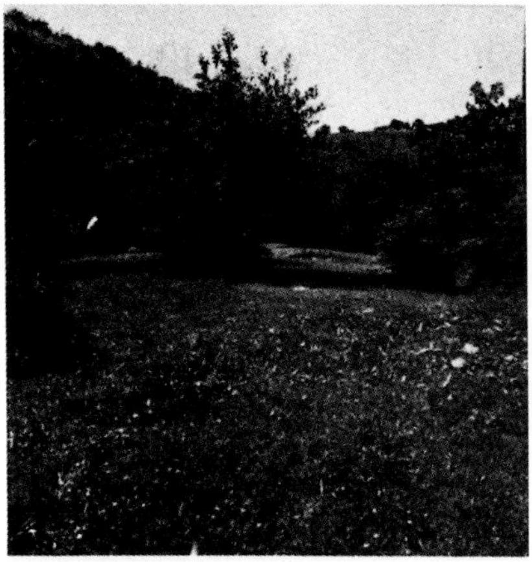

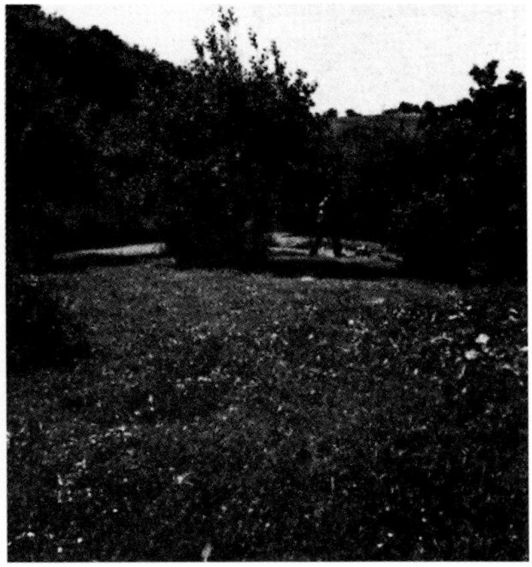

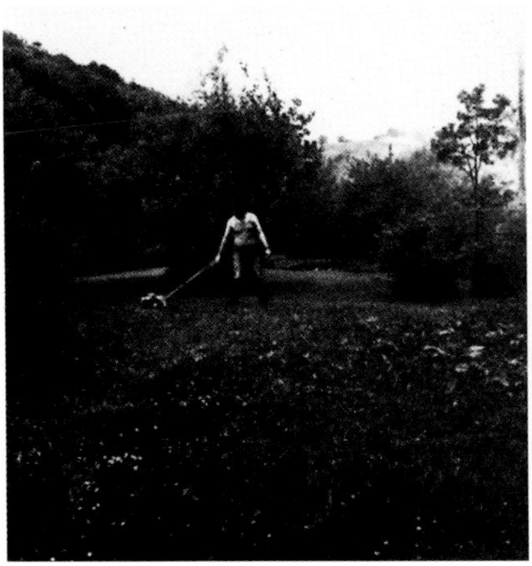

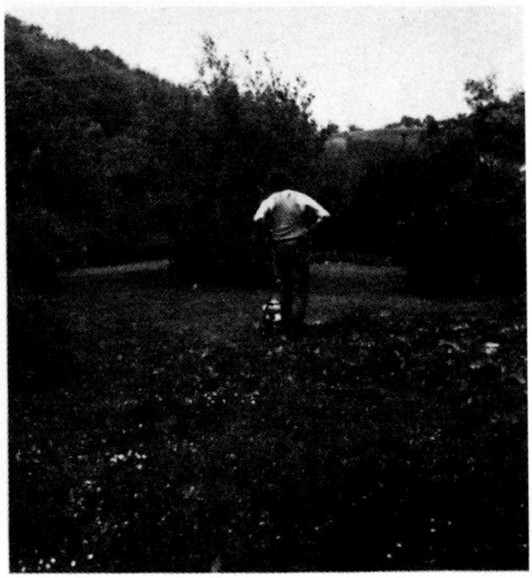

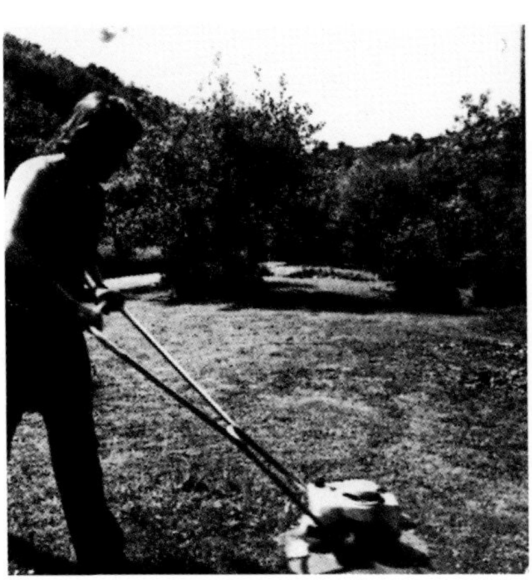

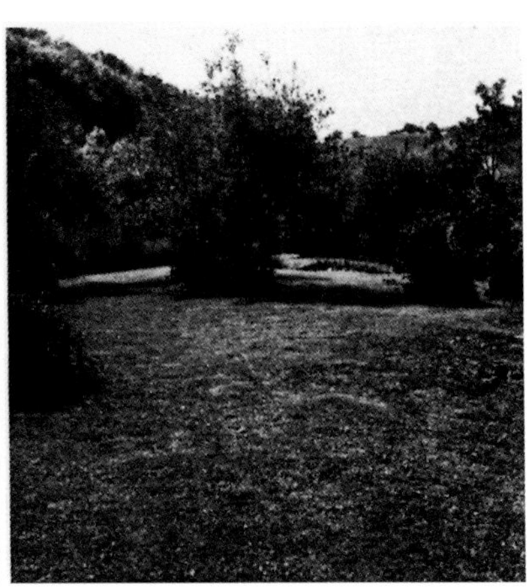

john baldessari

Easel Painting, 1972–73
Each finger on one of my hands is alternately stuck in yellow, then green, dry pigment. First it was fun, second it is a painting and a comment on painting.

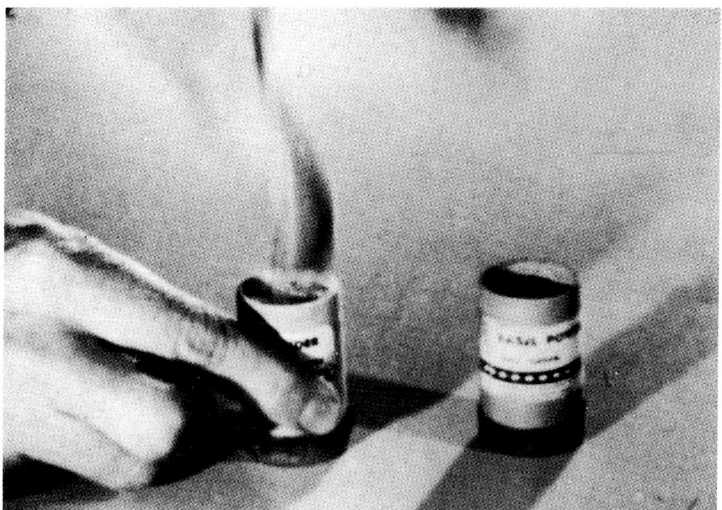

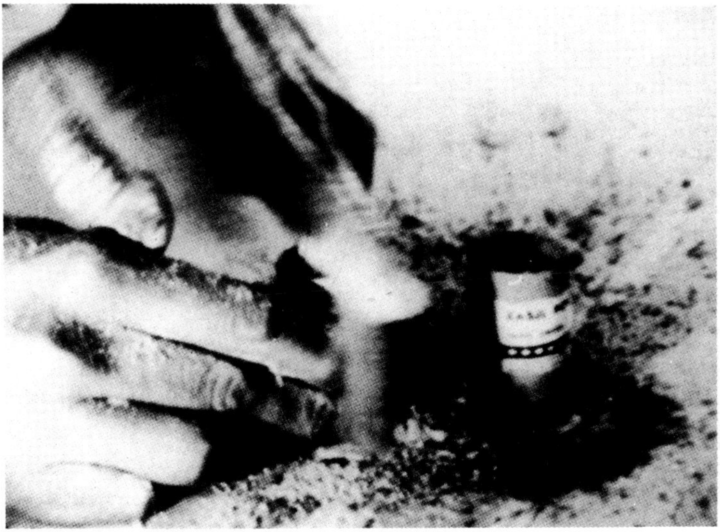

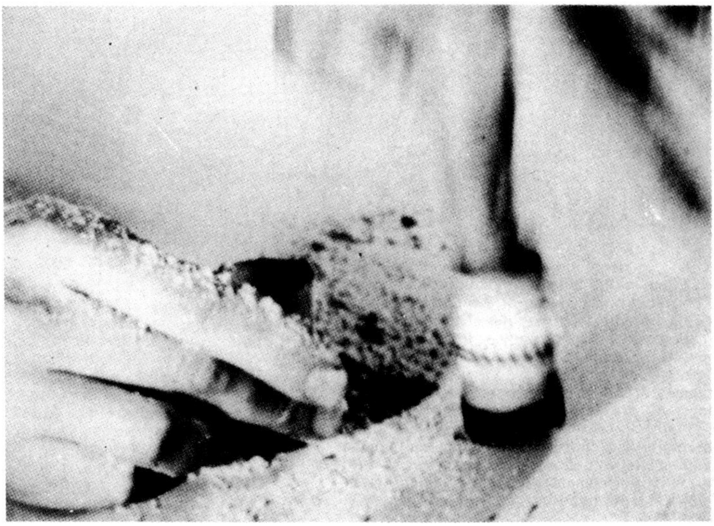

gianfranco baruchello

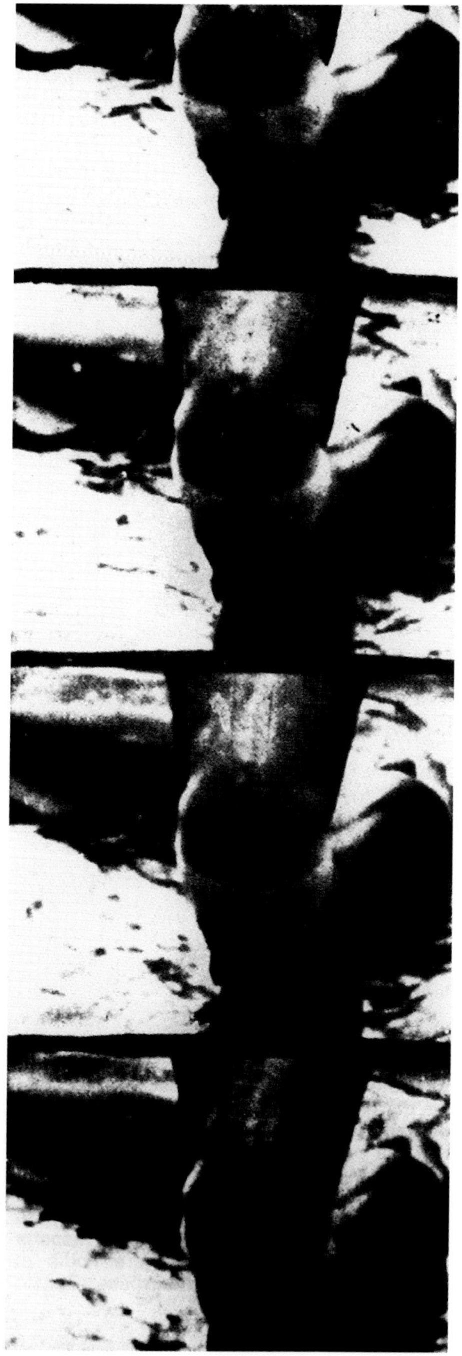

Perforce, 1968

The flesh of children, the bodies of children, children in the ritual mechanics of sacrifice. The ring-a-ring o' roses of the tiny bird disappears in a blaze of napalm. The negro floats motionless; nothing comes from death but death. The perverse melancholy of nothingness is still being sung here; the blame for catastrophe is still being shared; each time different holocausts are offered to corporeity; power is romantically exorcized. But there are other borders. And conscience won't wait for the intellectual, who does not know how to turn class hatred against the class to which he belongs. I write this today as I am revising *Perforce*.

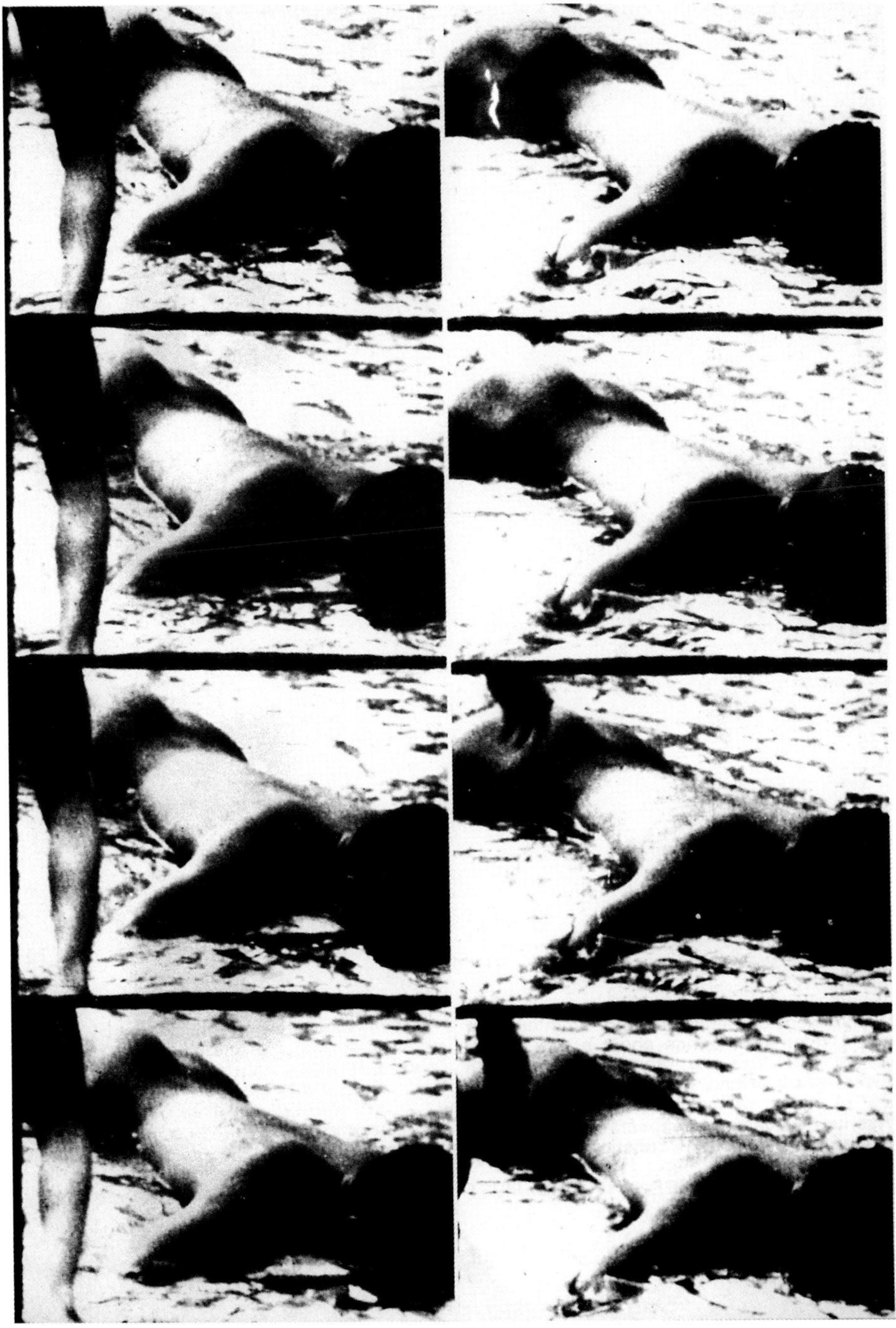

ben vautier

Declaration, 1973

I, Ben, consider that Body Art is interesting only insofar as it brings about a fundamental innovation and does not represent a series of tricks reflecting Marcel Duchamp's idea that "everything is art." This fundamental innovation appears when Body Art is involved in the transformation of the artist and his subjectivity.
IN ORDER TO CHANGE ART ONE MUST CHANGE MAN.

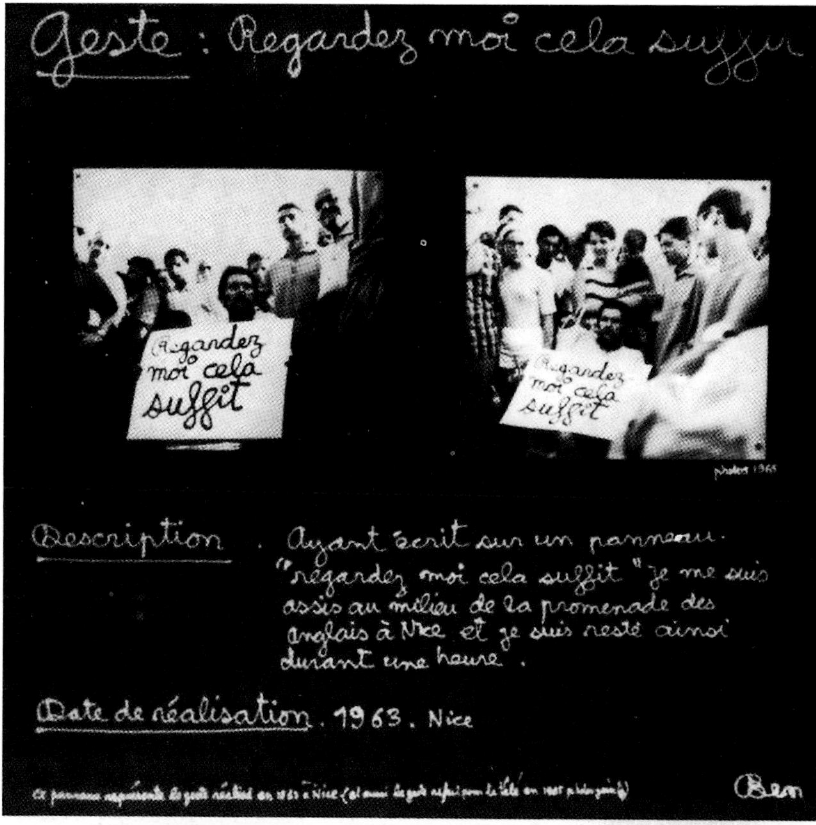
Geste : Regardez moi cela suffit
Regardez moi cela suffit
Regardez moi cela suffit
photos 1965
Description . Ayant écrit sur un panneau. "regardez moi cela suffit" je me suis assis au milieu de la promenade des anglais à Nice et je suis resté ainsi durant une heure.
Date de réalisation . 1963 . Nice
Ben

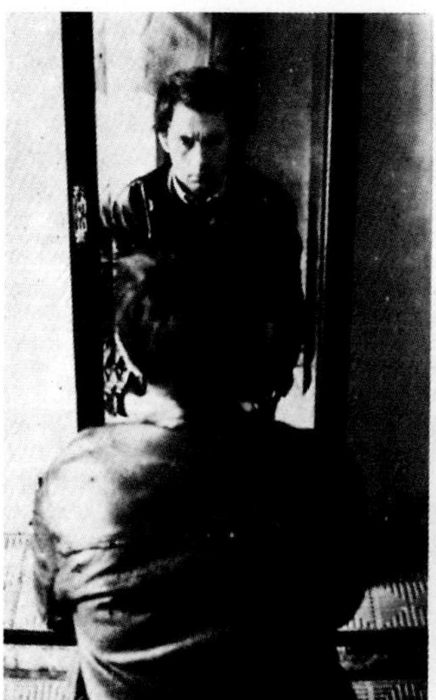

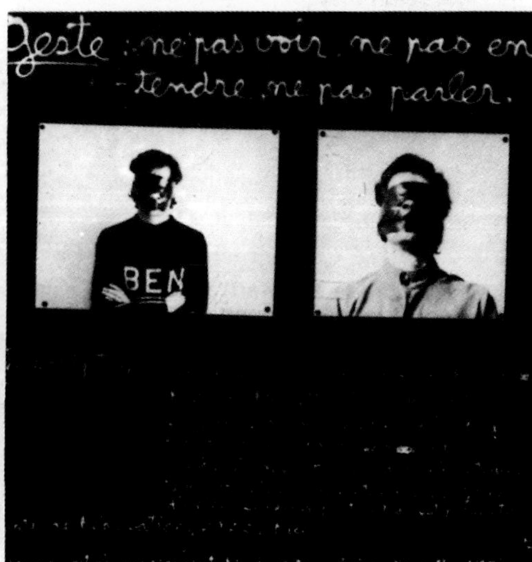
Geste : ne pas voir ne pas entendre ne pas parler.
BEN

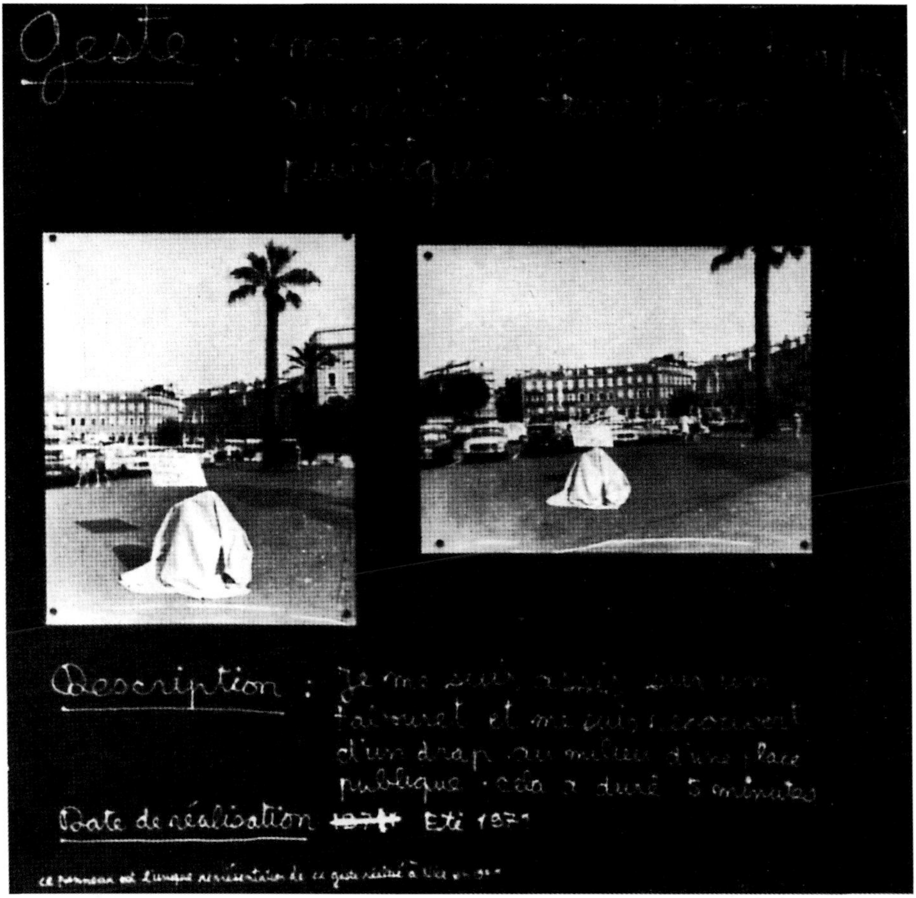
Geste
Description :
d'un drap au milieu d'une place
publique · cela a duré 5 minutes
Date de réalisation
Eté 197

valentina berardinone

Sequences from film "Urbana," 1973
The Hand as Phenomenon-Image
In the general context of my work the use of film, and in this, the use of the body (i.e. the hands), have a particular place. The basic theme of my artistic research is the happening—or what has happened.
By this I mean the recording of a modification to the given order, the attempt to make evident the dynamic ambiguity of the passage from a state of order to a state of disorder, which in its turn presents itself as an apparent order: the process can go on ad infinitum.
The use of film is inevitably involved in this theme of the "happening." I have chosen the hand as a recurrent basic element in my films, that is, a phenomenon-image which, in its historicity, could be a link between myself and the external world. That is why the hand is seen mainly as

gesture; it is not, as far as I am concerned, a morphologic element rediscovered as a place of shelter or as an intimistic situation, but as a projection of creativity outside myself.
The hand neurotically cleans the windowpane, it springs from under a step and reaches toward the light, it writes on a sheet of paper, it erases some writing, it is clenched, it throws a stone. These actions involve motions which are *happenings* and *knowledge* at the same time; the hand—the terminal part of the body, the one intended for contact with the things that surround us—makes gestures which synthesize the event (the hand itself being an event), turning itself into the protagonist and the catalyzer, becoming therefore a permanent reference point for every act of verification.

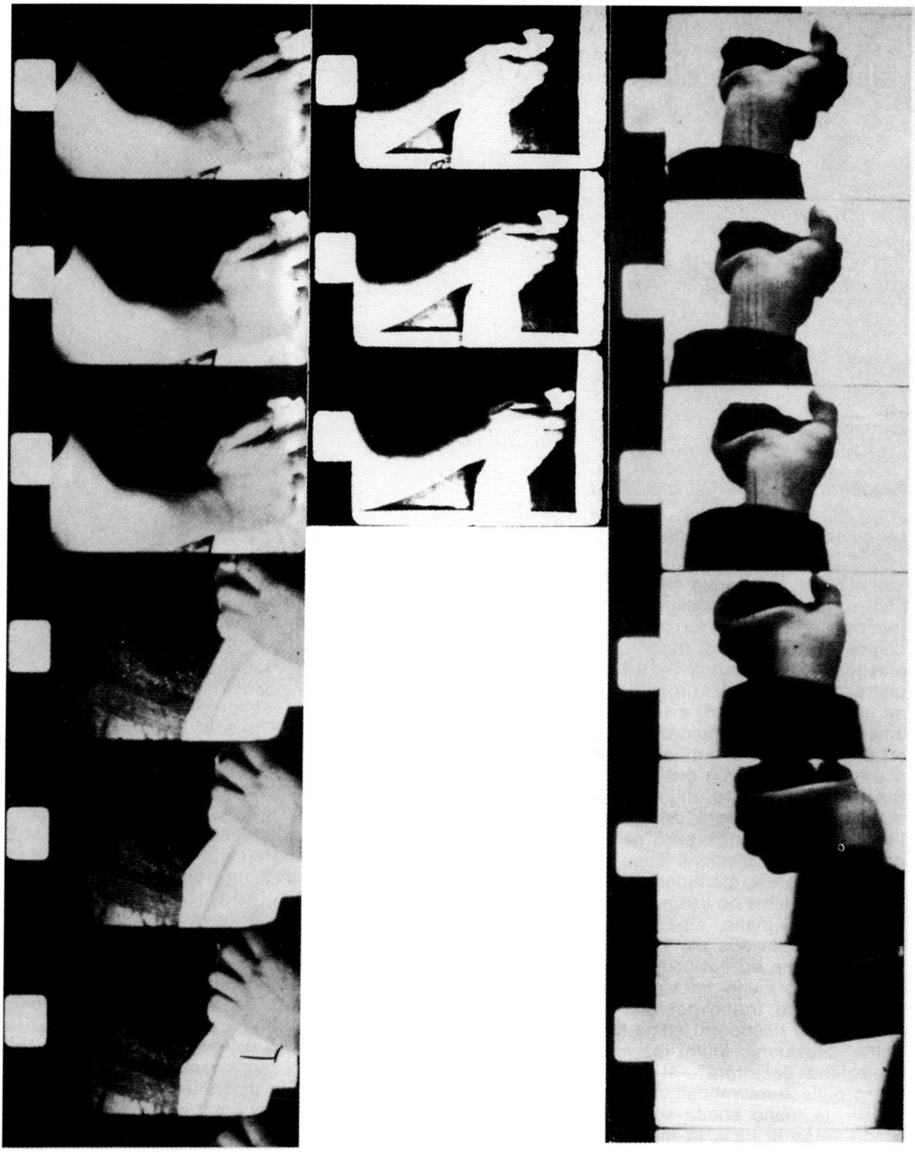

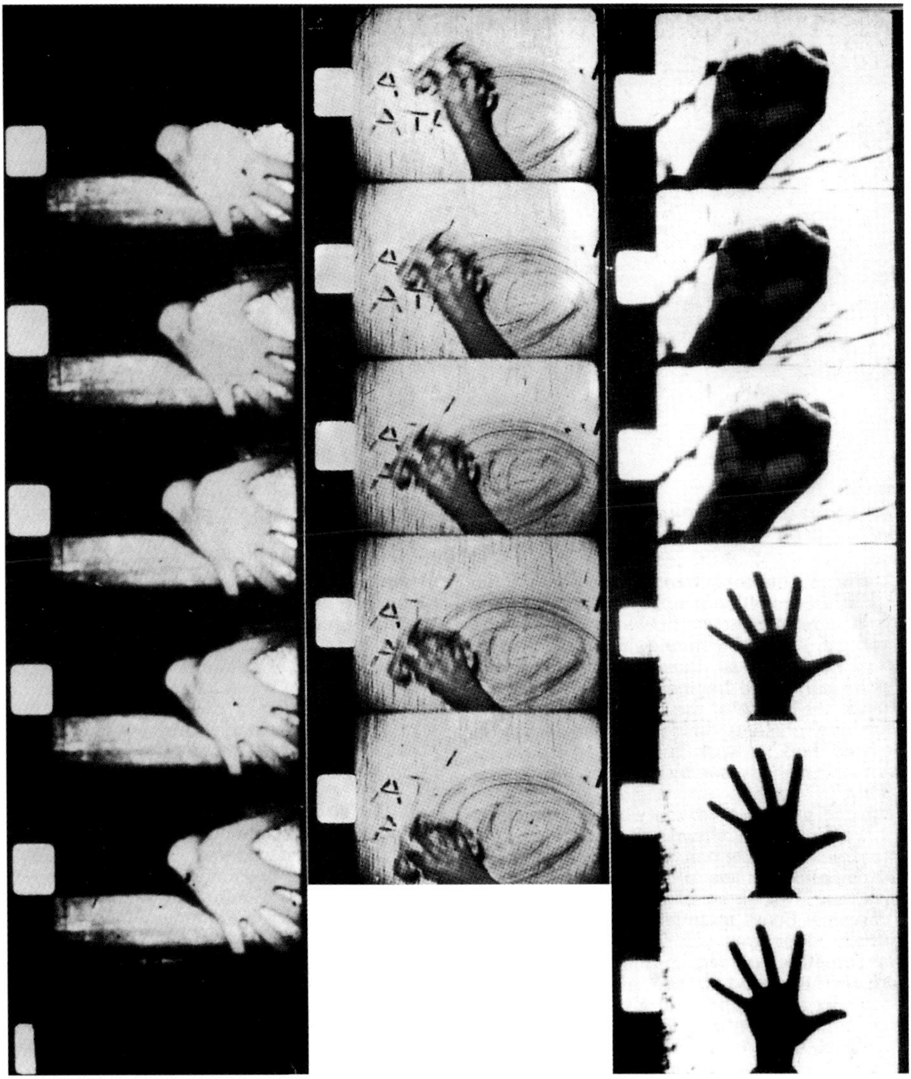

joseph beuys

Arena, 1970

Who knows how far I would have gone if I had been intelligent!

Arena can be considered Beuys' autobiographic work. It encompasses all the images of the most significant drawings and objects made by the artist during his first creative phase, but above all those which refer to his performances from the beginning of the sixties onward. *Arena*, the space of the tragedy in which the artist-hero presents himself, is an open work, a work in progress; Beuys intends to update it year by year for the rest of his life.

At present, the work is composed of 100 panels in aluminum and a sculpture in beeswax and copper. Each panel is 114 × 82 cm and contains, protected by thick plate glass, one or more photographs treated with Beuys' favorite materials—that is, wax, margarine, red or gray pigment, acid, sulphur, and so on. The sculpture, placed in the center of the work, consists of two piles of wax and copper slabs, and a plastic container filled with lubricating oil. The sculpture is the fulcrum of *Arena*, the symbol of a primary source of vital energy.

In June 1972, at the Modern Art Agency in Naples, Beuys did a performance with *Arena.* For almost three hours, lying on the floor of the gallery, with a plant (whose alchemic name is VITEX AGNUS CASTUS) tied on his head, Beuys passed his right hand smeared with oil over the slabs of copper (the conductor), until his body vibrated with energy like a body charged with electric current.

As he frequently repeats, "I am a transmitter, I emit!"

(Lucio Amelio for Beuys)

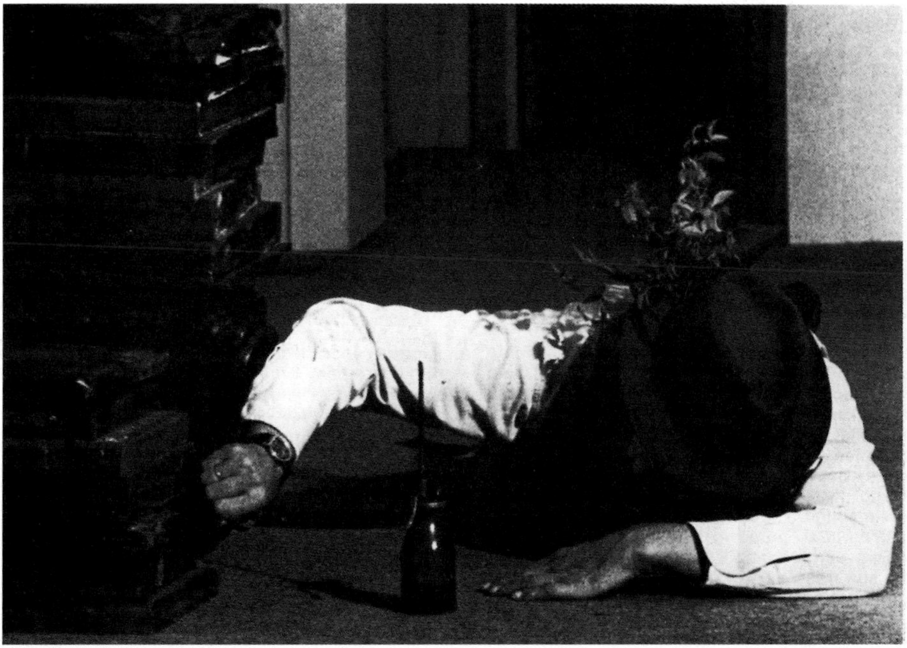

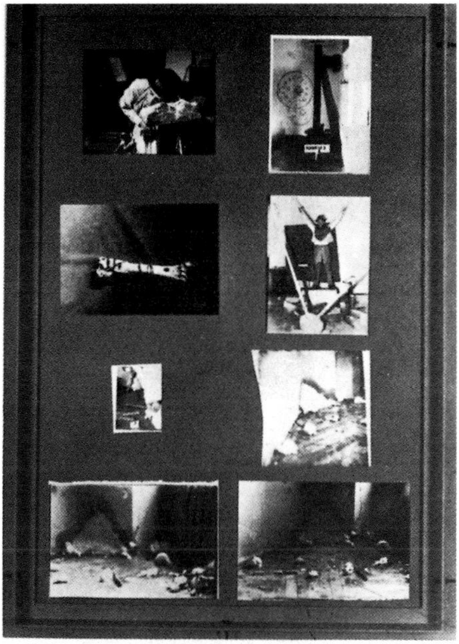

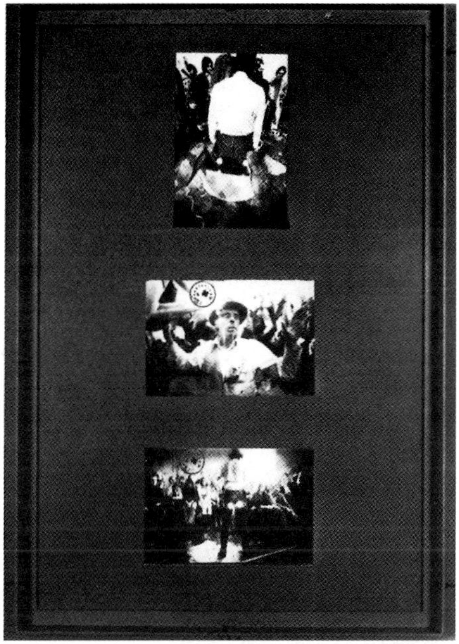

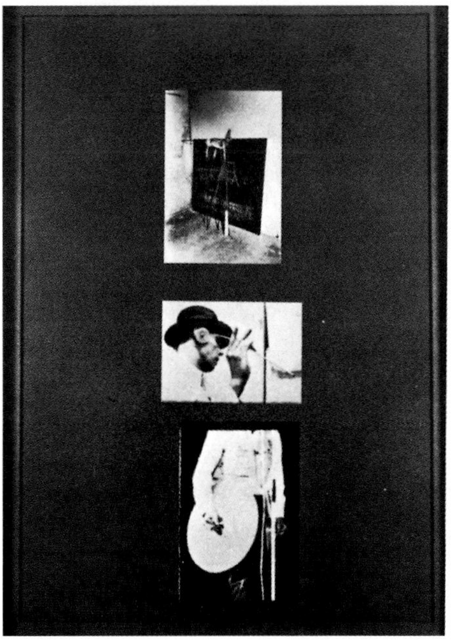

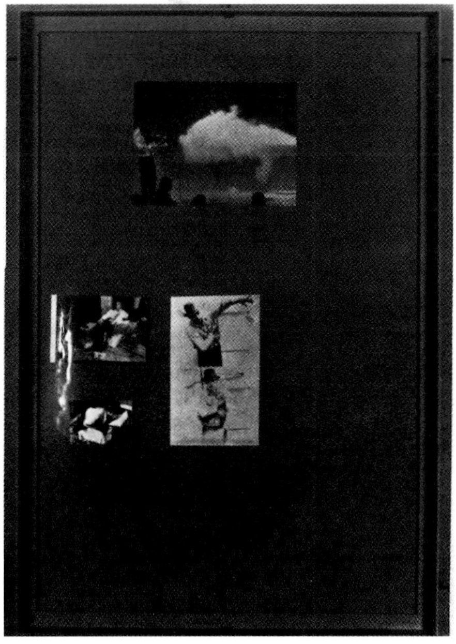

marcel broodthaers

London, November 15th, 1973
Dear Madam,
I don't know how to contribute to the book you are preparing. What I have done so far presents itself under a peculiarly baroque form. Every object (paintings, films and statements) places itself in different series which are not simply opposed to each other. These series try to follow and sometimes to precede the various artistic fashions of the last ten years. Art constitutes a platform on which I occupy a place, having the feeling I have nothing to say. (It would be a real pity if this proved to be wrong. Some of my strongly committed friends want to convince me of this.) However, here is the reproduction of a detail of a small painting I purchased in a curio shop which is located in the heart of that new Montmartre which the 6th arrondissement has become. This painting is the subject of a film and a book which will very shortly come out.
My best regards,

Marcel Broodthaers

N.B. I would be grateful if you didn't publish my biography, nor bibliography, or my age or even my place of residence; please limit my contribution to a double page according to the enclosed instructions.

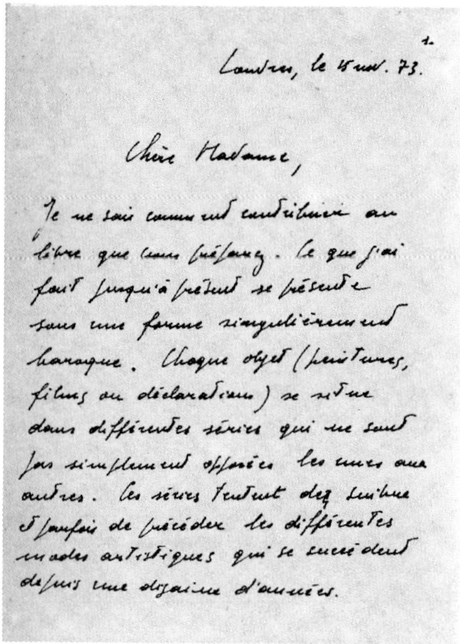
1.

Londres, le 15 nov. 73.

Chère Madame,

Je ne sais comment contribuer au livre que vous préparez. Ce que j'ai fait jusqu'à présent se présente sous une forme singulièrement baroque. Chaque objet (peintures, films ou déclarations) se situe dans différentes séries qui ne sont pas simplement opposées les unes aux autres. Les séries tentent de simuler et parfois de précéder les différentes modes artistiques qui se succèdent depuis une douzaine d'années.

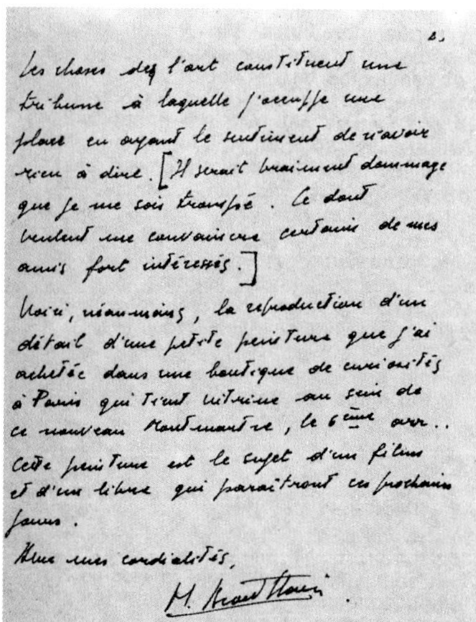
2.

Les choses de l'art constituent une tribune à laquelle j'occupe une place en ayant le sentiment de n'avoir rien à dire. [Il serait vraiment dommage que je me sois trompé. Ce dont veulent me convaincre certains de mes amis fort intéressés.]

Voici, néanmoins, la reproduction d'un détail d'une petite peinture que j'ai achetée dans une boutique de curiosités à Paris qui tient vitrine au sein de ce nouveau Montmartre, le 6ème arr.. Cette peinture est le sujet d'un film et d'un livre qui paraîtront ces prochains jours.

Avec mes cordialités,

M. Broodthaers.

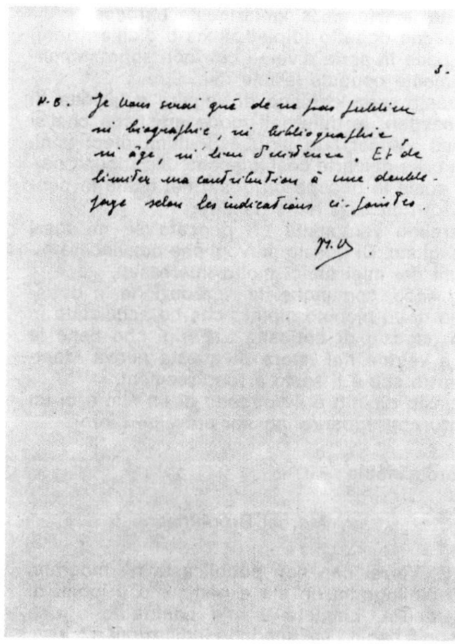
3.

N.B. Je vous serai gré de ne pas publier ni biographie, ni bibliographie, ni âge, ni lieu d'existence. Et de limiter ma contribution à une double-page selon les indications ci-jointes.

M.B.

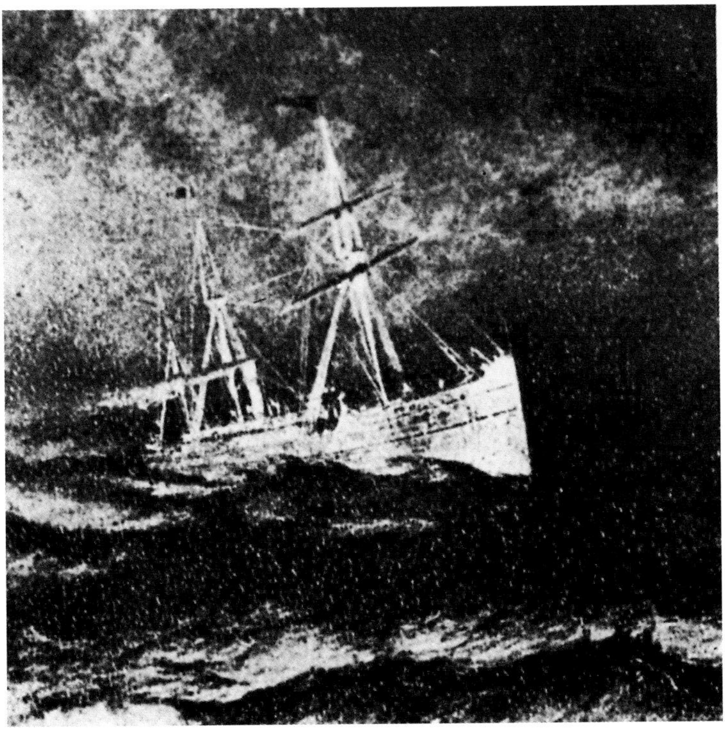

trisha brown

Group Primary Accumulation, 1973

… In the past five years I have been associated with the construction of mammoth props and technical systems that enable human beings to walk on walls, walk down a seven-story building or appear to be free falling or suspended in neutral space—works in which the main preoccupations are anti-gravity and ordinary movement appearing in extraordinary circumstances.

My current work—*Accumulation*—is a solo performance concerned solely with movements—no props, no music. The structure of the piece is rigid, the movement predetermined. Repetition has the effect of blurring the image, much as a word repeated over and over again loses its original meaning—ocean becoming notion, etc.

The performance is a live process of keeping vigil over the integrity of each gesture.

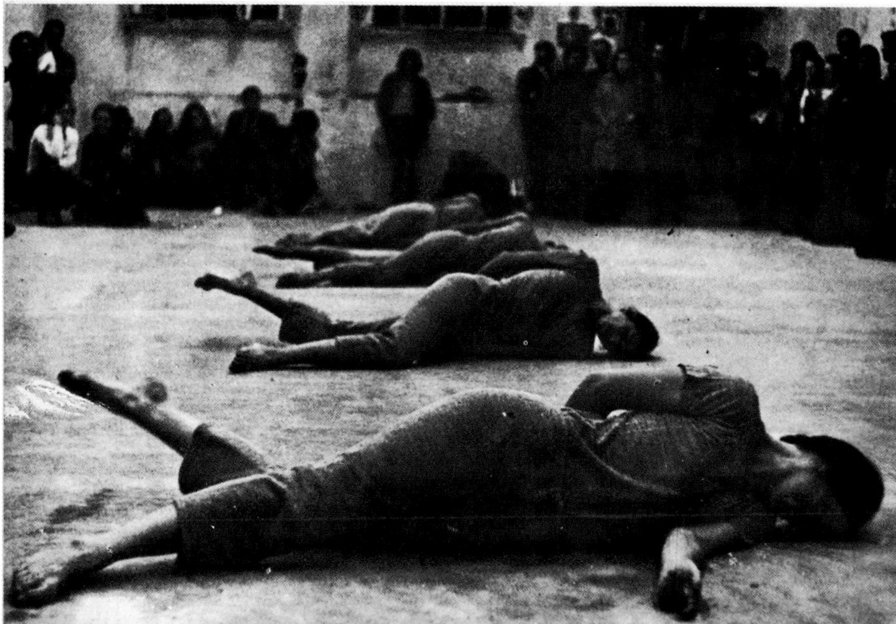

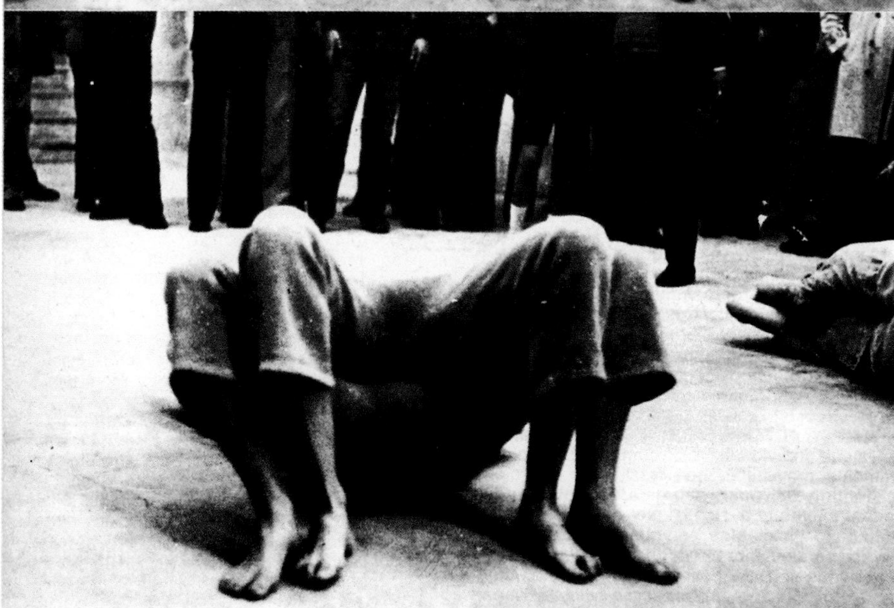

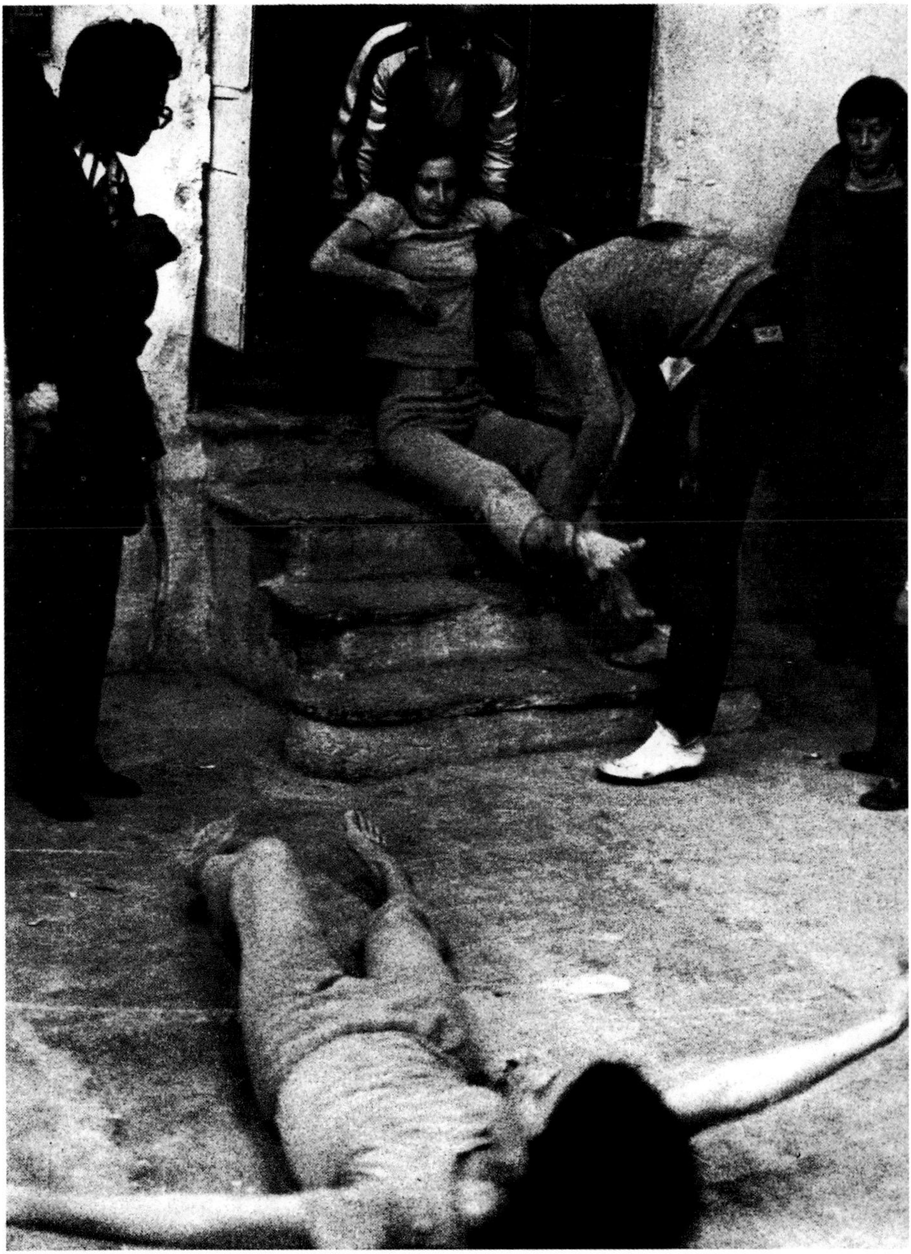

günter brus

Ana, 1964
A movable feast…
A happy, pleasant, languid life…
The water is flowing. A duck is swimming on the water.
The so-called undertow swirls around. Aquatic birds glide by quickly.
Far off, a pebble drops into the water: another undertow.
The sky is full of stars. The bespectacled ones are looking up.
Some think that the celestial bodies are dragged by art.
A double paragraph indicates Jupiter's bottom.
Strange, someone is lying over there, someone turns, he scratches
himself because he is itchy. A beautiful piece of horizon,
if one looks around.
Splintered night eyeglasses. Light penetrates inside them.
In front of the first zone
the one near the first man
is singing in the second row
a song for vagabonds
and this melody sounds
like the "consecration of reality."
What evidence! What a start for the artists who find themselves
in front of the door which is opening! And an anonymous participant
in the feast, in a dignified manner, arrests his neighbor:
a chain reaction!
(You didn't happen to hear about "little bodies"?…)

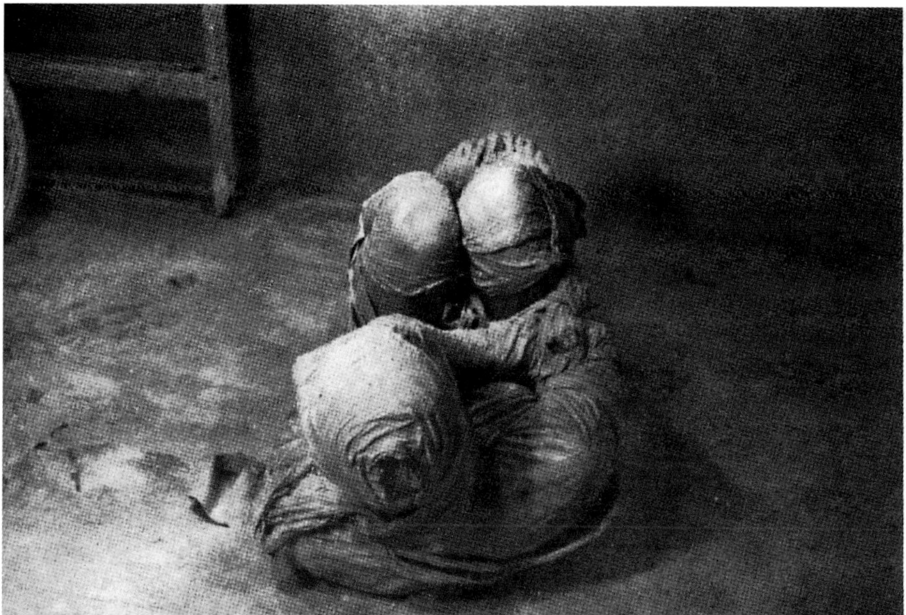

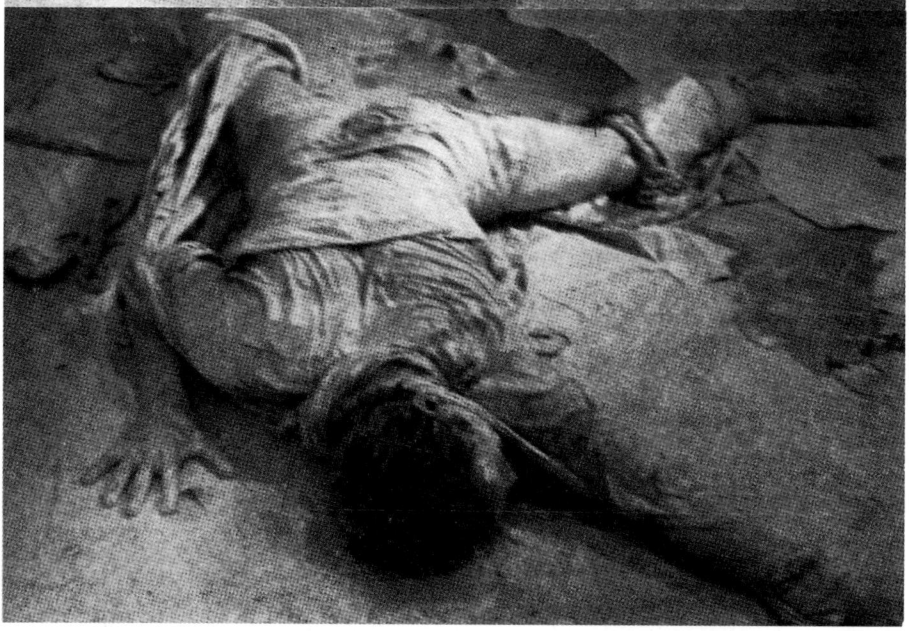

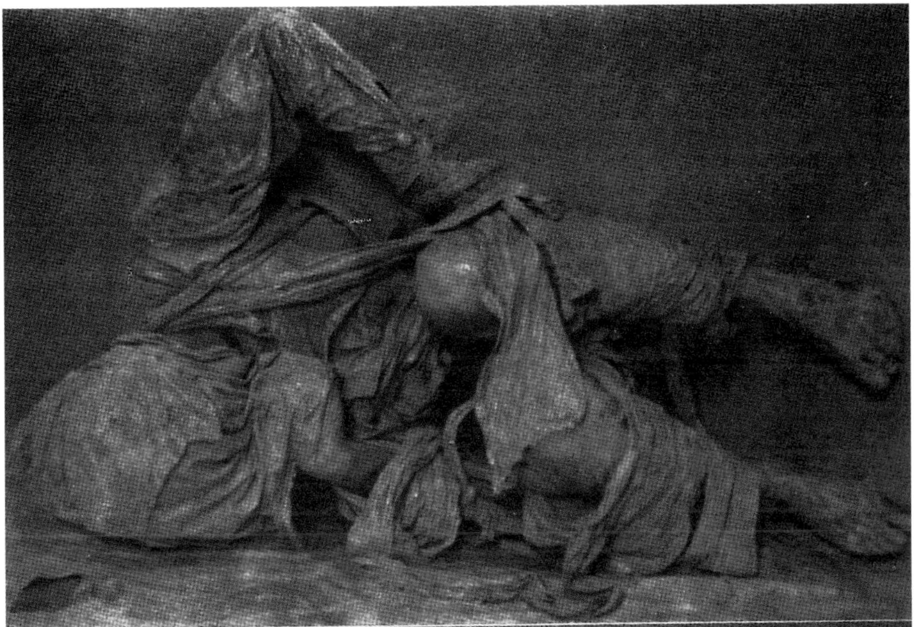

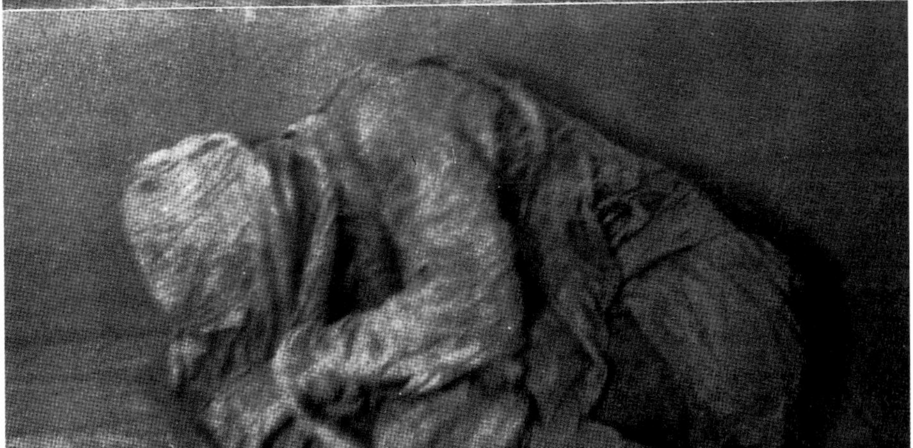

enrico bugli

The Search for the Ideal, 1972–73
Object to be acted upon: 54 wooden boards shaped by hand, tied with a 3 mm nylon cord, of unfinished fir, 20 × 220 × 1.8 cm; the length of the mounted object is 12 m, composed of two sections of 6 m each.

Use of object: two people undress themselves and place the object in various positions interacting with it, as the camera repeats the images of the performance on a 150 × 120 cm screen, placed 230 cm from the ground, to underline the tautology and the changes in their behavior, provoked and caused by the object.

The object is a pretext for stimulating behaviors which are completely different from what may be predicted from the spectator, who is an indispensable element in this true poetic monument to the useless. In this, although we can expect a natural pendular motion between cynicism and sincerity, we cannot exclude a point of transition where, as a matter of fact, the individual can try to force his own audience to judge him according to the fixed image of his so-called wickedness, which the object corroborates by constantly insinuating that the effectiveness of the interpretation proposed (see: tautology) is somehow illusory.

Besides, there is the old question of deception, which here becomes a suspicion of violent negation of the roles. The (physical) coercion is such, that once involved in the action, one becomes an actor, of necessity, offered to the sadism of the author. "Professions, for which the audience has a solid respect, often allow trespassing into cynicism, sometimes not to deceive their own audience (their statements can never be taken as valid ones), but because they can use this cynicism as a means to isolate the most intimate part of themselves from contact with the spectators." The latter are, in any case, misled by the double image, which comes as a commentary aside, but which ends up by being the only representative element—that is, a sadistic one.

The performance *The Search for the Ideal* lasts twenty minutes and is projected on a screen two meters high; in the dark behind the screen, two nude figures repeat the action of the film; the soundtrack by Caruso and me is obtained with two tape recorders which are placed in two corners at one hand of the room and run simultaneously.

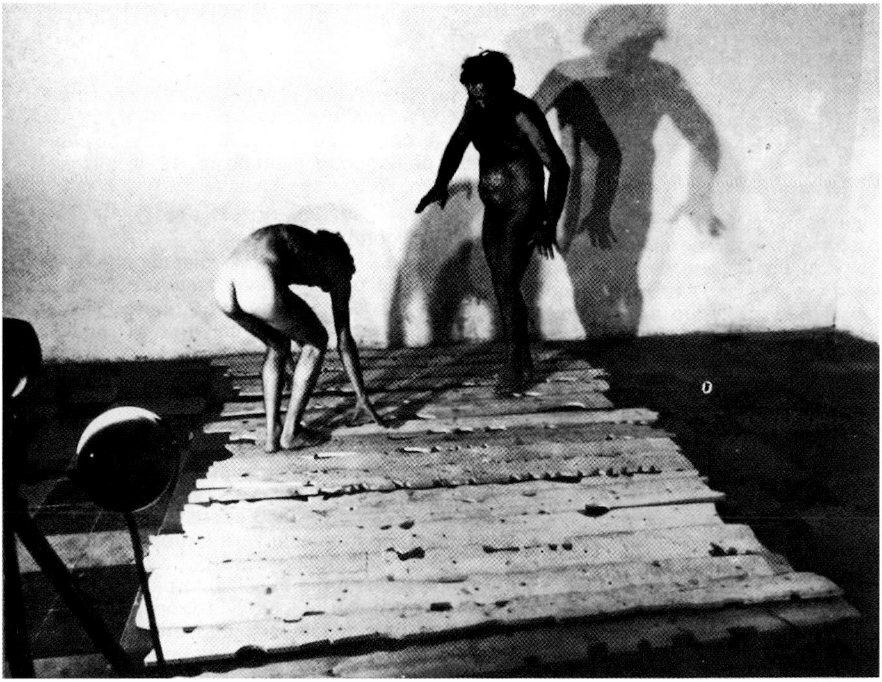

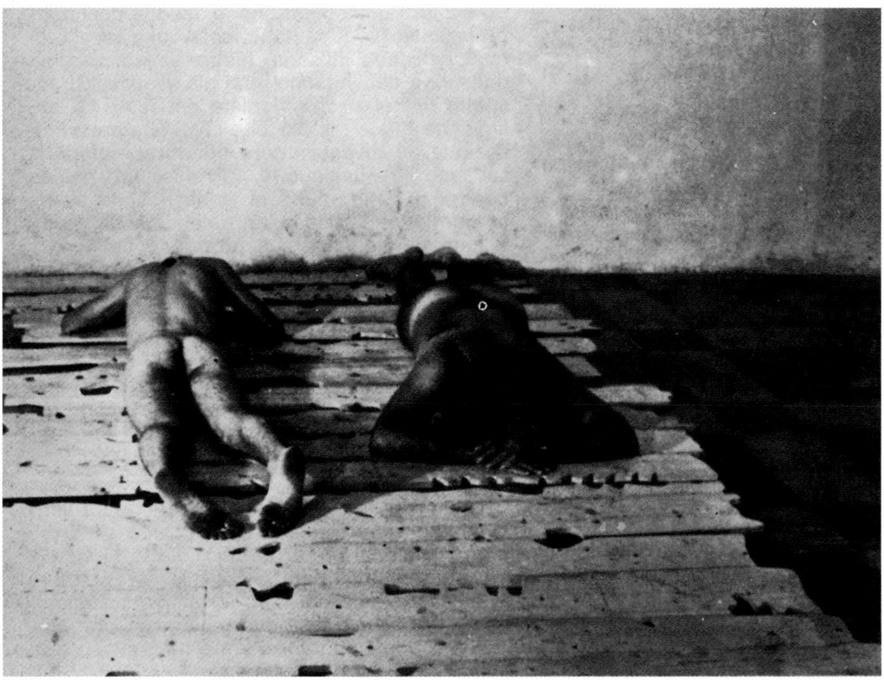

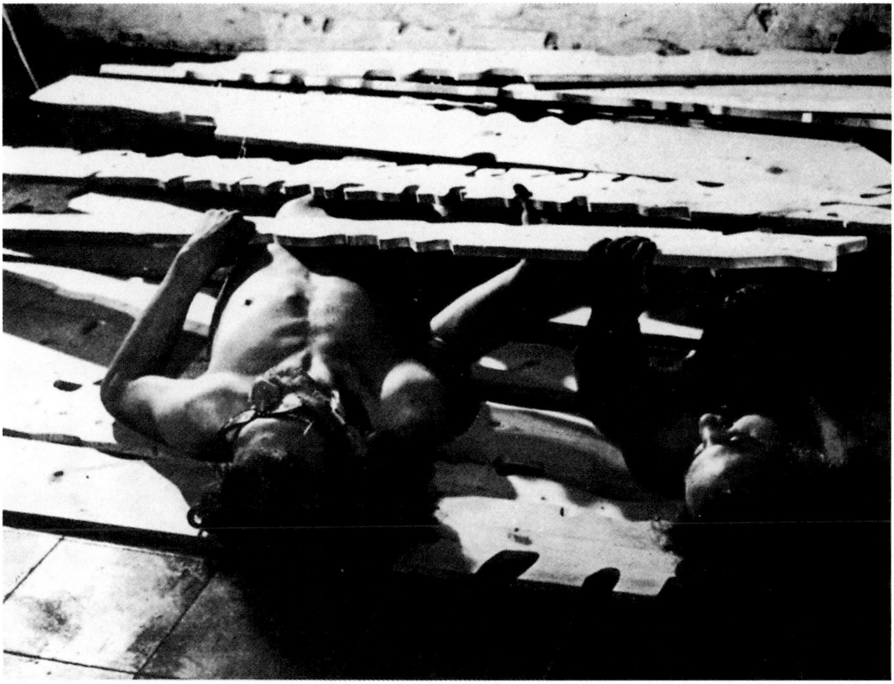

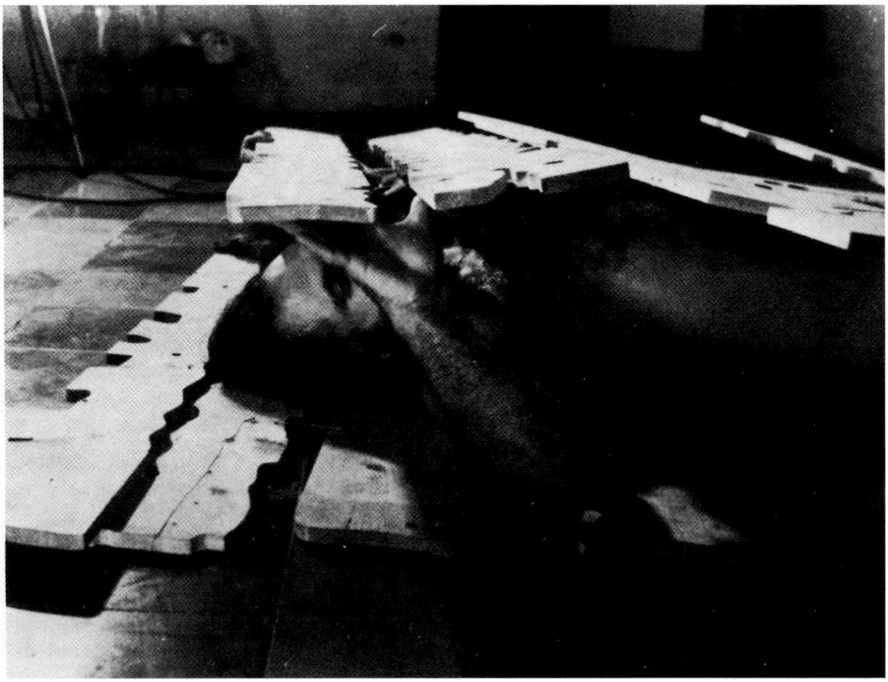

pierpaolo calzolari

Action, 1972
… as for the explanatory text for my action, I am sorry, but it is not my habit to accompany my work with texts.

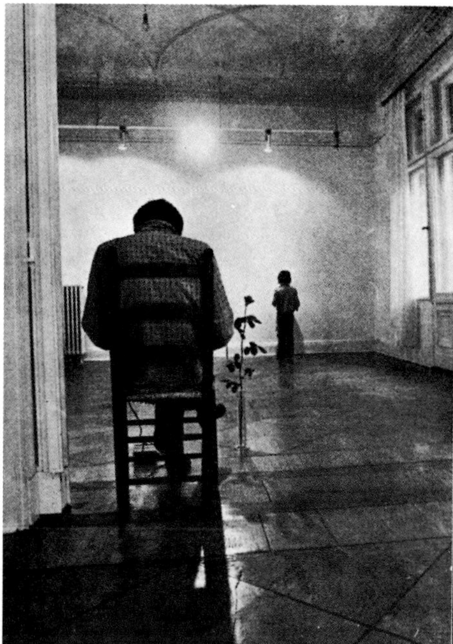

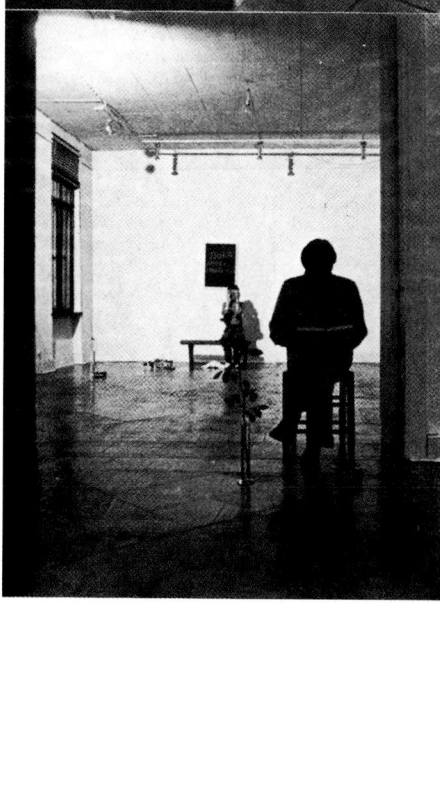

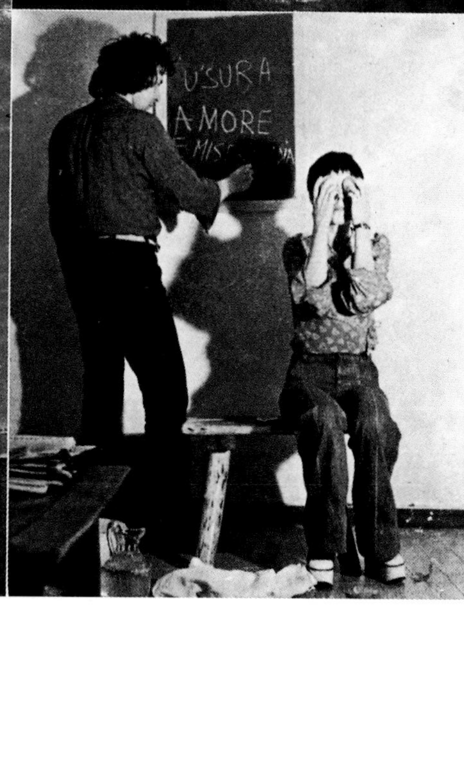
U'SURA
A MORE

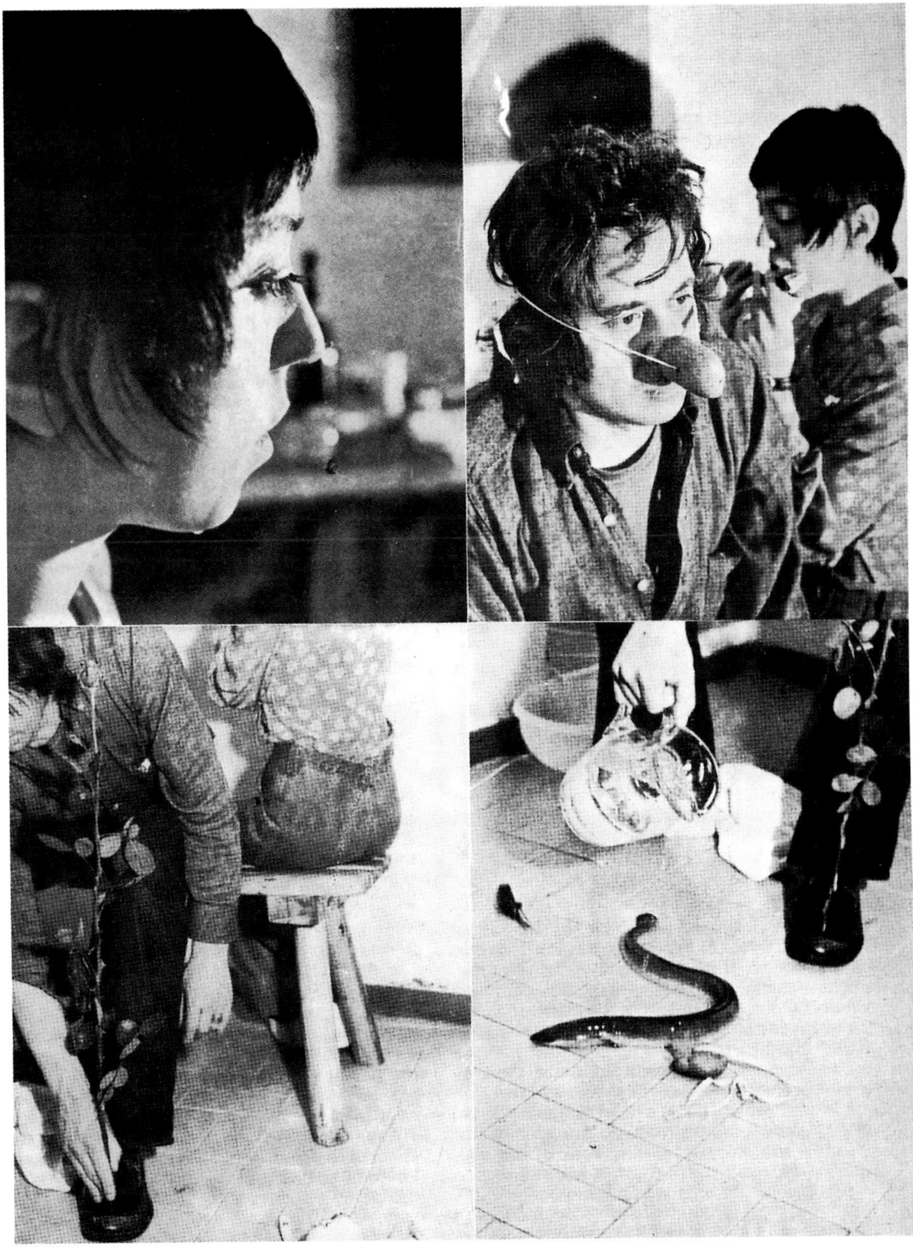

cioni carpi

I do not believe it is possible to talk about just one or two of my films (even if I omit a whole period, from 1960 to 1965, of experimental films) without also speaking of others which are their premise, or element of continuity. And particularly I would like to mention three films (*Dog*, *Rat*, *Puzzle*) of 3 to 4 minutes each, whose frames cannot be reproduced other than by projection, since the visually recognizable part of these films, which lasts a few seconds, is the key to their interpretation, that is, the element of shock which must act on the body of the spectator. So, I will start precisely with these non-reproducible films in which the recognizable sequences present situations of violence (with a meaning of bullying) that goes from the kind of violence which still leaves a margin for struggle, to total violence. In each of these three films the recognizable sequence is preceded and followed by about two minutes of imageless projection. It is inevitable that during the first part of "zero" projection the spectators' behavior will vary from individual to individual: from expectation, to boredom, to agitation, to irritation, to a hypnotic state, to thinking about one's own affairs, to hatred toward the artist, and so on. To sum up, this part of non-happening should help to detach spectators from the reality surrounding them, to free them from defined contexts, to make them available for any possibility. But from the very moment when these different inner attitudes recompose themselves thanks to the short recognizable sequence, the spectators' behavior should change by conforming to a common model through cognitive processes (curiosity, attention, reflection, etc.), since the received information of violence will be stored and elaborated by the

spectators according to homogeneous modes and quantities,
and the visual happening will be transformed into political awareness.
Therefore, during the second part of imageless projection the
spectators will have all the time they need to reflect, perhaps even upon
the impossibility of eluding the existential obligation—rather than the
nature of the existential problem—and the danger of evading objective
reality, which today seems to be merely a question of violence.
And these are truly active palimpsests.

Egg One Egg Zero, 1972
From a hole in the ground I unearth the last egg, I drink it,
I carefully bury its remains again. A situation of non-hope:
"to hope for something" must be replaced by "to fight for something"
(hope, as we know, is the last and the worst sin in Pandora's box).

Two Feet One Foot Underground, 1972
I dig a hole one foot deep and I bury my feet in it, I sit down
and I stop moving. An admission of impotence, of incapacity,
of insufficiency (but the admission is in itself awareness).
After the film was shot, the fact of having unearthed my feet,
although with a certain effort, was already a step in the right direction.
These films have no soundtrack, since sound must be taken for granted
(sea, wind, etc.), otherwise it would become an arbitrary and strongly
conditioning element, exactly as the "silence" is in the three films
described at the beginning.

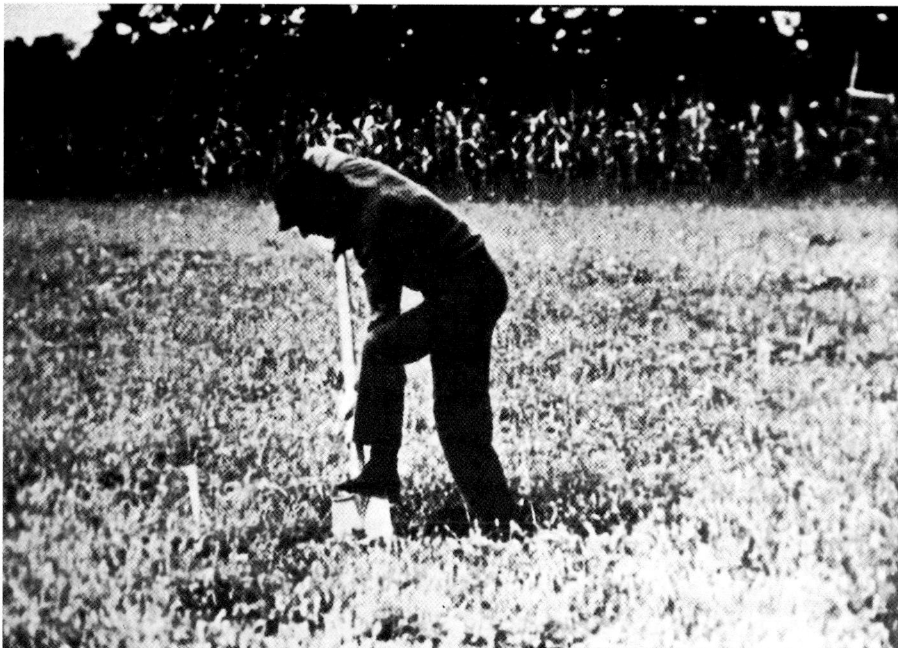

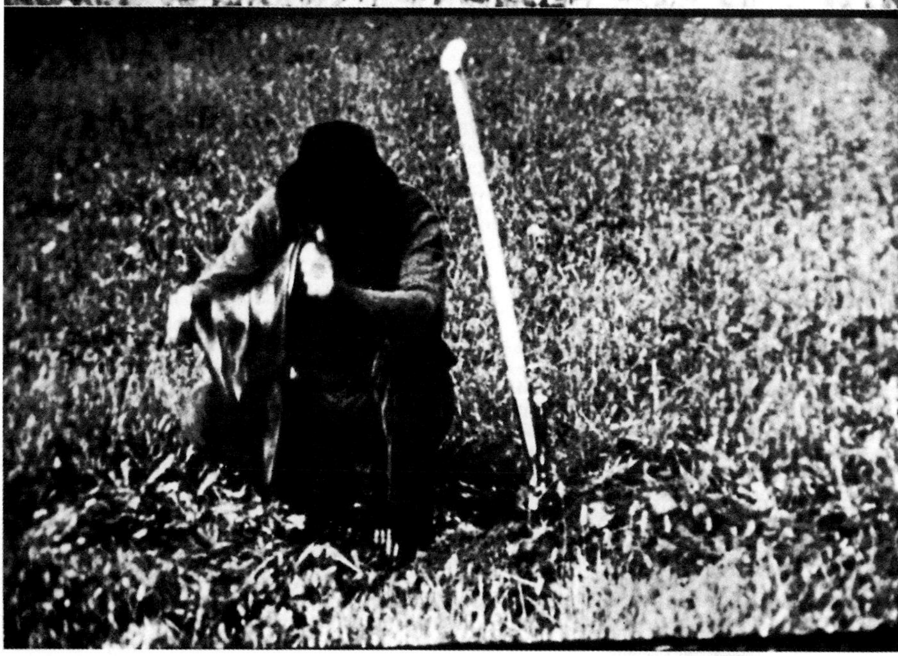

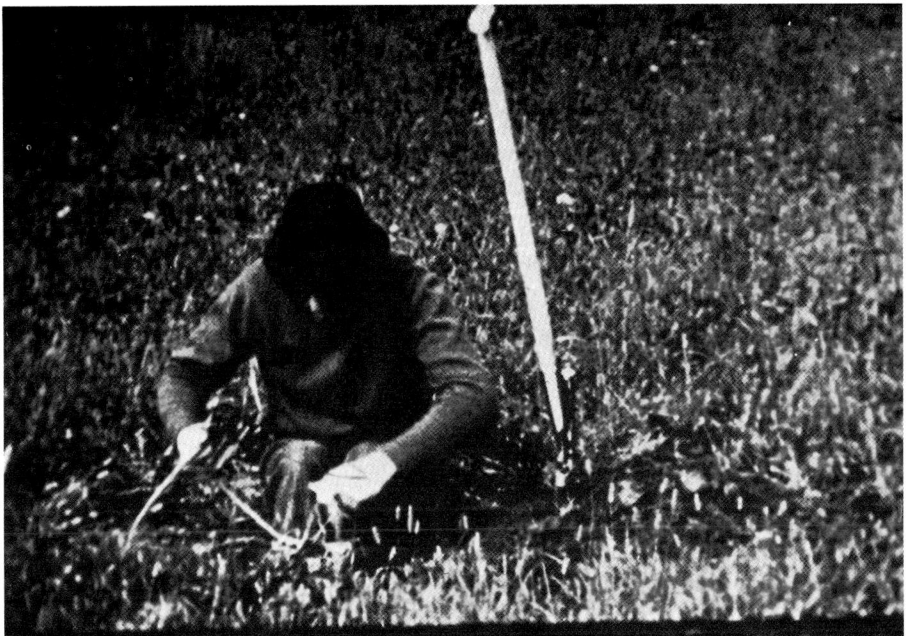

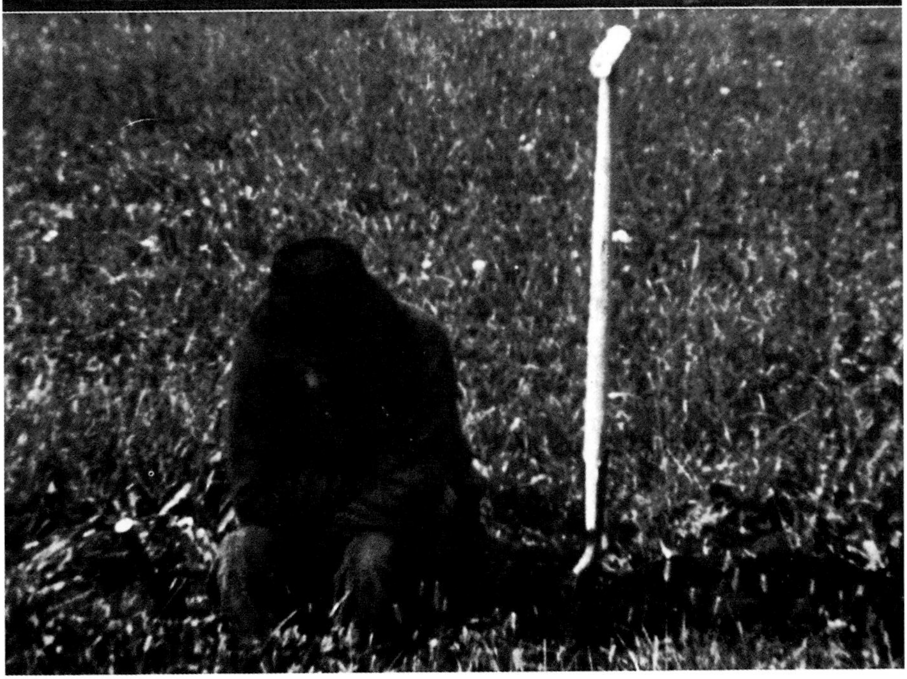

giuseppe chiari

Concert for Woman, 1968
Gestures on the Piano, 1972

I have written pieces for the human body such as *Concert for Woman* (1968) and *Doing Something with One's Body and the Wall* (1966). In the first one, the main part consists of soft, extremely varied noises which can be obtained by blowing into a woman's hair. In the second one, any variation whatsoever is right; as long as noises are produced by beating one's body against the wall.

However, I want to make it clear that as far as I am concerned the body is a thing like anything else. I have written pieces for the woman, but also for the bicycle, for the necklace, for the tape-recorder, for the TV set, for the city, for a sheet of paper, for a stone, for anything whatsoever. Perhaps the piece in which the human body has the most important function is *Gestures on the Piano*. By starting with the hypothesis that the keyboard of a piano is a long white strip, that man does not know the existence of the keys, that man though is aware that whatever gesture he makes, the keyboard will return it as a noise having the same expression, I proposed a whole technique of gestures.

And, in effect, during the years that I performed this piece, my hands, arms, shoulders, and face, had an opportunity to liberate themselves. The same effect was experienced by other performers like Frederic Rzewski, Giancarlo Cardini, Jean Charles François...

Perhaps this was a piece of gestures... a piece for hands, arms, face, shoulders... and the piano underlined only these gestures...

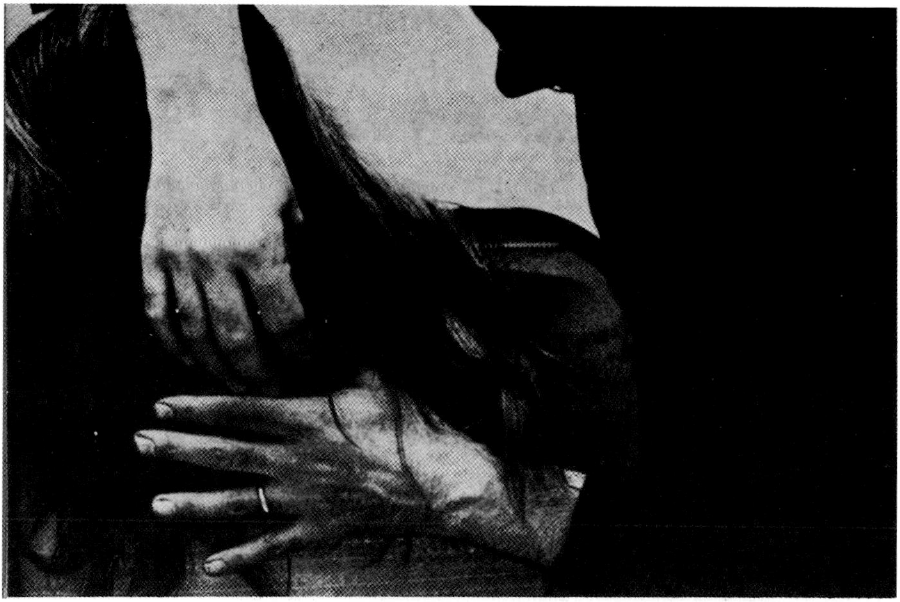

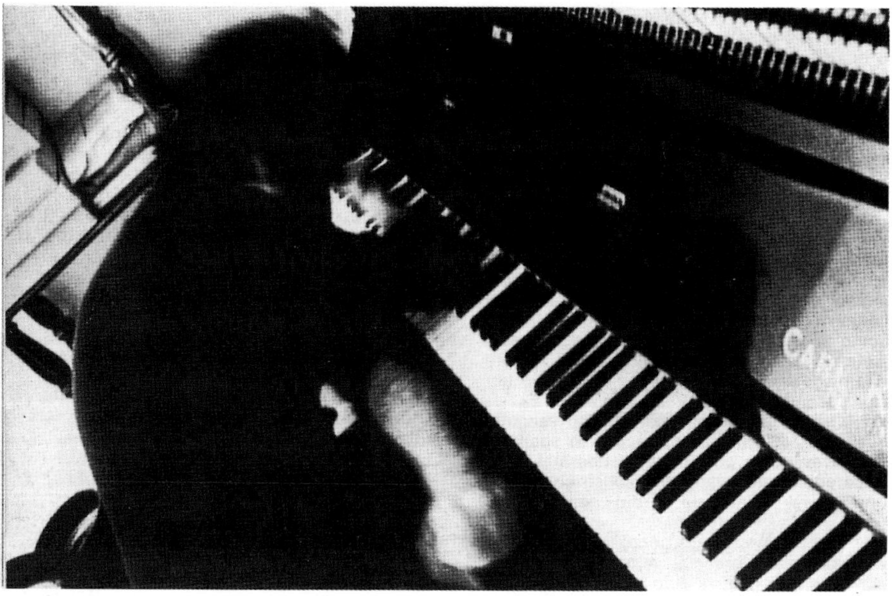

Top
Concert for Woman, 1968

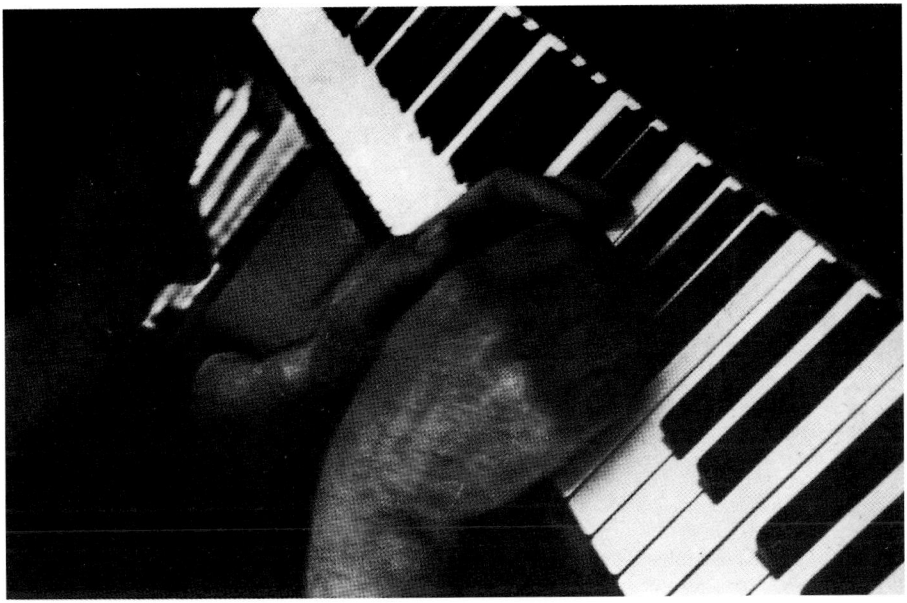

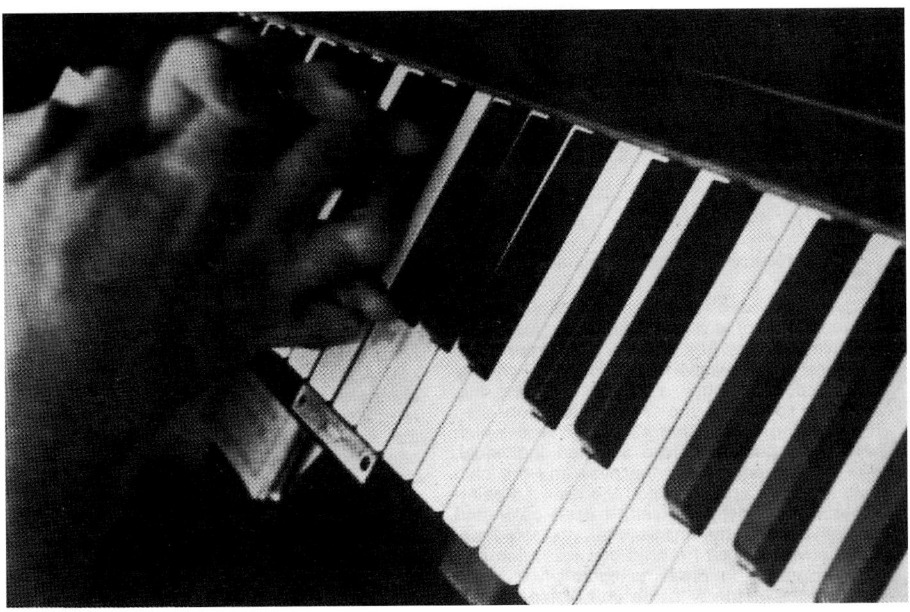

Gestures on the Piano,
1972

giorgio ciam

Attempt to Enrich Ciam's Personality, 1972
Sixteen canvases: one has the photographic reproduction of my face, the other fifteen, on which my image has been printed, reproduce a series of expressive faces for me: Fontana, Duchamp, Pistoletto, a typical murderer, etc. Roughly speaking, my intervention consisted in removing those parts of my face which were not common to the selected individual. The only constants are the eyes and the chin with the scar, around which the drawing/painting operation defined itself. I used color and pencil to obtain the images that interested me. The canvases must be viewed in succession and not separately, in order to establish a continuous comparison with the unit of measure.

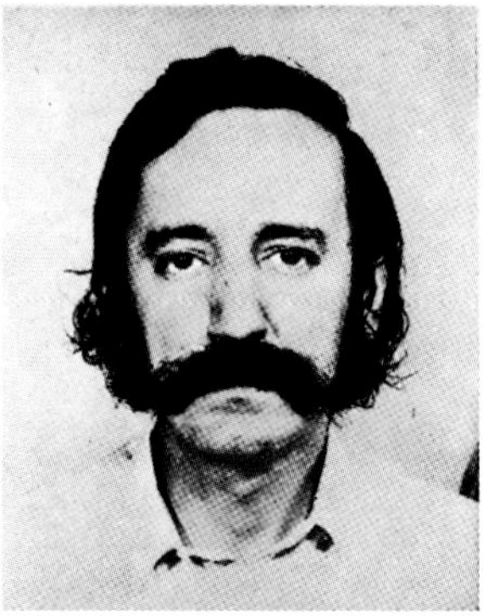
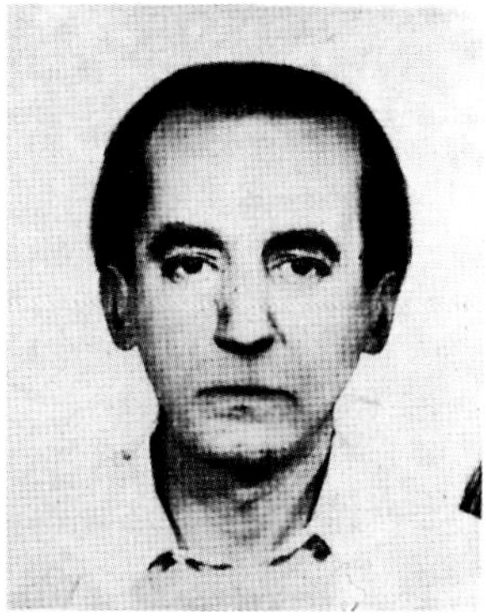
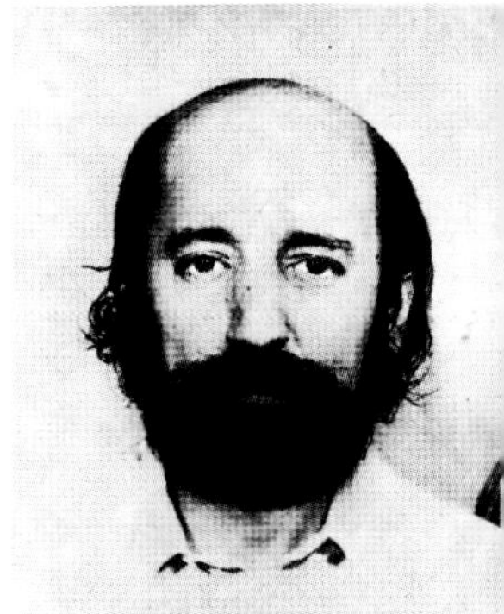
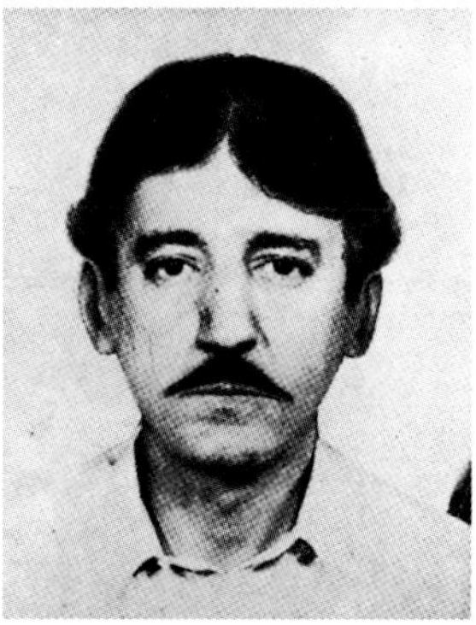
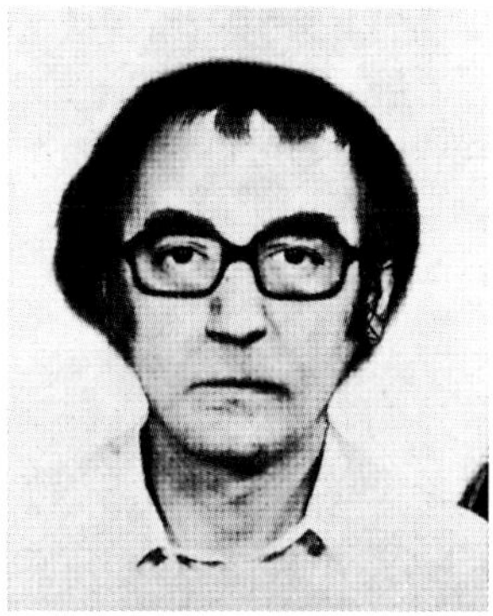
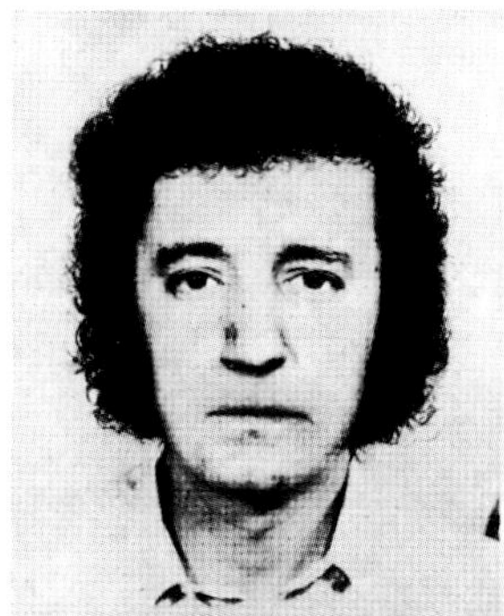
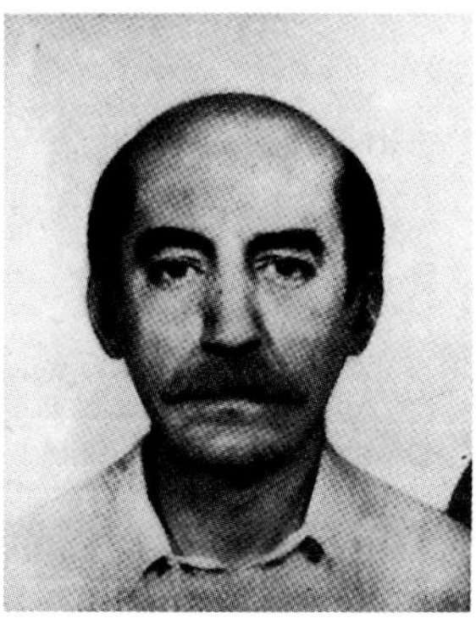
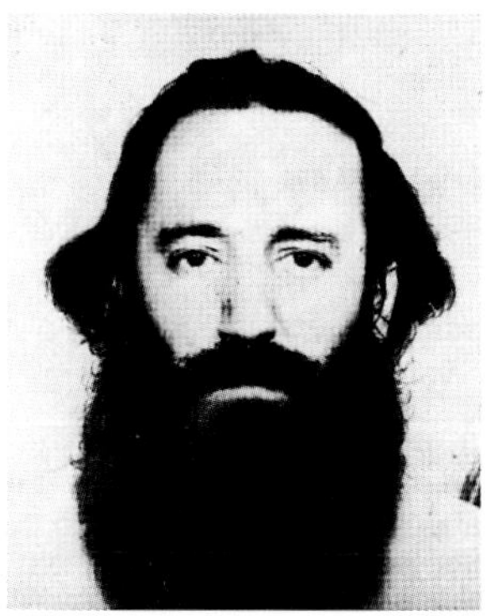
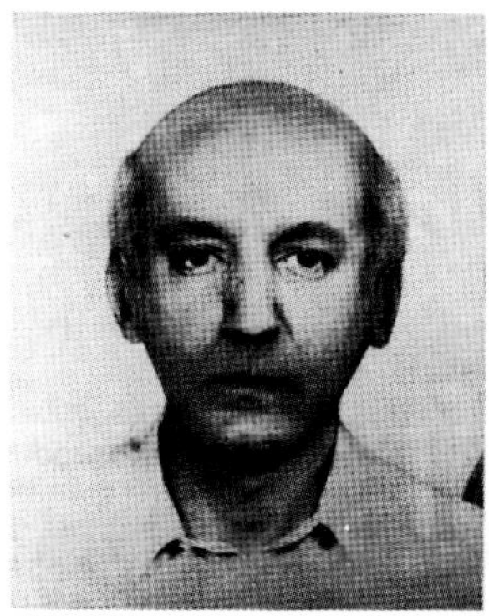

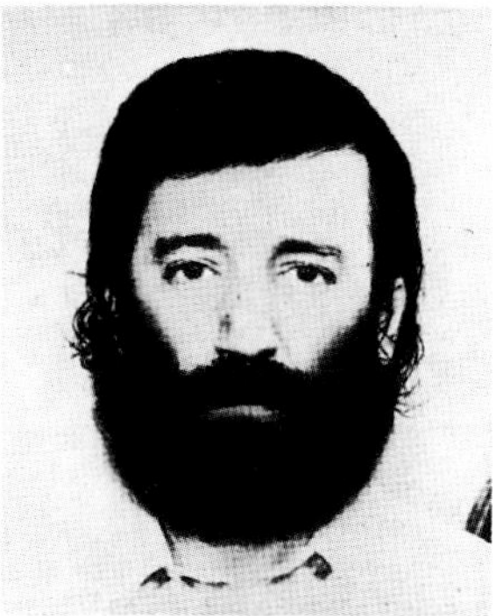

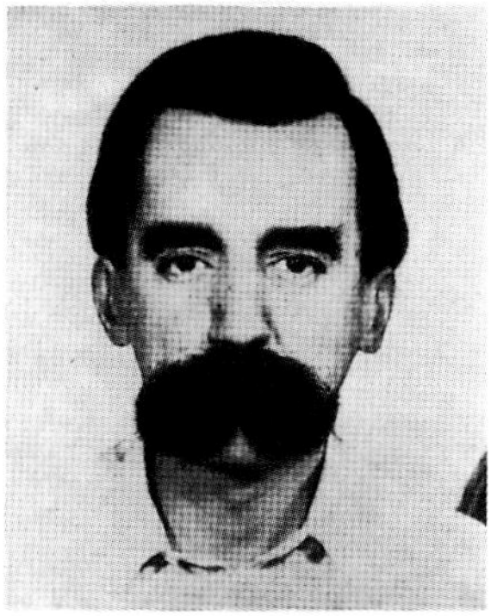

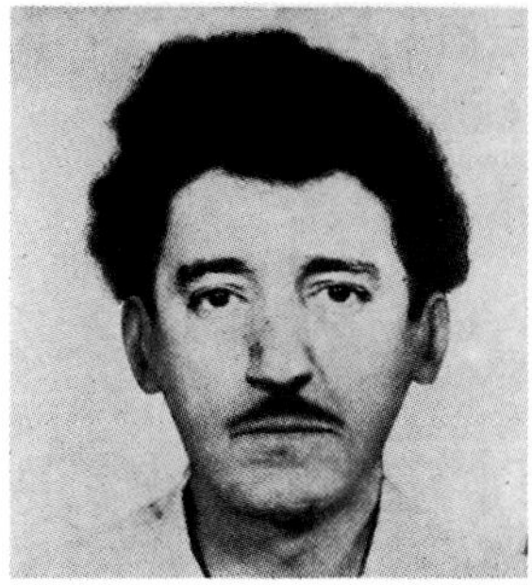

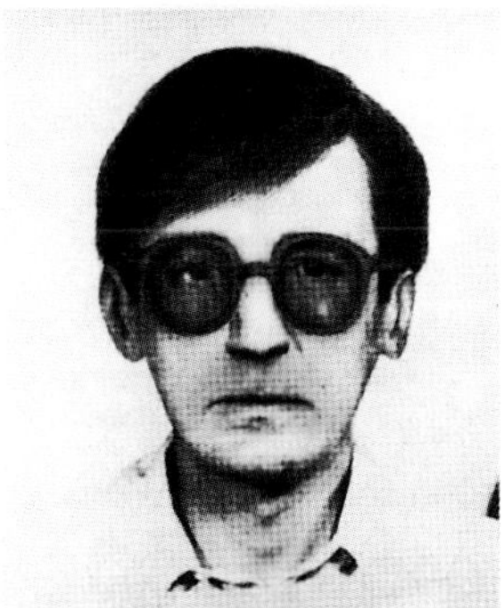

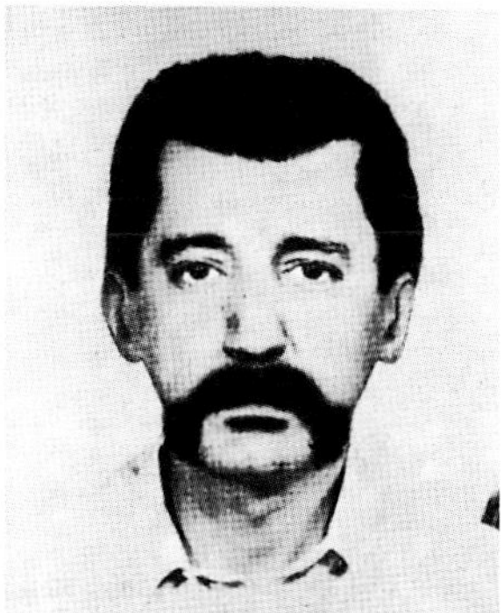

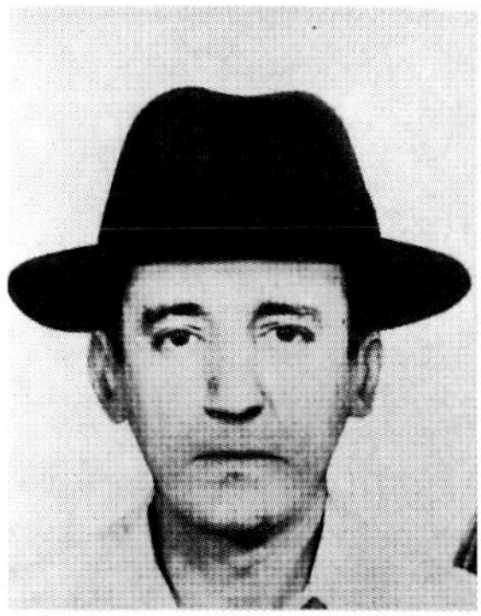

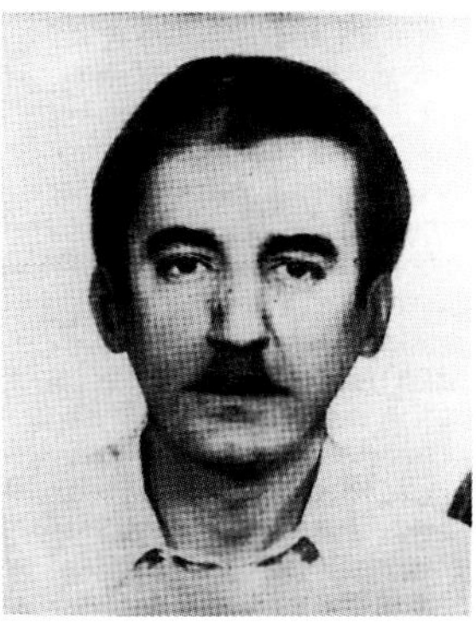

jole de freitas

"Introvert / penetrate
extrovert / penetrate
fear / do not penetrate"
Six photographic sequences, 1973
Using photography as a means of expression interests me inasmuch as it allows me to record the climate of my mental state. My body was photographed by myself; if another person had operated the camera the resulting image would not be that on which I alone must intervene at a given moment. Anybody else's perception would completely change the psychological meaning of the situation. I still need an intense release of feelings and I mean to record more than to document, through a planned image, certain moments which are part of an intimistic research, to reach a better understanding of myself. Such an aim was always present in all my prior activities: first with dance through corporeal expression, then with group analysis through verbal expression and presently by means of recording my image in particular psychic states.
The work I am presenting here, however, does not only involve the recording of what I call a psychic release, because the resulting images are supported by a rational organization which refers to the dialectics of language, as it appears from the contrast between images and words.

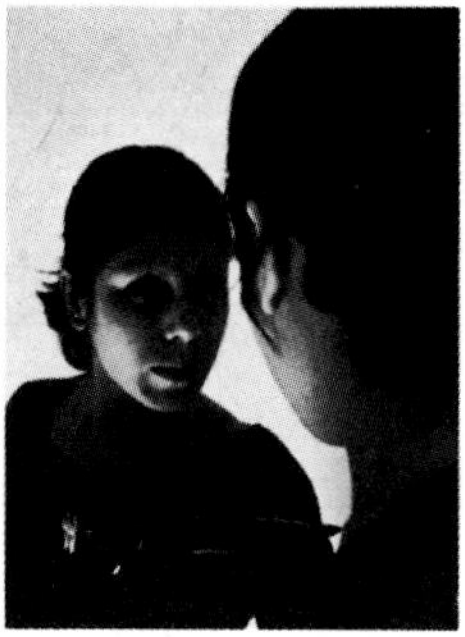

introvert

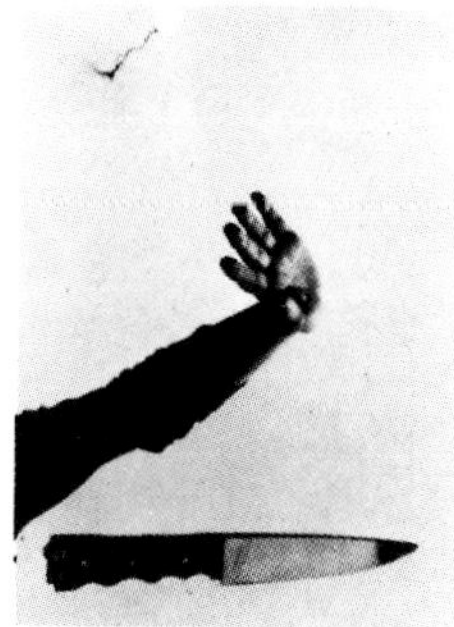

fear

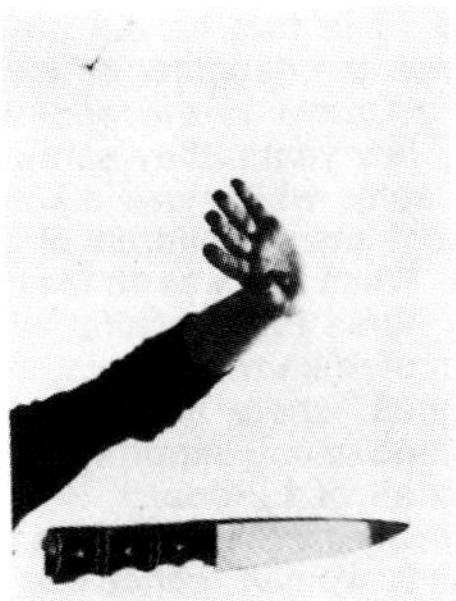

extrovert

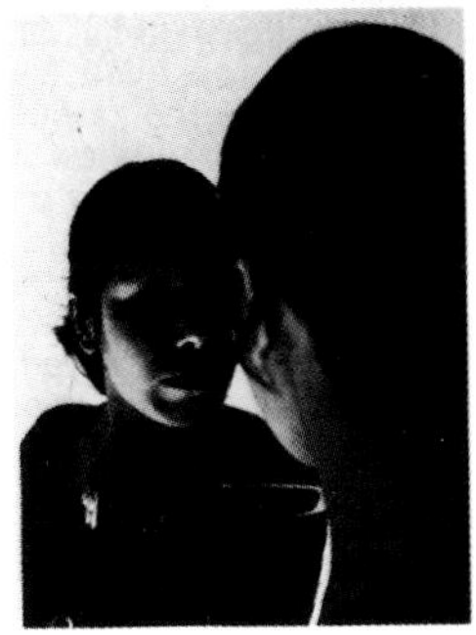

penetrate

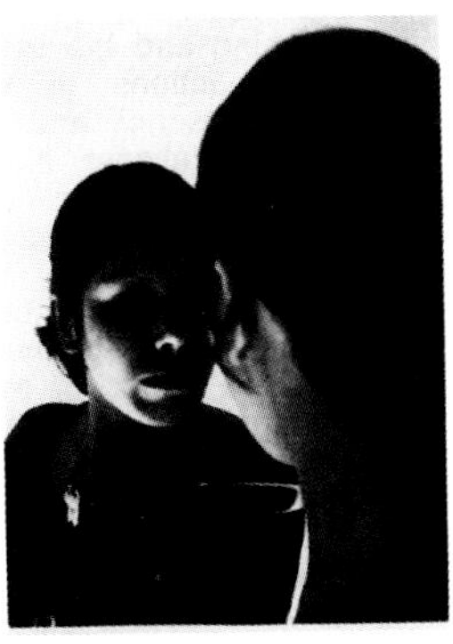

introvert

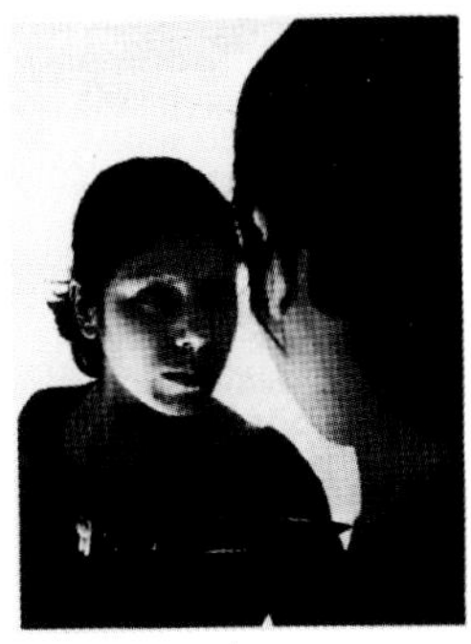

do not penetrate

giuseppe desiato

Rite no. 1, 1964–65

I was born in Naples in 1935 of an unknown father and Clementina Desiato. I became a painter because I did not want to become a tailor. My mother married a man who had four children when I was five years old.

My mother died a short time ago at the Cardarelli Hospital in Naples. I wanted to do something for her so that she would die later, since she was still young and because she had a curable sickness (elevated azotemia). During the preceding years, she used to tell me things about her life and I learned not who my father was —I never met him—but how he died (if in fact he did die).

My mother was the daughter of a parish priest (San Marco La Catola in the province of Foggia). After a few years, they sent her to the Buon Pastore of Naples, an orphanage for priests' and nuns' children. When she was 18 they found a job for her as a nurse in a hospital that looked after children of unknown fathers, in Forcella, Naples area, which was—and still is—the biggest center of smuggling in Europe. In that place my mother conceived me, though I still do not know whether with a tobacconist, a grocer or a doctor from the ward where she worked.

I only know that she was an intelligent woman finding herself in that situation only because of the system in which she lived.

The meaning of my work is not separate from the sum of problems

and experiences lived first by my mother and then by myself. I think that these situations are determined by the contradictions of the system in which we live. It is useless to try to construct only with reference to the future: it is important to take the past into account as well, and construct for the future through the past and the present.
My works have—and it can't be otherwise—meanings and feelings linking them to matters of lived and handed-down life. Personal and individual possibilities aside, it is always the force of logic and the weakness of contradictions in a system which decide and produce, in part, certain behaviors.
If an artist chooses to reduce or shorten the course of the path, without taking into account the rules of the system or even the progressive logic toward revolution, he does nothing but destroy the truth and reality which must be produced, lived and absorbed.
It is useless to improvise schemes and formulas in order to invent a new path. One must follow the course that I and others followed in order to go beyond the one of our predecessors.
The problem is certainly political. I quoted the facts related to myself because through them certain reasons and modes of artistic praxis can be shown.
I have never been able to have one-man shows because no one ever wanted to, or could show my things. I have only participated in group shows.

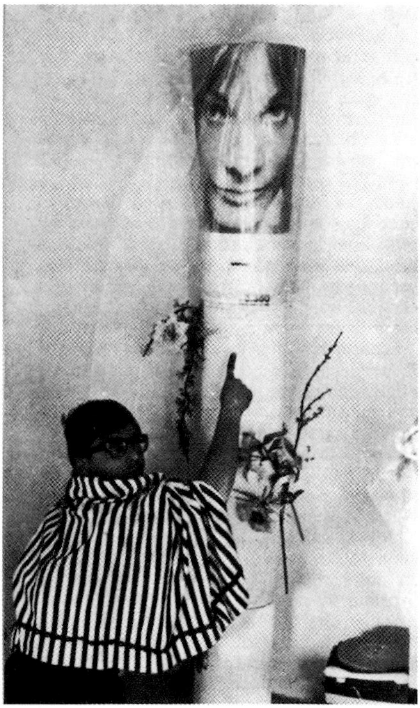

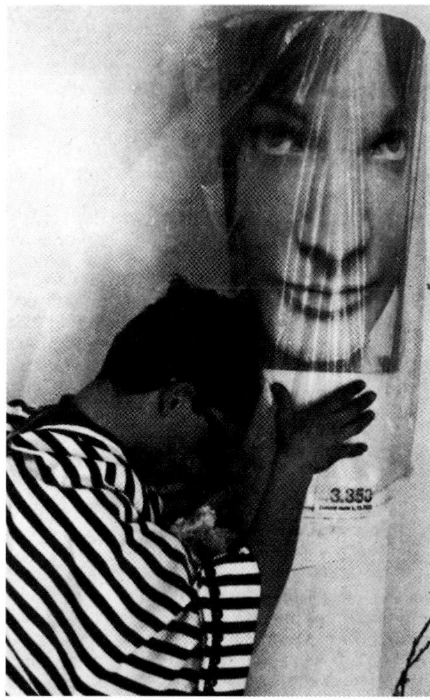
3.350

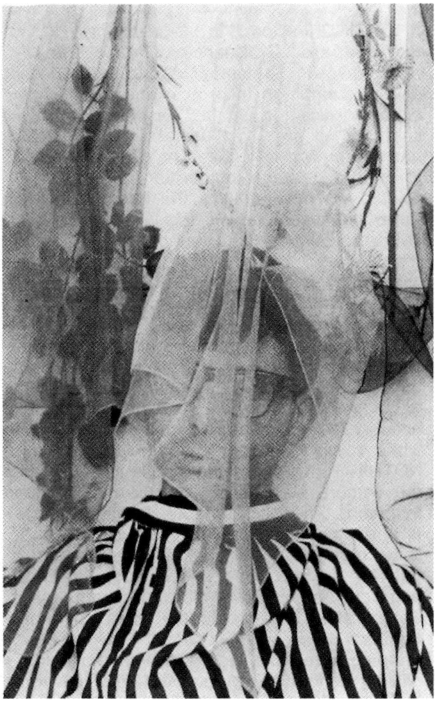

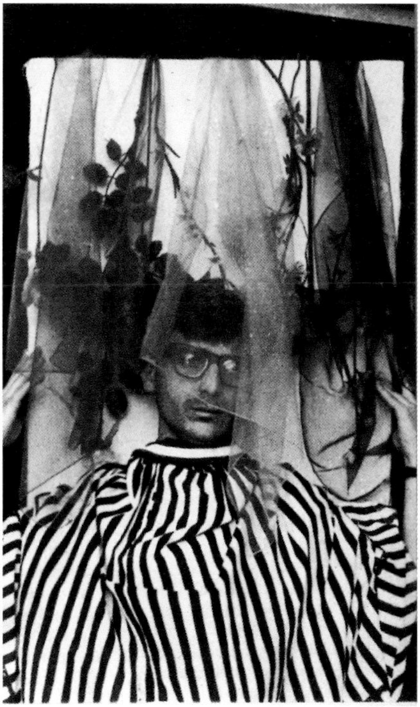

alain d'hooghe

Art / Garbage, 1970–73
Shooting: first part, in Liège in April 1970, at the Galerie du Croissant d'or—second part, near Wavre in September during the period of a lively campaign to protest against the city's expansion.
In fact, a bulldozer driver said to me: "It's useless, the population has finally won its cause, the city has decided to build a garbage incinerator."
Should we now analyze the intentions which led me to make a film three years ago? I arrive at the gallery with this old movie camera.
It's a child's game. We'll shoot a film. No screenplay. Nothing.
We ask people on the street, "Would you please drop off this garbage at the gallery, while..." Their indolence revolts us.
A heap of bricks, a construction they don't dare blow up. The camera is running through our veins. A dog has shitted in the gallery.
The smell of eyes popping out of heads. We are ready to roll on the ground while vomiting absolute words. In a word: NOTHING.
No screenplay, nothing.
Only then the camera starts shooting.
Like a profound initiation. The body shouts, twists, falters, explodes.
But life goes on. Far from art, no doubt, but it's life that counts.
We hang some garbage out of the windows, old underpants, chairs.

Empty bottles instead of the laundry. Space is in a state of chaos. One hears the grinding of teeth, regurgitating manure that's stirring and warming up, asphyxiating but nonetheless virginal, the flashing images of an epoch which is passing from the liquid to the solid state. The spirit forms a rind and cheese is not absent from art. Camembert, brie, bleu… skull bones growing moldy invade everything. There's no art at this moment. There's only life. There's a phallus breathing in the air. Perhaps there's the idea of Heliogabalus who's about to arrive. The phallus feels heavy above the testicles. Art is a big temptation. Or rather poetry. One makes love badly and is happy there is art in order to complete his ejaculation, in the absolute sense. Then one day, a woman and I, making love—but we don't care any longer, our bodies clutched and rolled up, dismay in the depths of our eyes. The camera like a cold black dagger that gives us the shivers… It's a jump into a car for initiates (about whom we'll speak later), a car that darkens space, the latter seems to have been struck by a brain tumor. In the slippery night, where frogs are vomited… it's the embarking of a woman still quite naked, a camera-priapus, a length of film, the brain of a spectral man who is shivering. We must shoot a film. It's no use insisting. All have understood that everything started in the places where we are shooting. Nothing was foreseen.

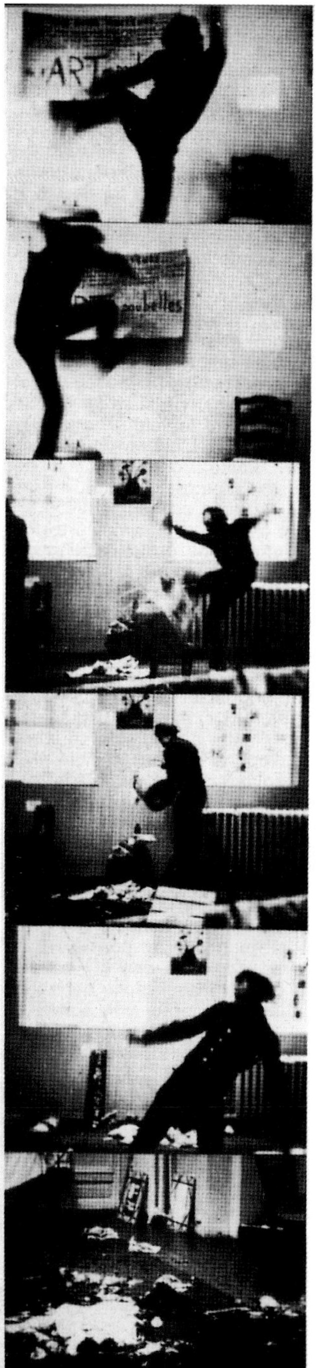
ART
poubelles

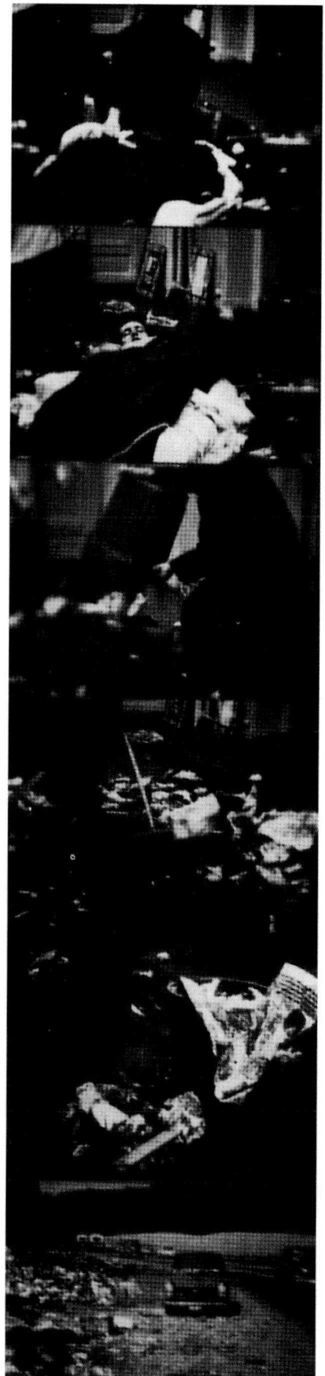

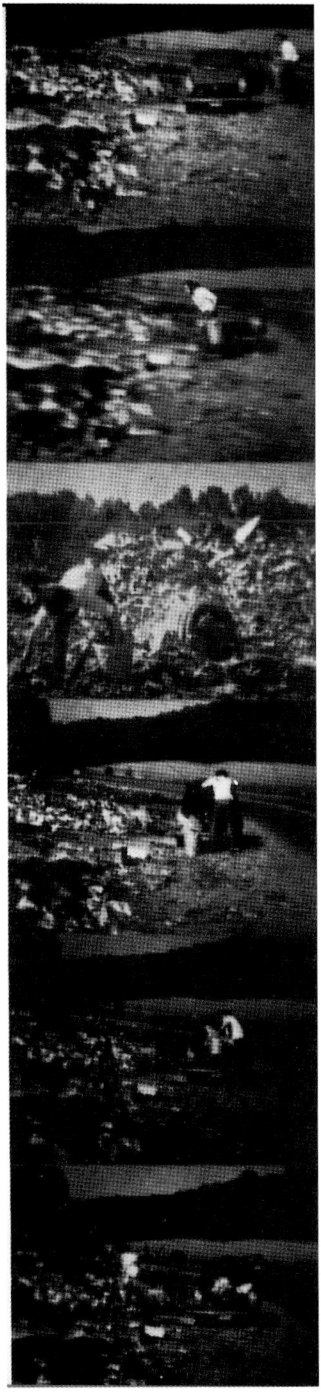

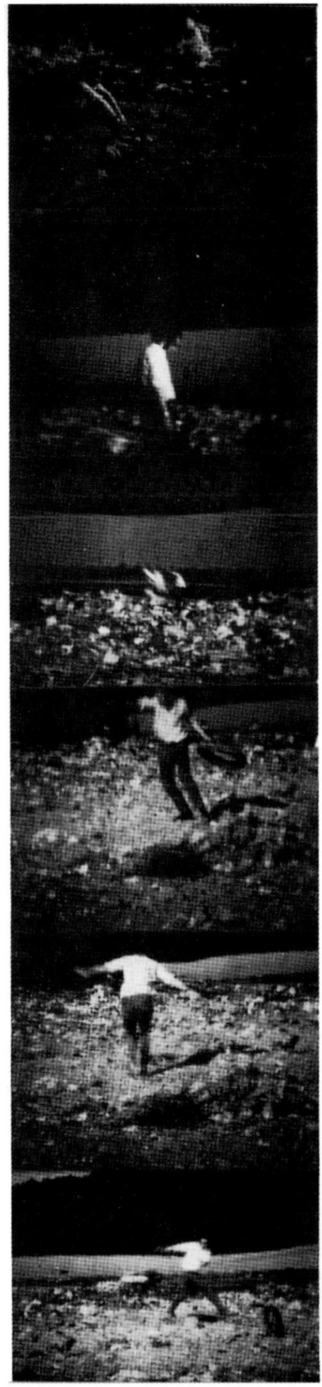

terry fox

yield, 1973

I am sending 8 photographs from my latest work, at the University Art Museum, Berkeley. This was a two-month exhibition (September 4–October 21) that involved two rooms. I enclose a drawing of the floor plan of this space, with my actions indicated. This exhibition and the actions were based on my investigations into the labyrinth at Chartres. I made a model of the large space in my studio and photographed small objects in it through a magnifying glass, including an eyetooth and an apple, a plaster model of the labyrinth at Chartres, a tube of bread and a vial of blood. These photographs were blown up to 2 by 3 feet and 22 of them were placed close together completely around the smaller room (B). A blackboard with a drawing of the curtain in the larger room was placed on its back in the small room and the objects used in the photographs were on this blackboard (A) corresponding to the actions to follow in the large room. This is the first room the visitor saw and served to slow him down and place his emotional state and critical facilities at the service of the larger room, in that the actions to occur there were very slow and trancelike and analogous to the labyrinth. The visitor left this room and walked through four 50 foot tubes of blood, urine, milk and water (C) to the large room. Here I had constructed a 12 foot high curtain out of translucent muslin (D); this curtain was 40 feet long and completely covered this room, which had a solid wall of windows (G). The curtain was in the shape of a body and had a cul-de-sac at one end and a passage, through glass doors (E), to the balcony outside (F) where the viewer could watch the action in the sealed space (H) which

he could not enter. It was in this hermetically sealed space that I made my actions together with my twin brother, Larry Fox, who photographed everything.
The action took 3 days: 4 hours the first, 2 hours the second and 3 hours the final day. They were continuous and each action began where the previous one left off. The first was done in the daytime and the next two were done at sunset into darkness with the aid of a spotlight.
On the first day I created a ribcage of lines of flour laid on the floor and then a trough made with my fingers, then I filled this trough with water transferred from a metal bowl through my mouth, drop by drop. This method was used to make all paste lines. Then the excess flour was blown away.
The second day I made a line (vertebrae) from the ribcage to the pelvis. Here I had a 8 foot square mirror on the floor. I made the pelvis by laying flour on the mirror, which reflected this image on the curtain. I added a mirrored bowl for the socket of the pelvis and blew smoke in it.
The third day I made a line out from the sternum to the metal bowl (1) which contained dried flour, and blew smoke. I continued this line to the mirrored bowl, which had formed a penicillin mold, and blew smoke. I continued this line to the enamel bowl at the window. Here I made a loaf of bread and laid a spoon against the bowl. I caused the bread to rise by holding a heating bowl above it. The bread rose and caused the spoon to rise.

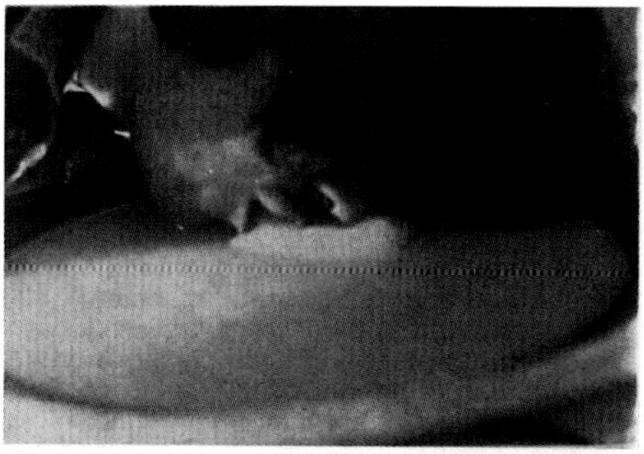
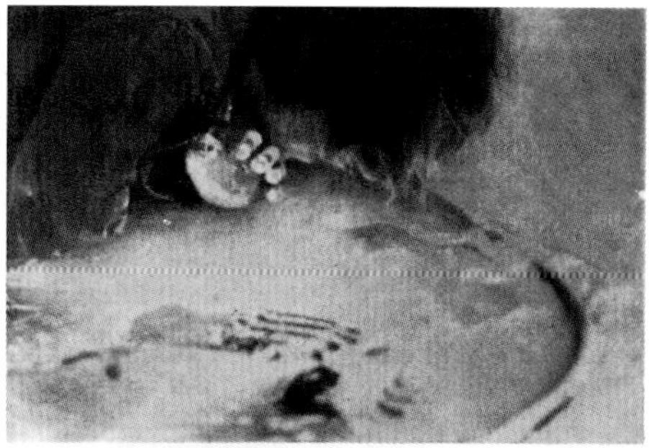
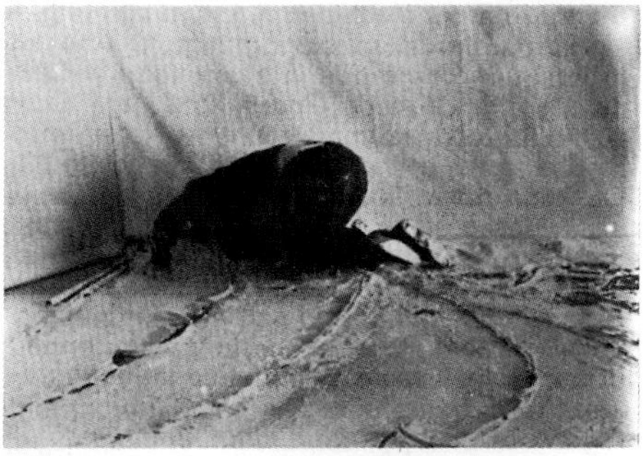
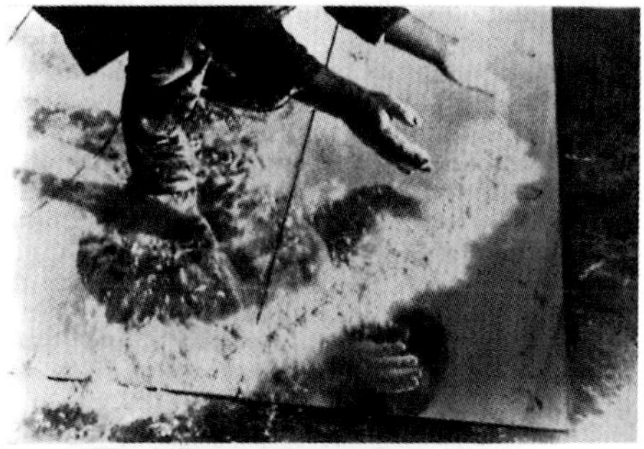
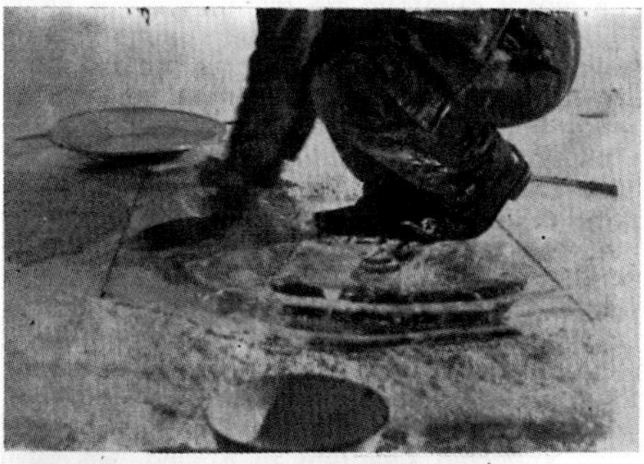
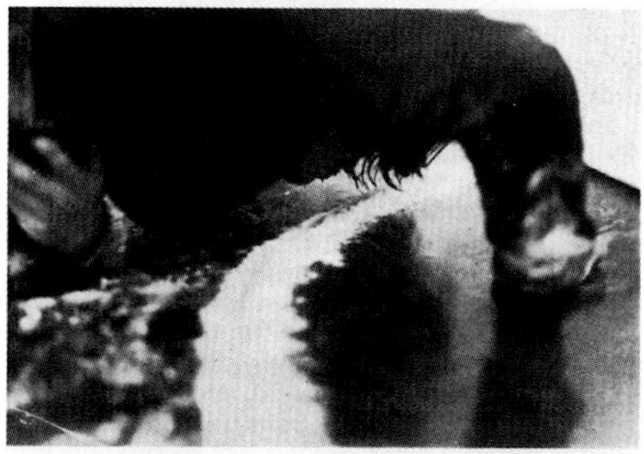
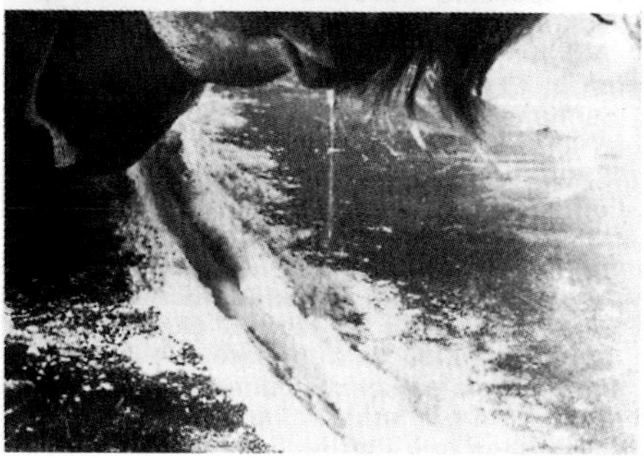
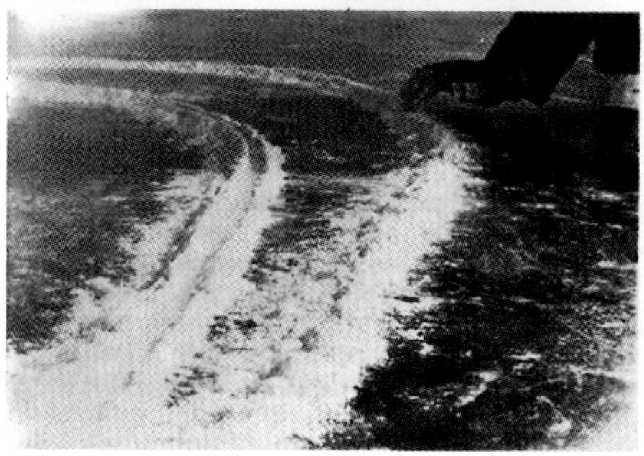

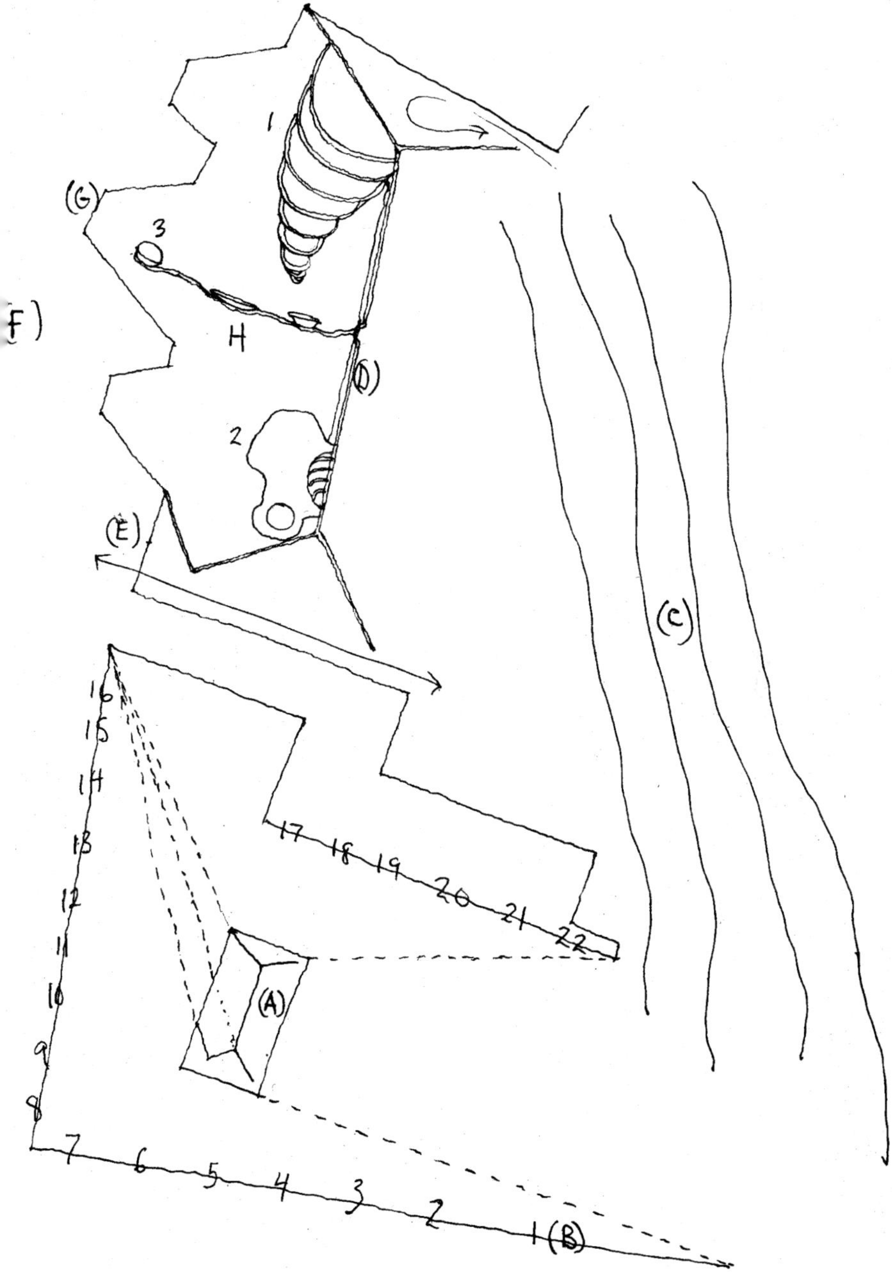
(G)
1
3
H
F)
(D)
2
(E)
(C)
(A)
16
15
14
13
12
11
10
9
8
7
6
5
4
3
2
1(B)
17
18
19
20
21
22

howard fried

Chainsmoke - Flavor Mint - Portrait by Rumor, 1972
Object... Howard Fried's transmitted image.
Object modifier... Howard Fried.
Subject... the transmission of Howard Fried's image.
Subject modifier... Anne Evans.

Out of Sight Out of Mind
The psychological tone originally transmitted by the physical presence of the object modifier decreased in fidelity or was distorted by the passage of time and eroded by the friction-like correspondence of the subject modifier and the time spent in the presence of each of the objects (the portraits). This process reached a stage where the psychological tone displayed by the object seemed to the object

modifier to be somewhat less than nineteen times more reflective of the subject modifier's psychological stage than that of the original object; much less, the object modifier. The twentieth then seems to be a mask, or rather functions as a camouflage for the subject modifier's reaction to her encounter with a particular structure of time rather than her encounter with the object modifier—whose image is the object.

I commissioned Anne Evans, an ex-portrait artist to do twenty portraits for me. The first was a portrait of me. The second, a portrait of the first portrait; the third a portrait of the second portrait… and so on. I was present while the first portrait was executed, I posed for it. I was not present while any of the subsequent nineteen were executed.

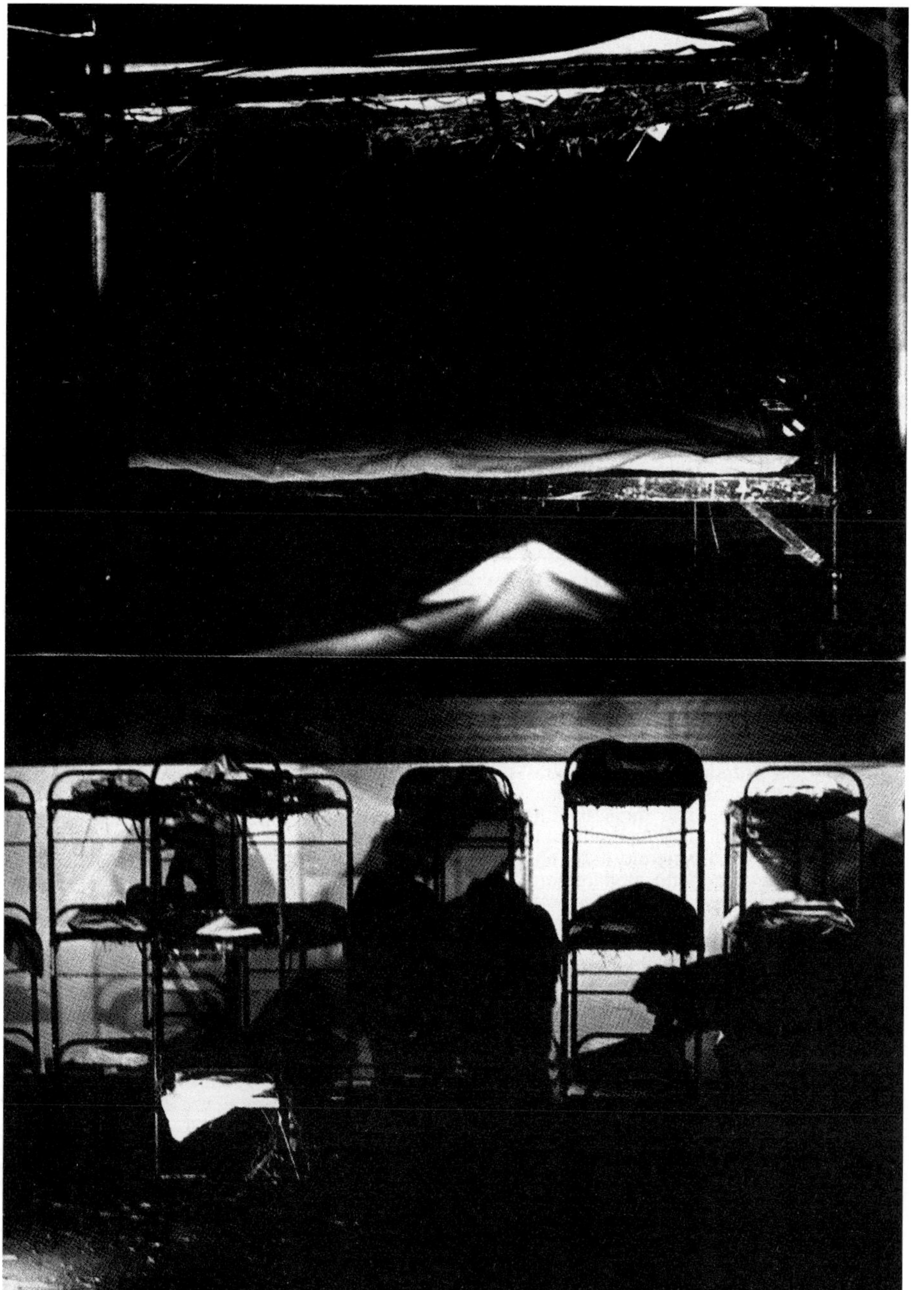

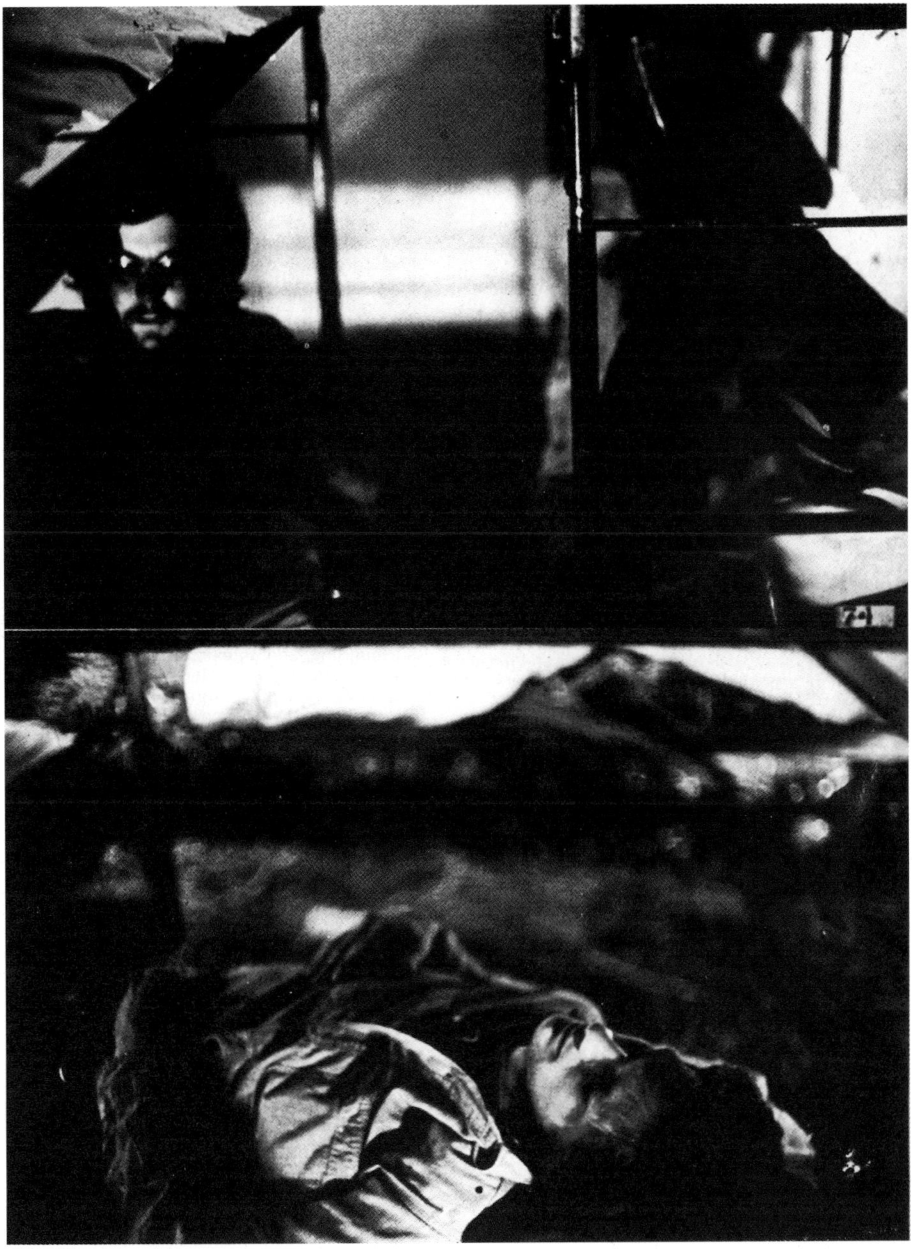

gilbert & george

Oh, the Grand Old Duke of York, 1972
(no UP, no DOWN)

> Oh, the Grand Old Duke of York
> He had ten thousand men
> And he marched them up to the top of the hill
> And he marched them down again
> And when they were up, they were up
> And when they were down, they were down
> And when they were only half way up
> They were neither up nor down.

Being living sculptures is our life blood, our destiny, our romance, our disaster, our light and life. As day breaks over us, we rise into our vacuum and the cold morning light filters dustily through the window. We put on our shoes for the coming walk. Our limbs begin to stir and form actions of looseness, as though without gravity they bounce about for the new day. The head afloat on top levels on the horizon of our thought. Our hearts pound with fresh blood and emotion and again we find ourselves standing there all nerved up in body and mind. Often we will glide across the room, drawn by the window's void. Our eyes are glued to this frame of light. Our mind points ever to our decay. The big happening outside the window floods our vision like a passing film. It leaves us without impressions, giving up only silence and repetitive relaxation. Nothing can touch us or take us out of ourselves. It is a continuous sculpture. Our minds float off into time, visiting fragments of words heard, faces seen, feelings felt, faces loved. We take occasional sips from our water glasses. Consciousness comes along and goes away, slipping from dreaming space into old concrete awareness. The whole room is filled with the mass and weight of our own history, at time it sees us chained to our chairs and then it will appear like large music, surrounding and intoxicating. We feel briefly but seriously for our fellow artistmen. More than ever complete with our physical, for a time with legs crossed, or arms folded until the elbows ache, a throat is cleared gently but effectively, we then stand for relief pushed up against the wall. Sometimes the room with its size and form and precision of our clarity, its one vase of flowers, its large desk-blackboard of our doing, our two dear, faithful green chairs, the black telephone, linked with the World's art-network.

Ring and ring again
Make us happy ever again
Stay as silent as the desk
And be as free and let it be.

The neat ash tray steadily fills with relaxful butts, beside it a fresh yellow packet of cigarettes. Very often the room makes us hurt with real bodily pressure. From time to time we are taken head-first from this room called "Art for All" out and away, sometimes driven, sometimes drawn to breathe again amongst the people. We stroll with specialised embarrassment and our purpose is only to take the sunshine. The people are all living near to beauty, passing by. Walking is the eternity of our living movement, it can never tell us of end, it is for nothing but the time passing unnoticed. We give ourselves to this walking and so the houses come towards us and then away behind. We would like to tell of our great pleasure in seeing the early flowers and blossoms, they seem to have a young fresh youth, so fine and coloured. We remark the trees with their tight bursting buds. As our legs take us jauntily along we come to a place where we pause for a cup of poison-nervous tea. We sit over it chatting a little of the normal afternoon when all is usual and well. Nothing breathtaking will occur here, but in the darkness of a picture house, where time is killed, the world explodes realistically into giant action stories, men are killed, women are loved, mountains are blown up, night falls, Volcanoes erupt, john wayne rides again and caesar speaks anew to people. All this until the reel is done and viewers drift blinking and reeling out into the bright city. And we happily go back to Our art where only tiredness and searching play big roles, where all is thin on the ground, where greatness is made at the stroke of a brush, where something and nothing are both qualities. Art is for all the only hope for the making way for the Modern world to enjoy the sophistication of decadent living expression. It is our strong belief that in Art there is living, and where there's life there's Hope. It is for this reason that we have dedicated our hands, legs, pens, speech and our own dear heads to progress and understanding in art.

Art my Life and Art my Way
See us painting in mud and clay
See us dancing and smiling too
Let us hope that Art is true.

And then maybe we will see ourselves in a garden, soft and sitting, watching the sun as it gently lowers itself down behind the horizon, taking with it all its golden light and warmth. For a little while the garden keeps some of the day's warm-strength. The two men-sculptures use up this last pleasure, but soon the chill of evening creeps over all, we hear no insect, the birds begin to settle down from the day's frolics and we feel it must soon be time to stretch a leg and make our way between the rich beds of flowers, over the spongy lawns to return to solid state of buildings with their sensible doors and windows. On our way we pause on the embankment to take in the glory that is the Thames and Westminster. Slowly the lamps are lighted and night presumes upon the evening. We like it very much. We like it because we are so stupid, artistic and shy. Because we have come from nowhere and where we go nobody knows. We feel the total mystery of each man-laid brick. We are just down at the river feeling around. As the shades of night are falling around our neighbourhood we stroll because we know full well that another sculpture day is over.

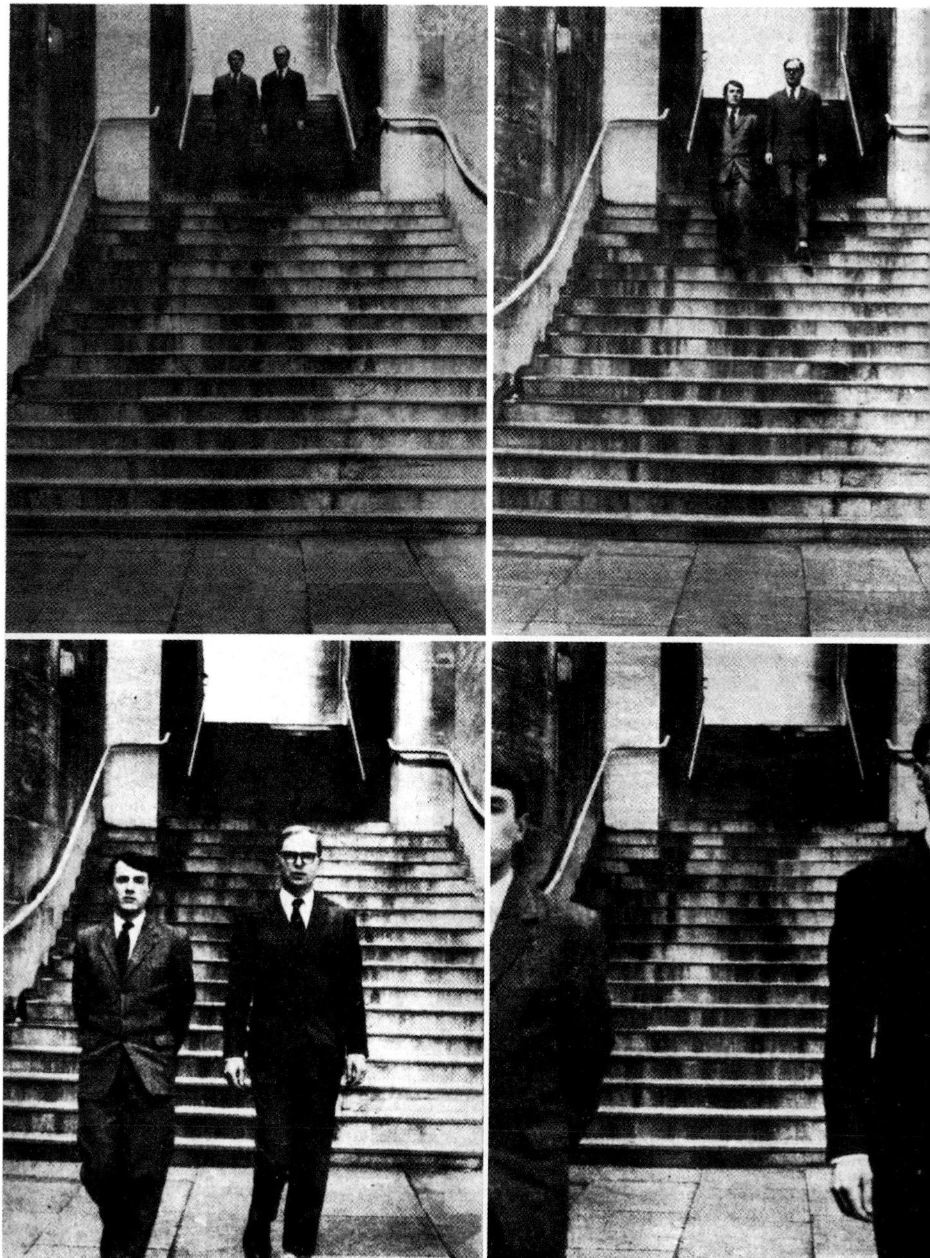

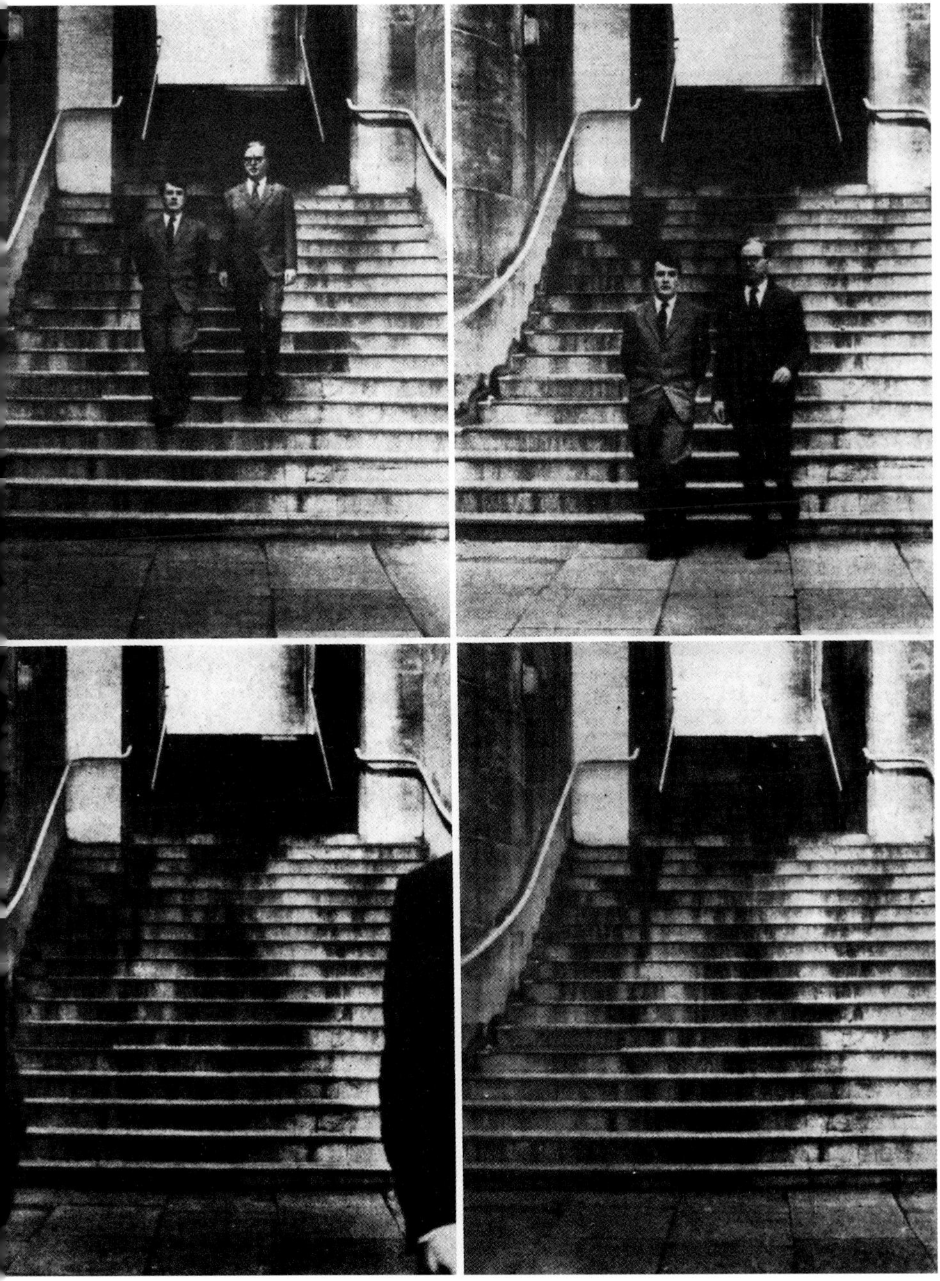

dan graham

Body Press, 1970–73

Two film makers stand (within a surrounding and completely mirrorized cylinder), body trunk stationary, hands holding and pressing a camera's back end flush to, while slowly rotating it about the surface cylinder of their individual bodies. One rotation circumscribes the body's contour, spiralling slightly upward with the next turn. With successive rotations, the body surface areas are completely covered by the back of the camera(s) until the cameraman's eye level is reached; then a reverse mapping downward begins until the original starting point is reached. The rotations are at corresponding speeds; when each camera is rotated to each body's rear, it is facing and filming the other as they are exchanged, so the camera's "identity" "changes hands" and each performer is handling a new camera. The cameras are of different size. In the process, the performers are to concentrate on the coexistent, simultaneous identity of the camera describing them and their body. To the spectator, the camera may or may not read as an extension of the body's identity.

Optically, the two cameras film the image reflected on the mirror, which is the image of the surface(s) of the lens, the camera's visible sides, the body of the performer, and (possibly) his eyes on the mirror. The camera's angle of orientation/view of area of the mirror's reflective image is determined by the placement of the camera on the body contour at a given moment. (The camera might be pressed against the chest but such an upward angle shows head and eyes).
Projection of film: the films are projected at the same time on two loop projectors, very large size, on two opposite, but close, room walls.
A member of the audience (man or woman) might identify with one image or the other from the same camera or can identify with one body or the other, shifting his/her view each time to face the other screen when cameras are exchanged.
To the spectator the camera's optical vantage is the skin—there is no space. The performer's musculature is also "seen" pressing into the surface of the body (pulling inside out). At the same time, kinesthetically, the handling of the camera can be "felt" by the spectator as surface tension for the hidden side of the camera presses and slides against the skin it covers at a particular moment.

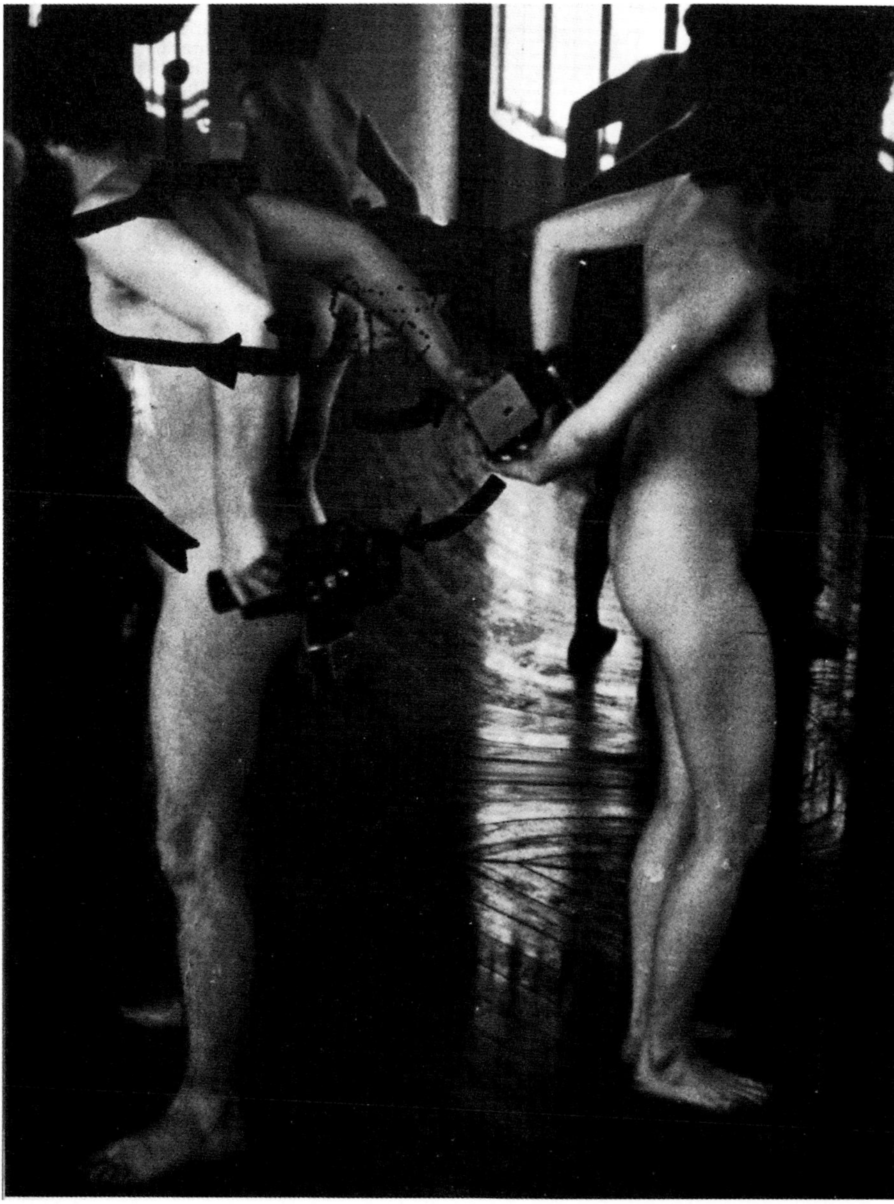

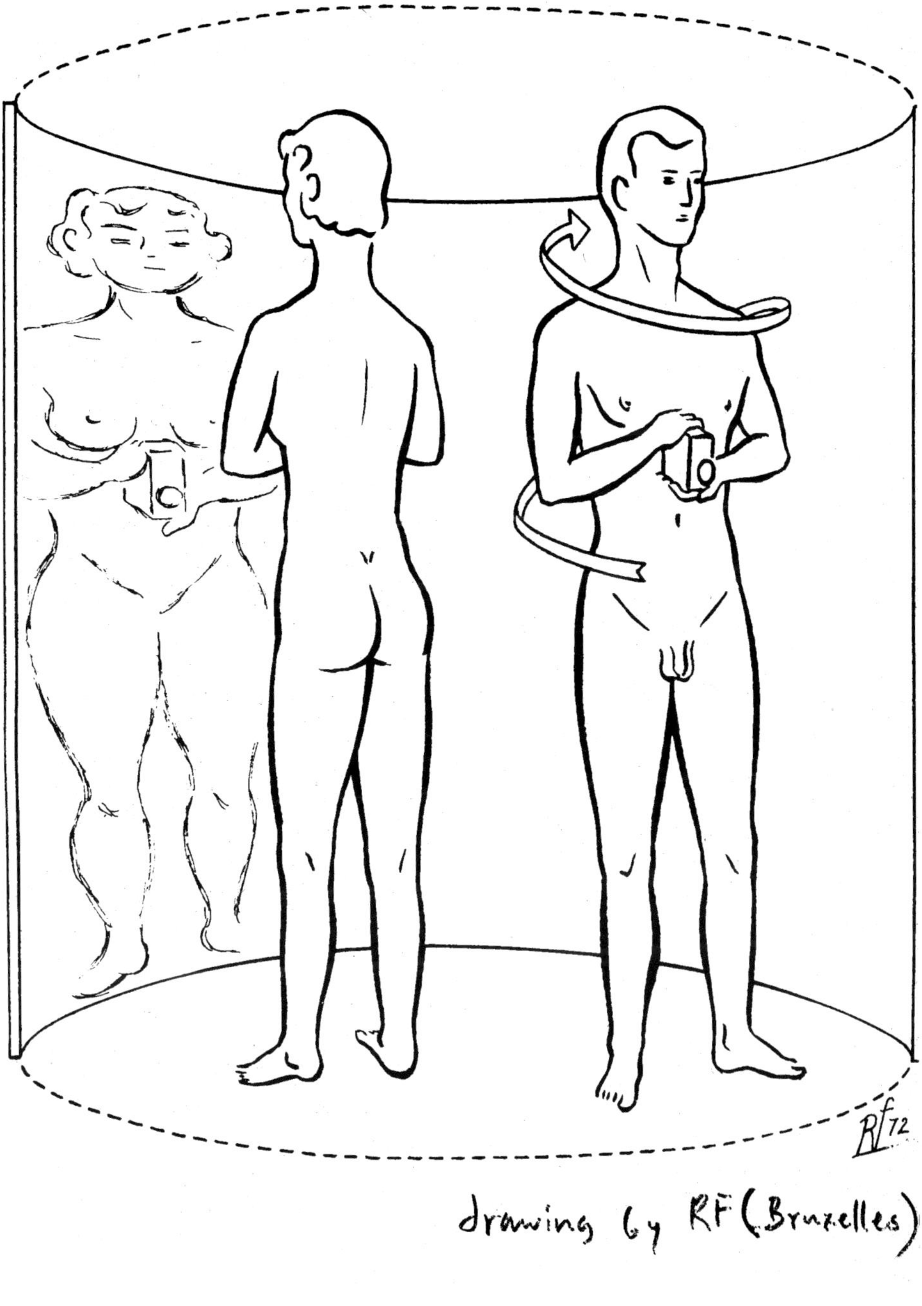

drawing by RF (Bruxelles)

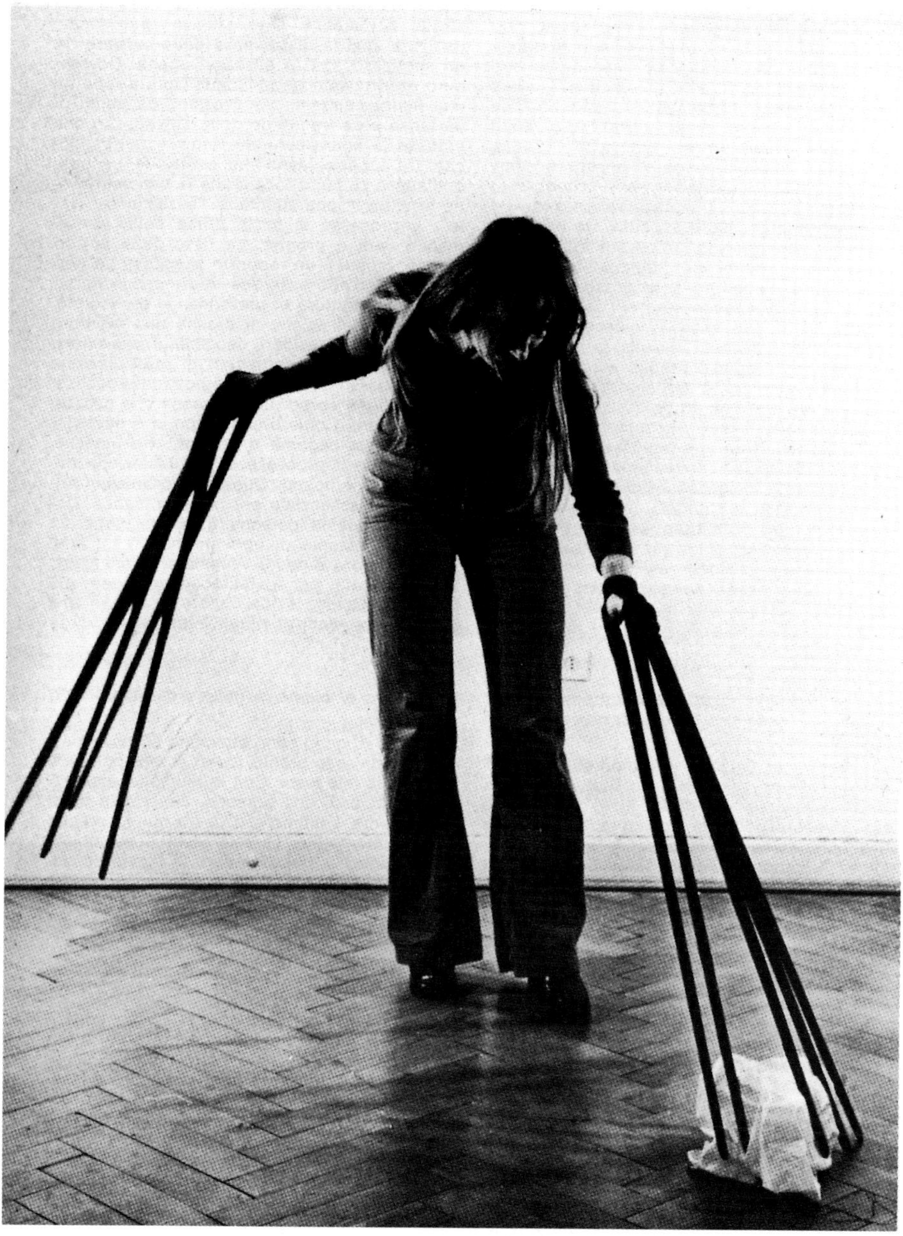

Finger-gloves, 1972

Cockfeather Mask for Dieter, 1973

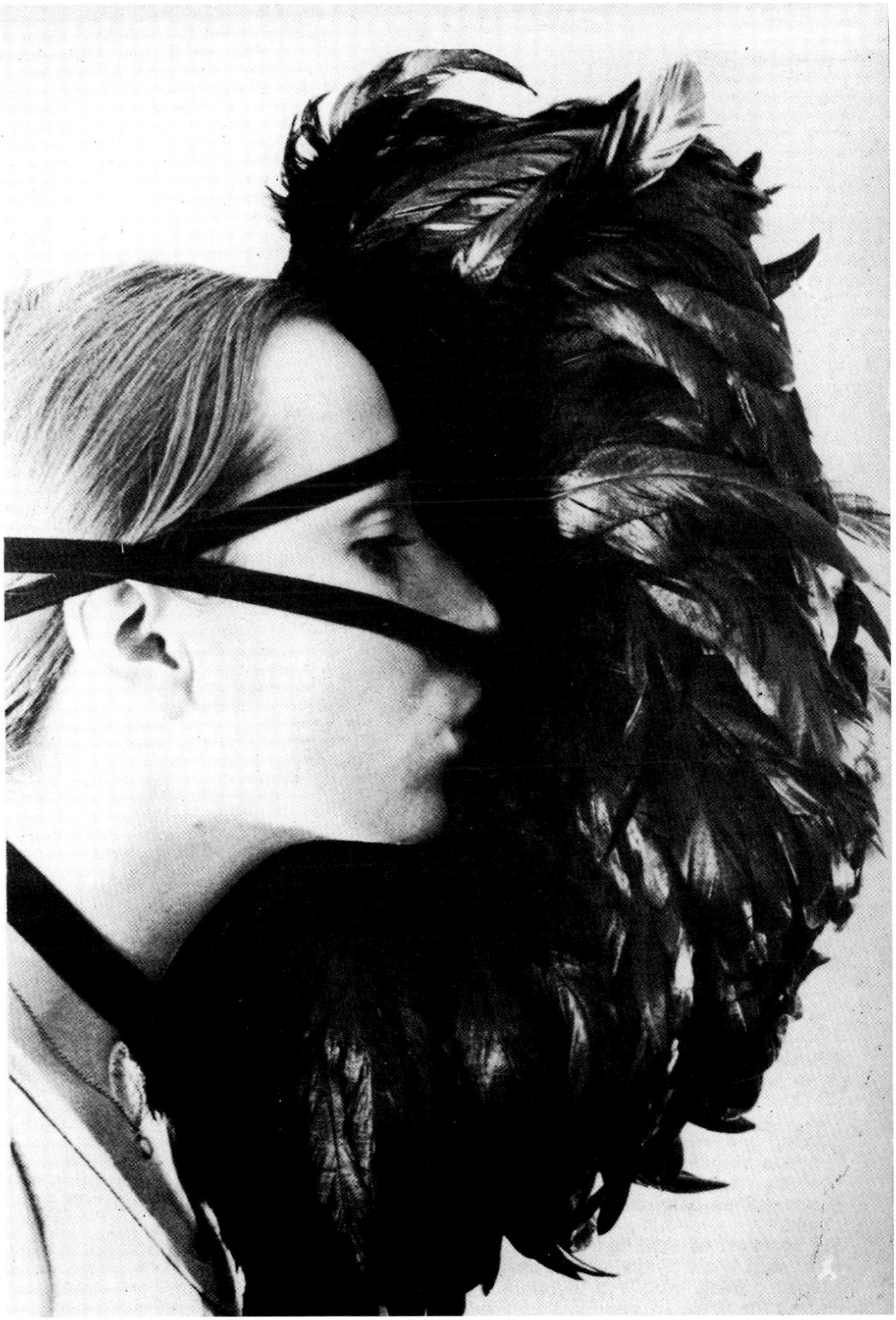

enrico job

Bodymap, 1974

The *Bodymap* is composed of about one thousand photographs; the skin of the artist's own body has been subdivided in black pencilled squares of 4.50 cm for the body and 2.50 cm for the head. The squares have subsequently been photographed and enlarged twice their actual size and then pasted on wooden panels to recompose the original body in a gigantic puzzle. It appears as a skinned man: a flat animal carpet.

The intention of *Bodymap*, like that of any other map, is the reduction to a single dimension of a living thing, and therefore it works against the double time-space dimension.

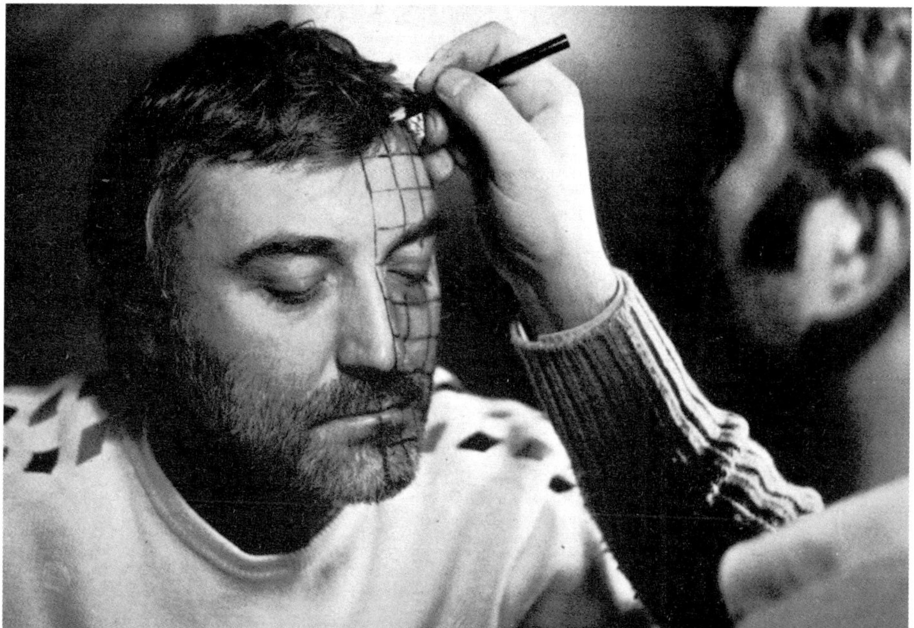

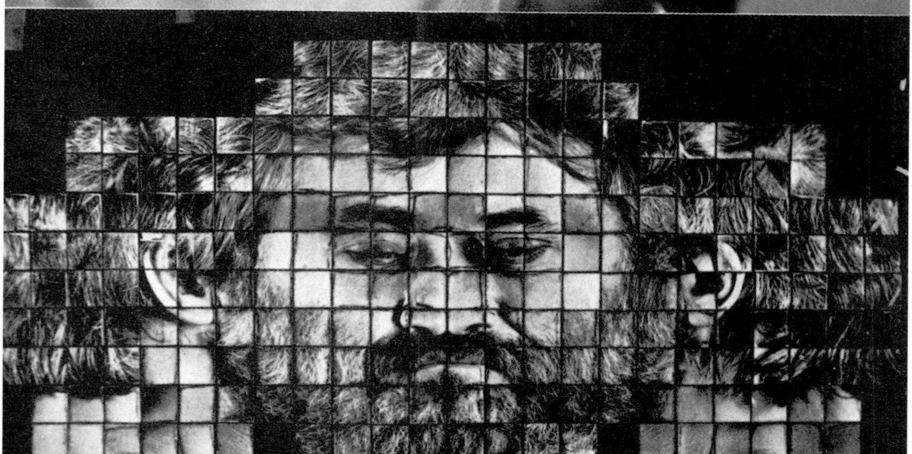

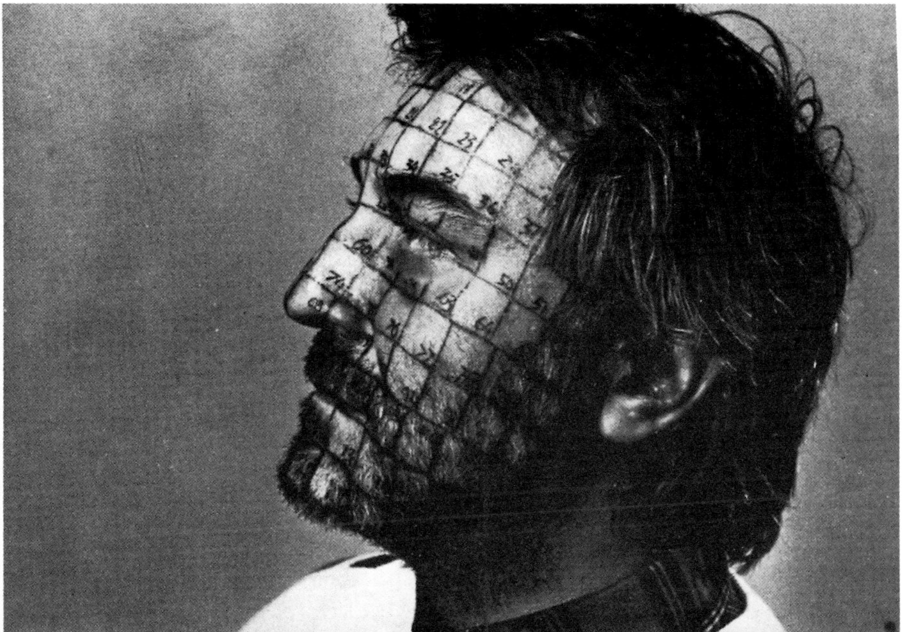

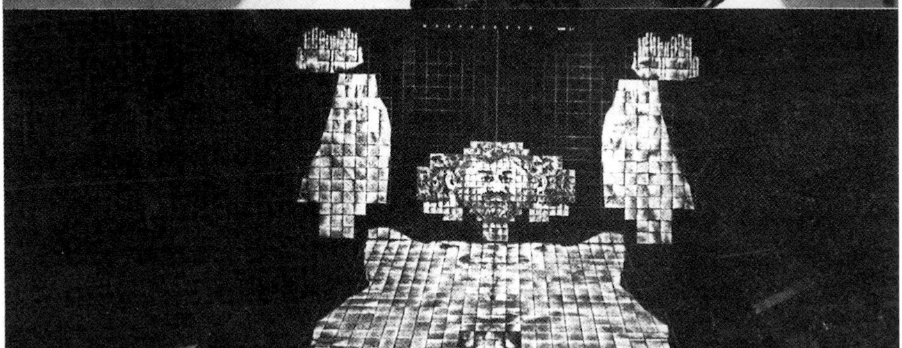

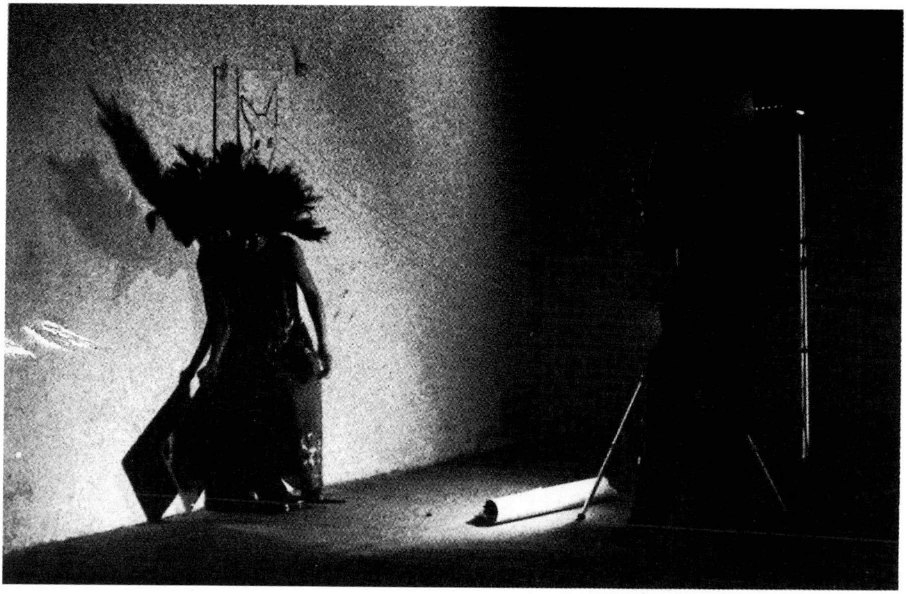

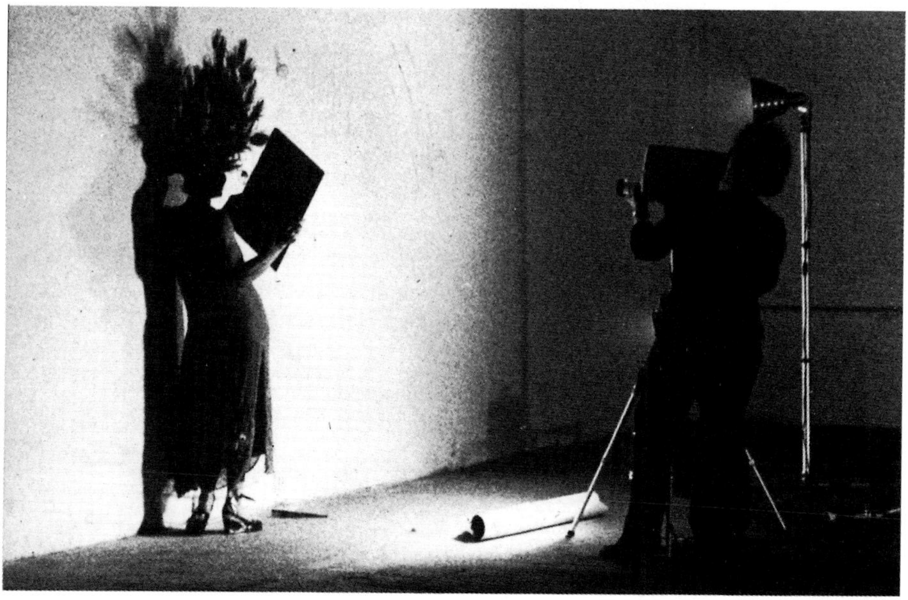

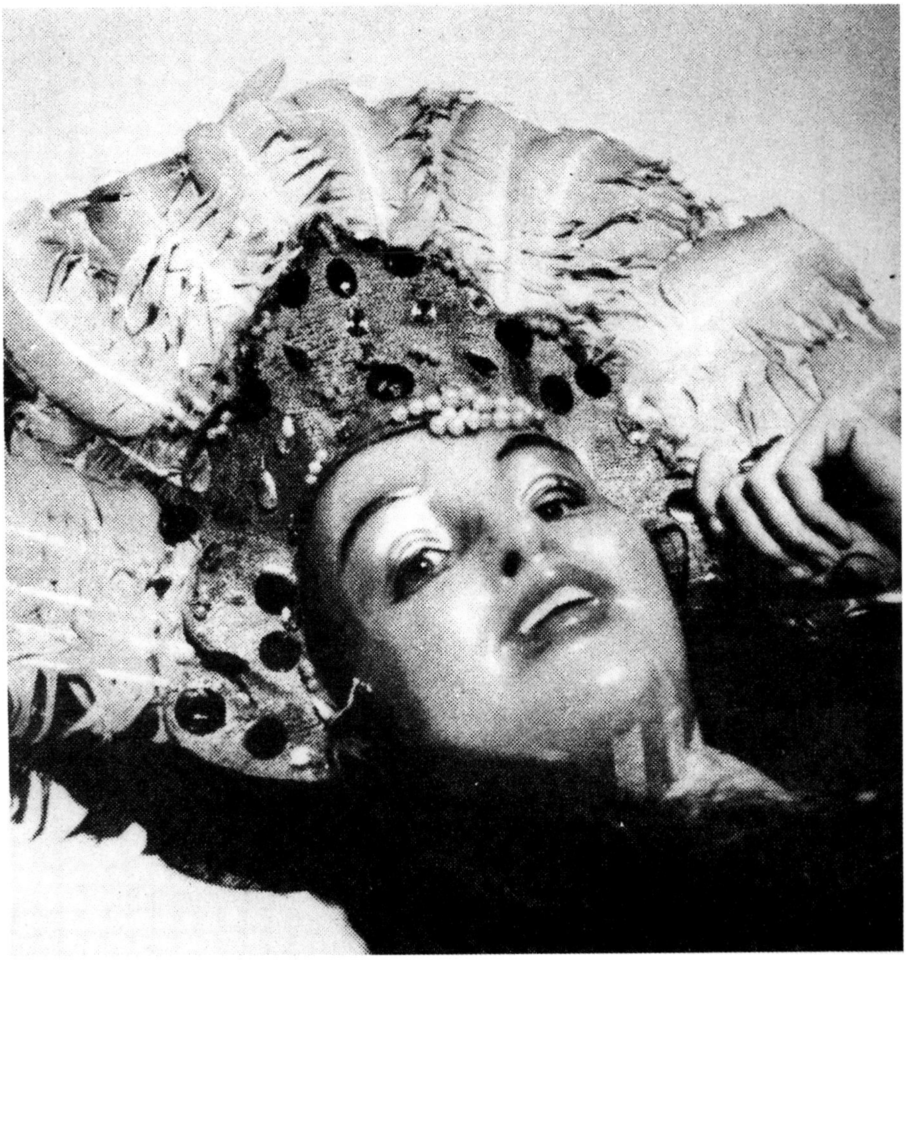

michel journiac

Homage to Freud, 1972

Body Contract, 1972

Change your body into a work of art.

Contract A: you settle for painting—your skeleton is lacquered white.

Contract B: you settle for an object—your skeleton is dressed in your clothes.

Contract C: you settle for a sociological factor: the gold standards—your skeleton is gold plated.

Conditions: 1—bequeath your body to Journiac.
2—die.

HOMMAGE A FREUD

CONSTAT CRITIQUE D'UNE MYTHOLOGIE TRAVESTIE

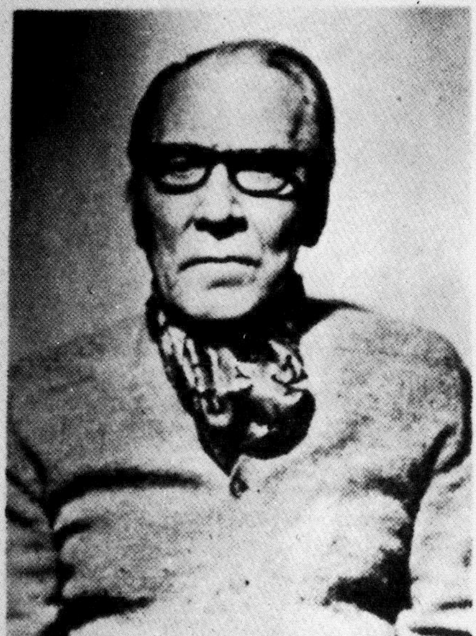

PERE : Robert Journiac travesti en Robert Journiac

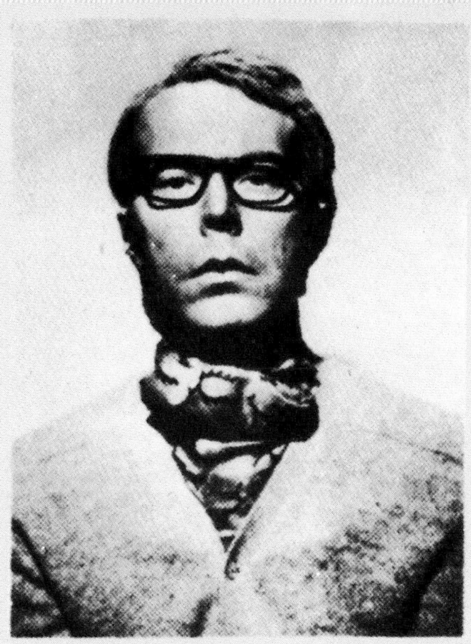

FILS : Michel Journiac travesti en Robert Journiac

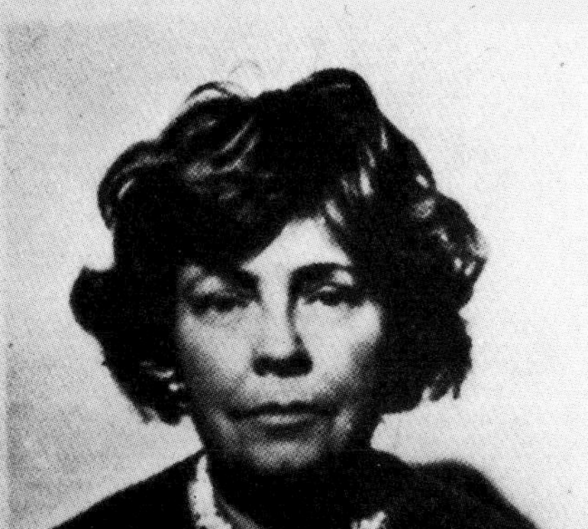

MERE : Renée Journiac travestie en Renée Journiac

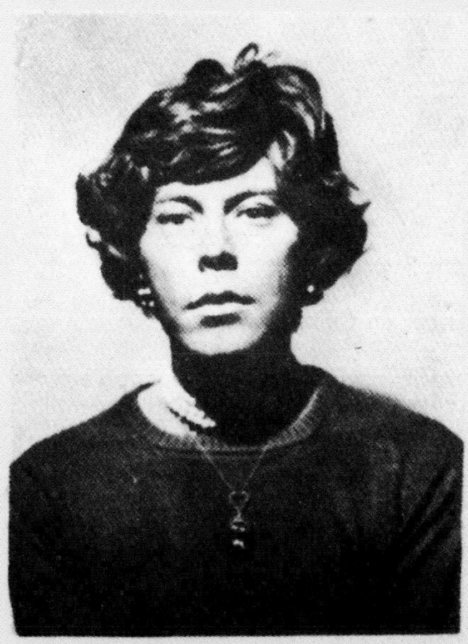

FILS : Michel Journiac travesti en Renée Journiac

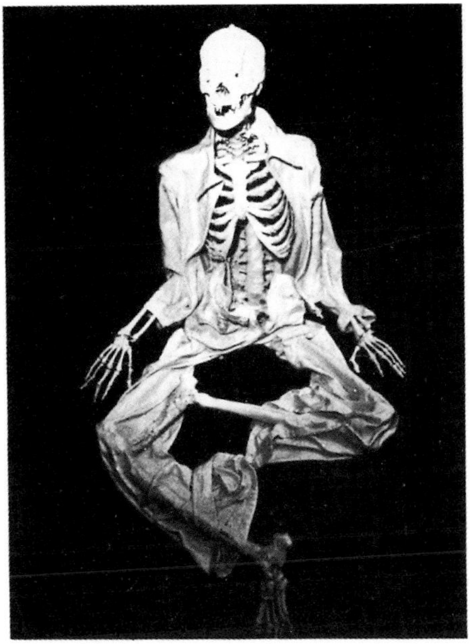

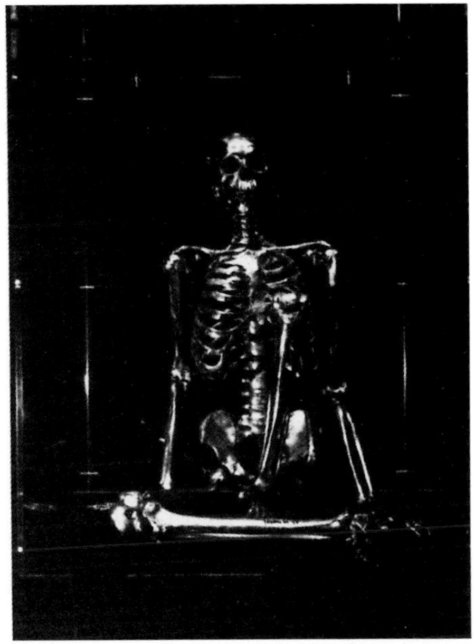

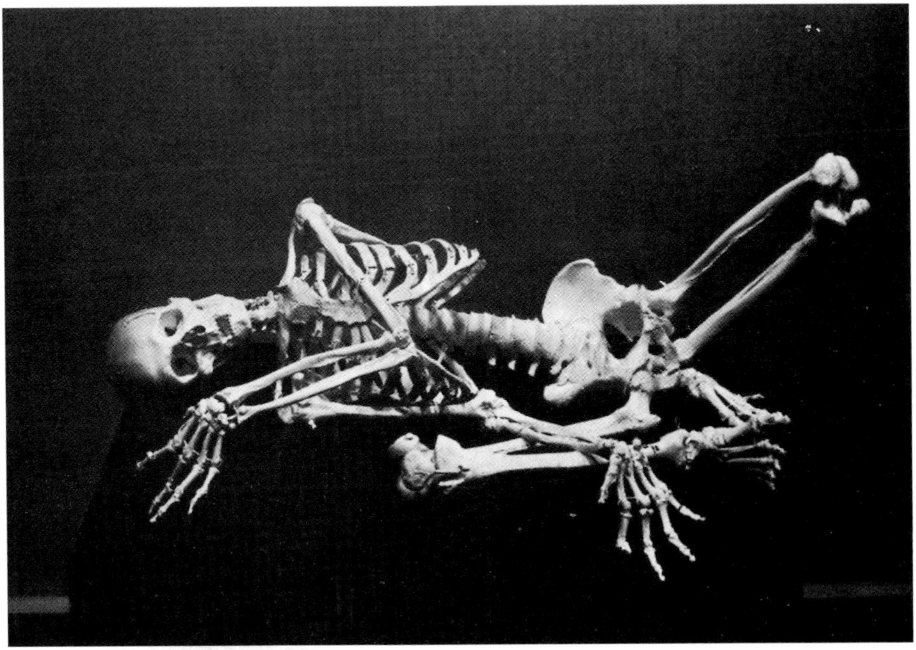

Homage to Freud,
1972

Body Contract,
1972

ketty la rocca

You, you, 1972–73

my work attempts to redeem the image for itself / by materializing the challenge to metaphor, a challenge already lost, but in a declared manner, / in fact I do not narrate, I limit myself to go over again, to draw, to write the outlines with the only possible sign: handwriting / handwriting, alienating and partial moment which already pre-announces itself as historical, although always unique, my only gesture there / "you, you" tries to hamper the visual and mental process / and to reduce the language to a simple bit of information / and to make immediately clear the asymptote of alienation / "you" also means I, I do not have alternatives, I save myself within my own hysteria, with the not repeatable of writing myself / by making microscopic the living the otherness outside myself / by being an example to myself of alienation / but not of perversion / thus, my work is not the seat of my affections / it is not the partial, therefore, / but the denunciation made against my stereotypes / it is not the warm placenta with which to wrap myself / but cruelty as new and only will, / outside of this force one is able to do so much / like saying / "deer are fast, Indians are fast, Indians are deer" / and to lose oneself in the narcissism of paralogism.

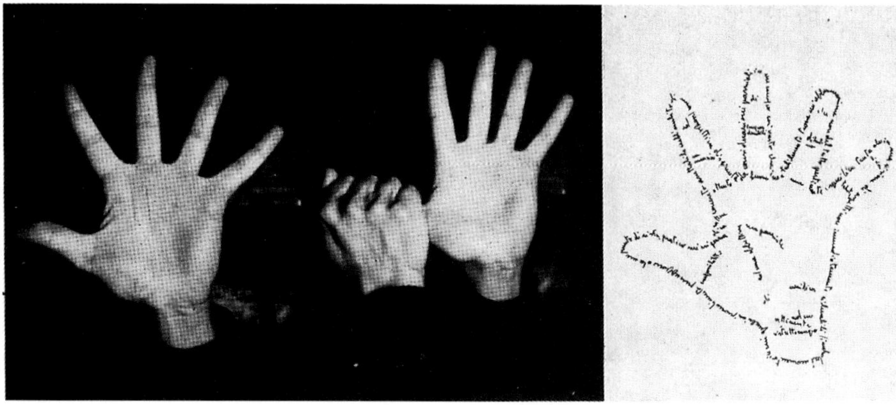

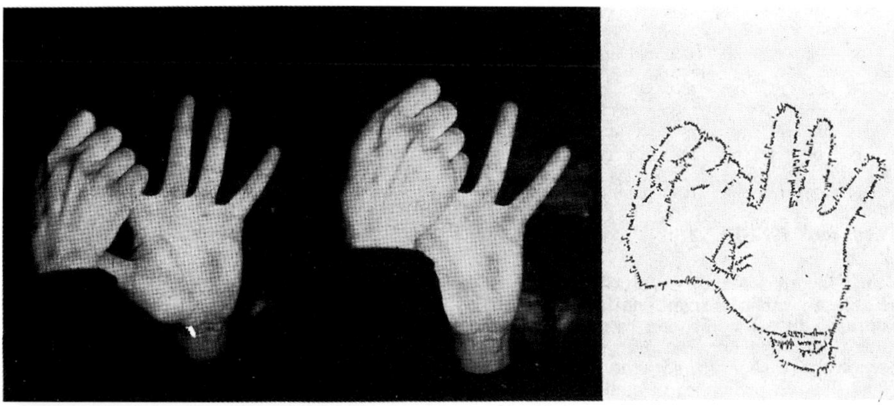

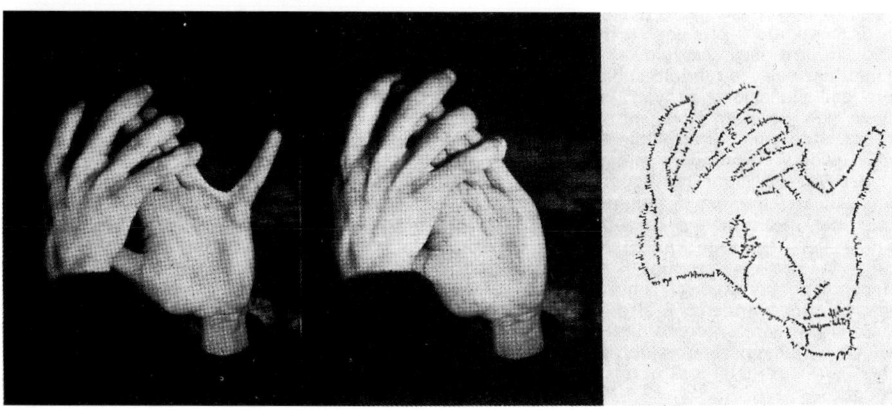

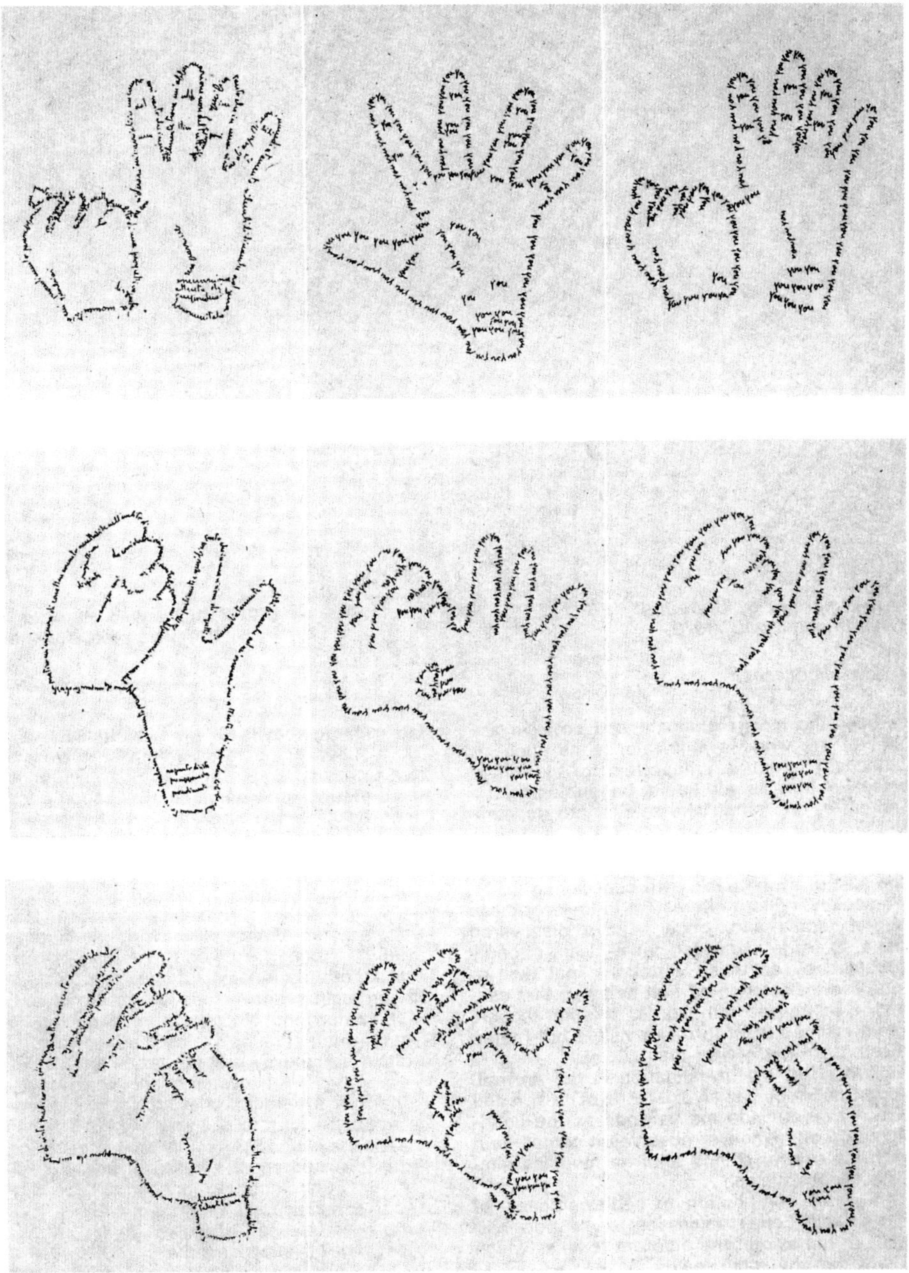

urs lüthi

A Self Portrait by Urs Lüthi, 1973
This is About You, 1973
A Few Mindflashes
Perhaps the most significant and creative aspect of my work is ambivalence as such... Objectivity is not very important for me: all is objective just as all could be subjective... Therefore, one must take reality into account and actually my awareness of the real, depending on my mood, has thousands of facets... I believe that these facets are in fact, the sum of every man's own conscience...
Personally, I find it interesting to look for these secret facets and, once I have discovered them, to try to visualize them. I am strongly attracted by all those vibrations that live inside every existence as well as by all that cannot be expressed with words. It is not, though, great events I want to make visible but rather, the reason that moves them...
The result of my investigation is the portrait. A portrait which has an existence of its own and which lives outside me as soon as the floodlights go off. Whoever observes it compares it with his own existence until he modifies himself, divides himself...
This is my contribution to self-awareness, of one's limits, one's excesses, one's possibilities... and also of the different realities which live within the same reality...

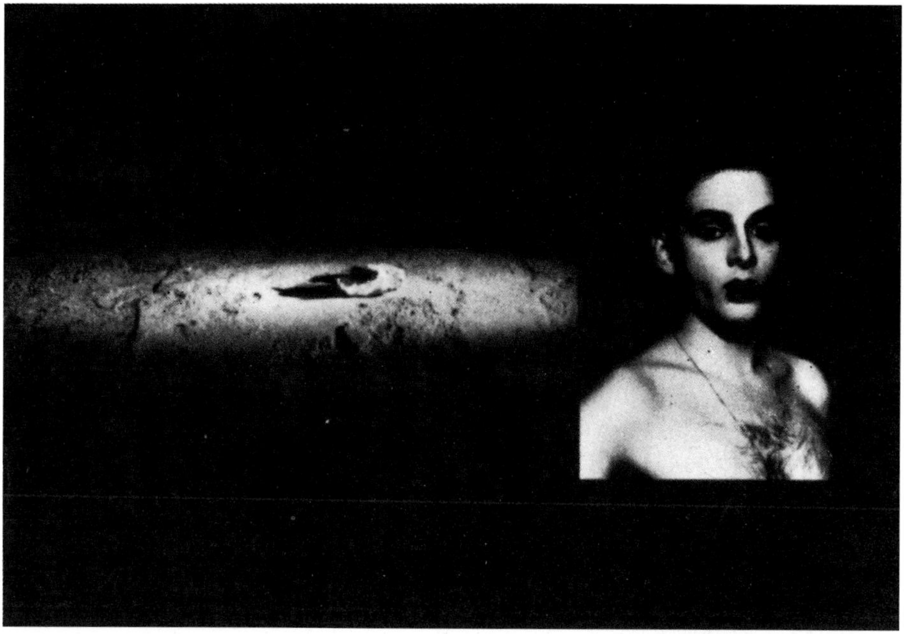

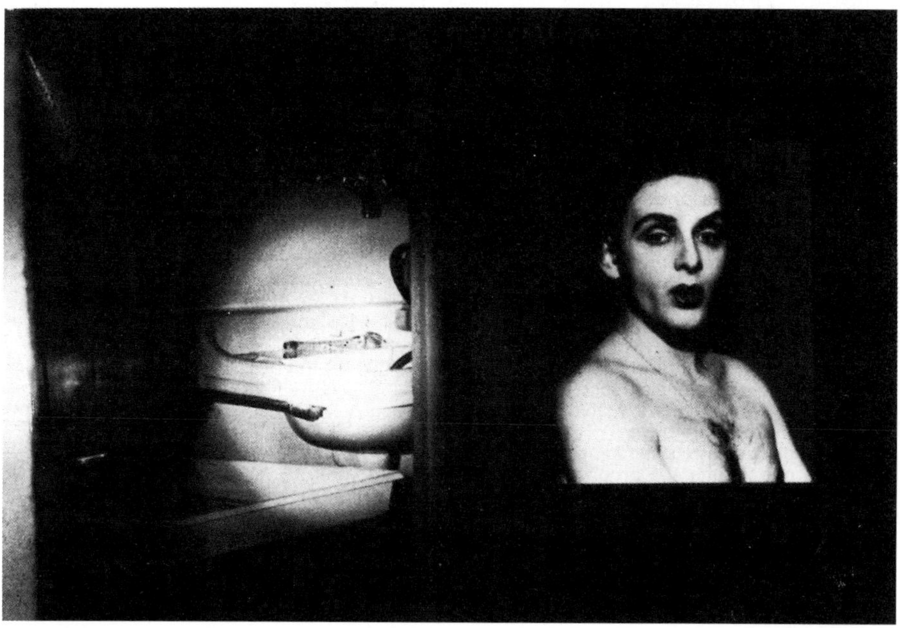

A Self Portrait by Urs Lüthi, 1973

This is About You, 1973

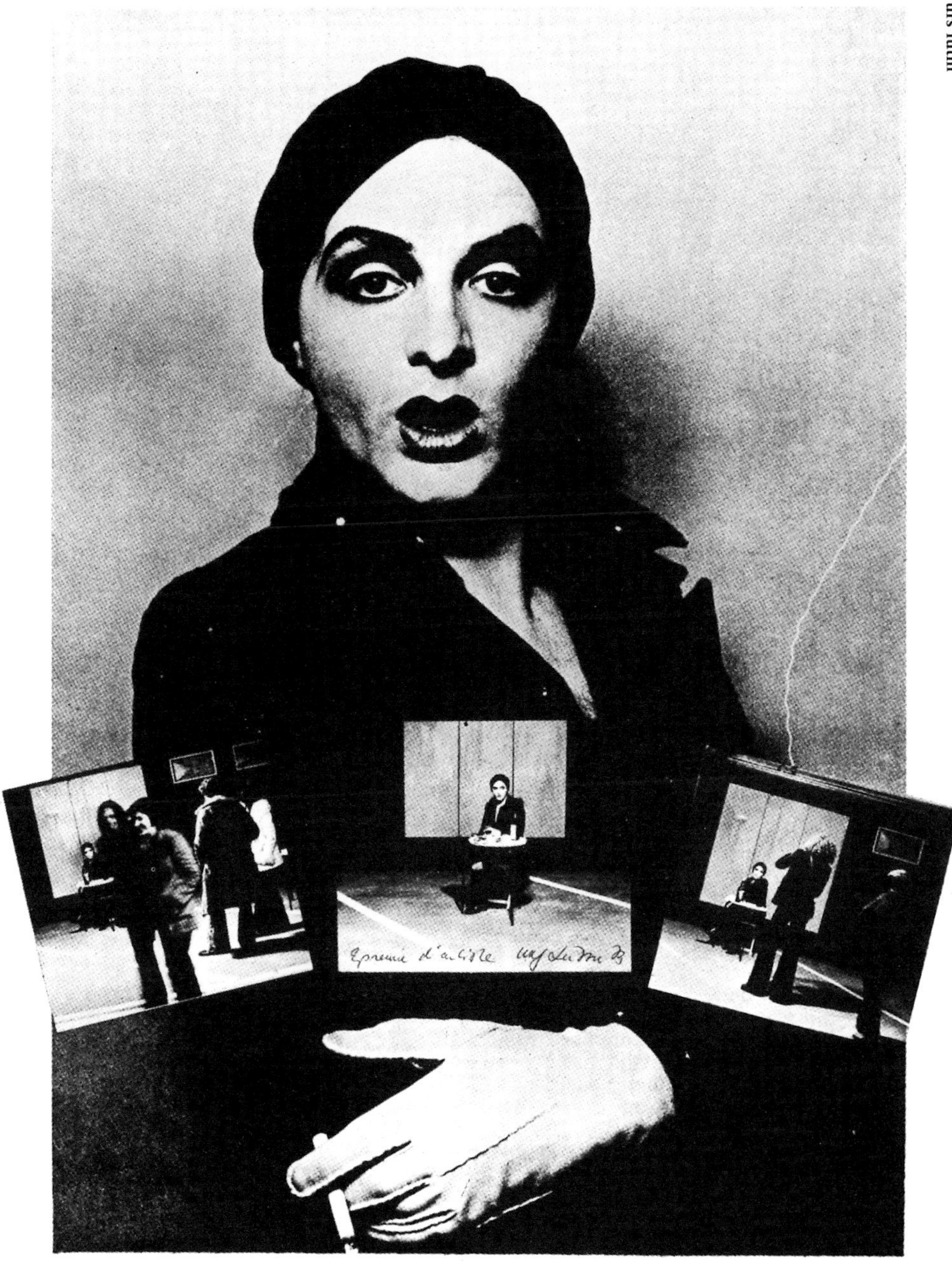

THIS IS ABOUT YOU

elio mariani

Ambiences, 1972–73

The ambience, the body, the embraces. The before and the after. The empty ambience is "the before," the body, the embraces "the after." The before represents the basic premise, the departure of all things, our desire, the expectations, the hypothesis of possible actions; the after is their conclusion, the necessary end to be reached, from an unstable balance (departure) to a verifiable one (arrival). The analysis of the bodies' behavior through their embraces is the most natural, logical investigation of the function the body itself assumes in a process of self-identification, almost a realization of the self, of the relationship with reality. All my operations of recording and intervention are photographically executed, enlarged and then transferred onto sensitized canvas.

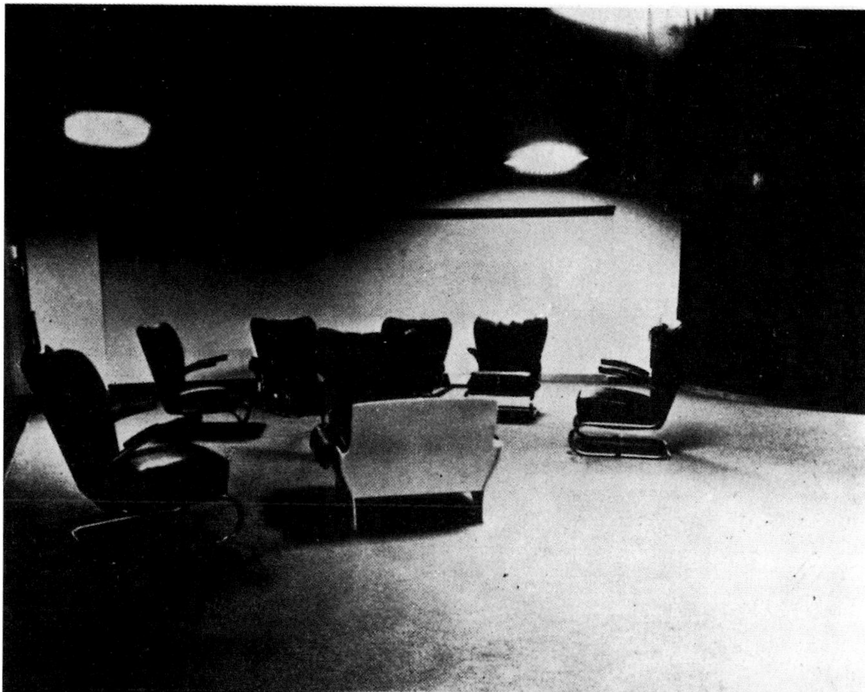

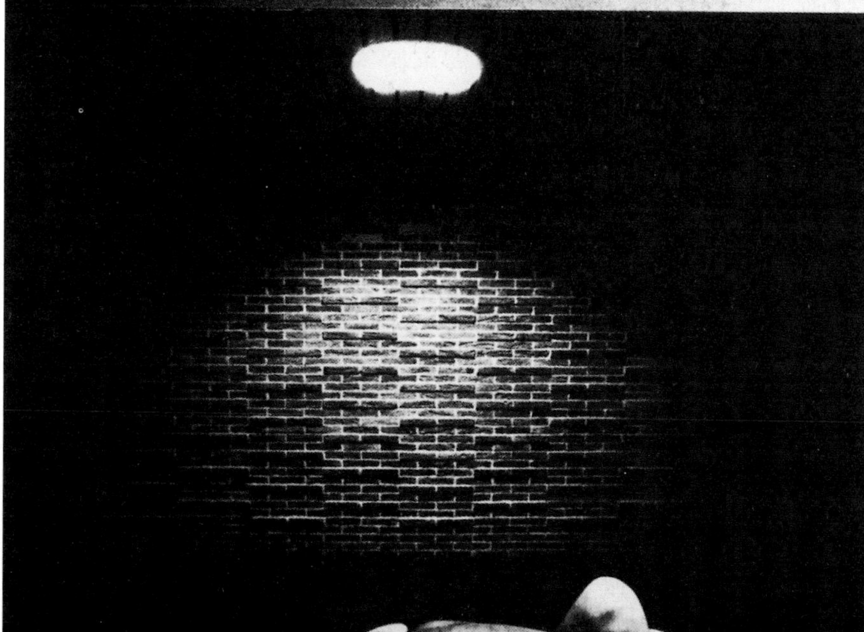

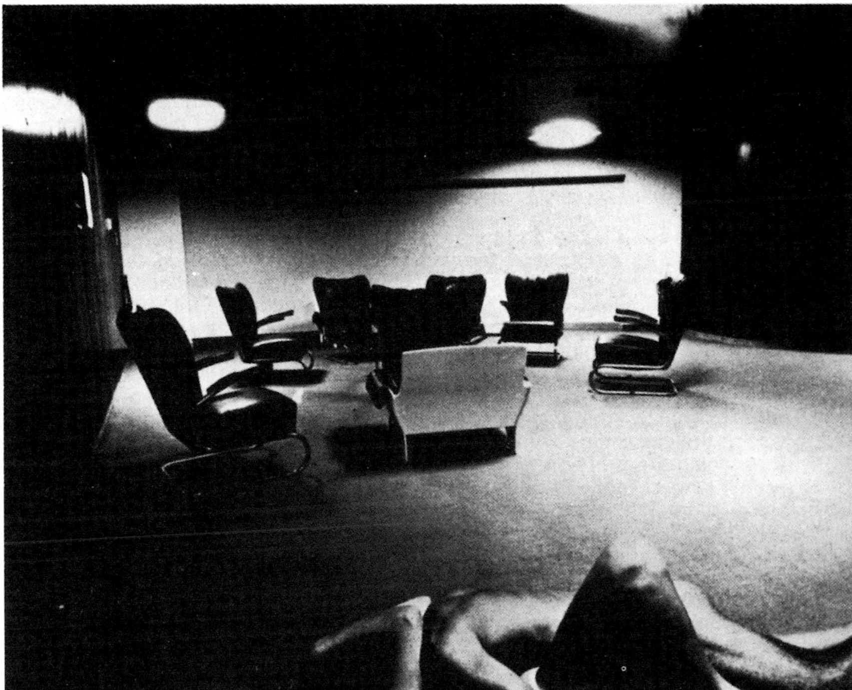

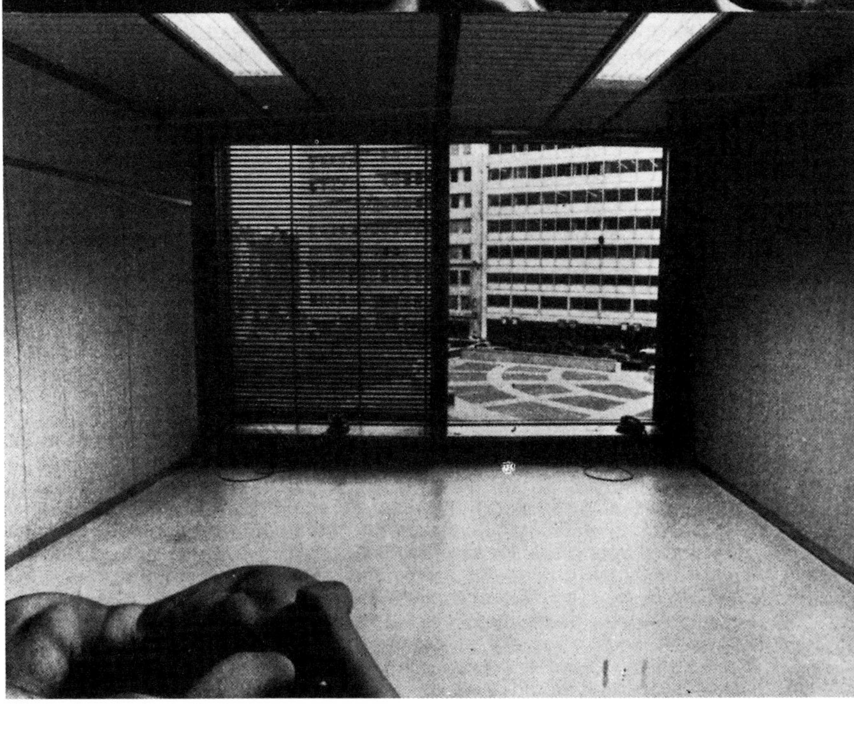

tom marioni

Action, 1969
From 1969 on I have made performances.
I was interested in the act that took place because there was no static object as a result. The only static object might be a case of empty beer bottles for one thing, left as a record of some kind of activity.
In 1969 I had to have a way to exhibit because I felt like exhibiting. It was too politically complicated to try to exhibit my work and be a curator at the same time for a combination of reasons which are probably obvious. So I had to exhibit under another name. I created a fictitious character, Allan Fish. And when it was no longer necessary to be concerned about those things, then I announced, by way of a transformation piece, that I was Allan Fish. *The Act of Drinking Beer With Friends is the Highest Form of Art* was the first Allan Fish one-man show. It took place at the Oakland Museum. I invited 21 of my friends to come and drink beer at the museum. And 16 people were there. All of the people were sculptors except for Werner Jepson, the music composer. We got drunk in the museum together and the debris that was left over was exhibited as documentation of that activity—empty beer cans and cigarette butts, just morning after kind of debris. It was to exaggerate the concept of the act being the art and the documentation being just a record of the real activity.
Last summer I did a piece called *Allan Fish Drinks a Case of Beer*, which had to do with creating a situation, an environment, while becoming increasingly more intoxicated over about an eight hour period. The Reese Pailey Gallery bought a case of Becks beer for me. I put it in the refrigerator, and had the refrigerator in the gallery. I had all the things in the gallery that I needed to be comfortable.

I had a TV set, my easy chair, a tape recorder, a refrigerator, and a can opener hanging down on a string from the ceiling. To separate myself from people that came into the gallery, I ran thread at about a 30° angle across the room. The thread was white for the first foot, and then it was black across the room, and then it was white for the last foot against the wall. It looked like thin black lines floating, the kind of lines you see on your TV screen when you get disturbance.
I tried to create an image with lines across it that would serve as a barrier. The lines also served as a screen, a projection of everything that was in the room, tending to make it all two-dimensional, as in a painting. I also had my conga drum there. I played my conga drum while the tape recorder, the radio, and the television set and the phonograph records were all playing simultaneously. I had a barrage of noise. Later in the day, as I was very drunk, those were the kinds of sounds I needed to keep me going. At a point when I was very drunk, I drew lines on the right side of my face and the left side of my face that suggested the contours of my own face moving around the left side of my face, so that it appeared, as in Futurist paintings, that I was moving fast when I couldn't move fast. To compensate, I drew these lines to make it look like I was moving faster than I was.
I went to Scotland and did five pieces, one each day for five days at the Demarco Gallery in Edinburgh. I amplified the sound of making drawings.
The first day I did a drumming piece which was made up of four 45 minute segments of drumming. Forty-five minutes was the length of

the tape on my cassette recorder. I recorded 45 minutes of drumming with steel drum brushes on a sheet of blue plastic. Then I put the tape recorder inside the drum and drummed a duet with myself for the second 45-minute section. Then I repeated the process for two 45-minute segments after that. At the end of the day I kept the plastic as a drawing of that day. The second day was a Saturday, and it was the day of the biggest soccer game of the year on TV. I realized that people would stay at home to watch the event rather than come to the gallery, so I asked the gallery to rent a color TV and show the game between Scotland and England. I had a refrigerator full of free beer in the gallery available to people. I lettered the words "free beer" on the outside of the refrigerator and had the refrigerator facing the TV, one at each end of the room. The third day was a Sunday.
I did a violin piece. I played my violin and did a drawing with the rosin from the bow. I cut a piece of brown paper to fit underneath the strings, and I bowed one harmonic note for 25 minutes.
Then as the bow went across the string, the rosin drifted off the string down onto the piece of paper. On Monday, I did a vertical line drawing until the pencil was used up. I put the microphone in the corner of the room under the paper. The paper was stapled to the wall and ran down and across the floor like a giant scroll. It was a roll of tracing paper. I stood on the paper in my stockinged feet and drew a line with the pencil from under my legs to the corner of the room and then up the wall as far as I could reach.

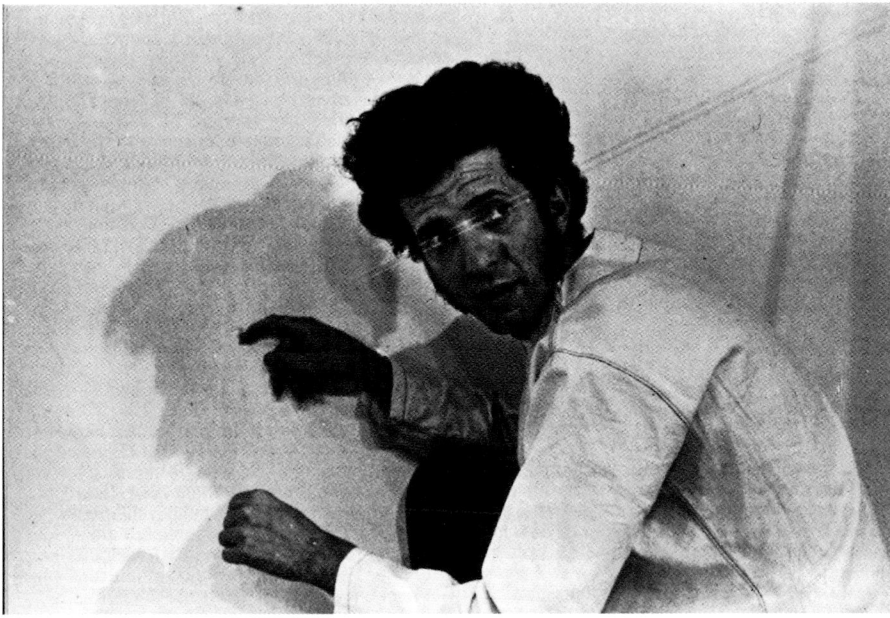

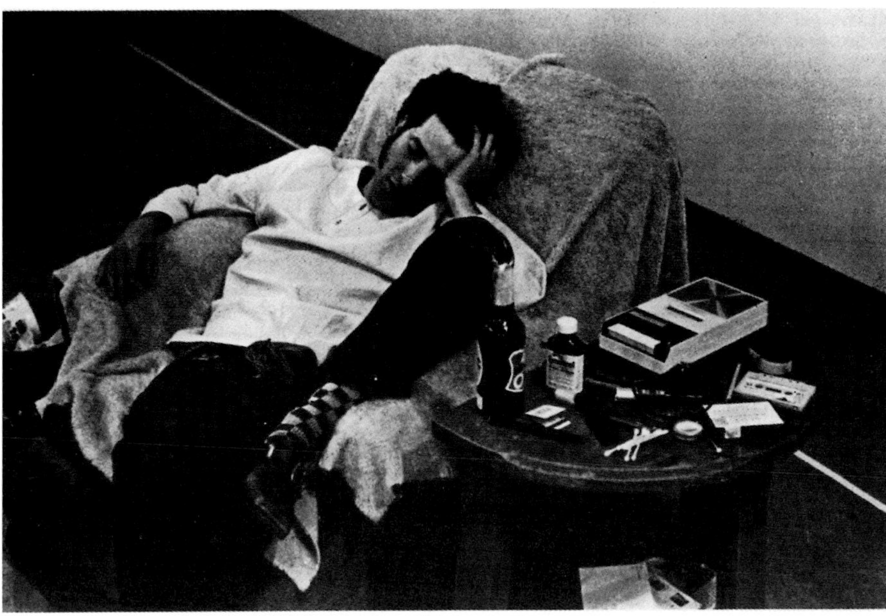

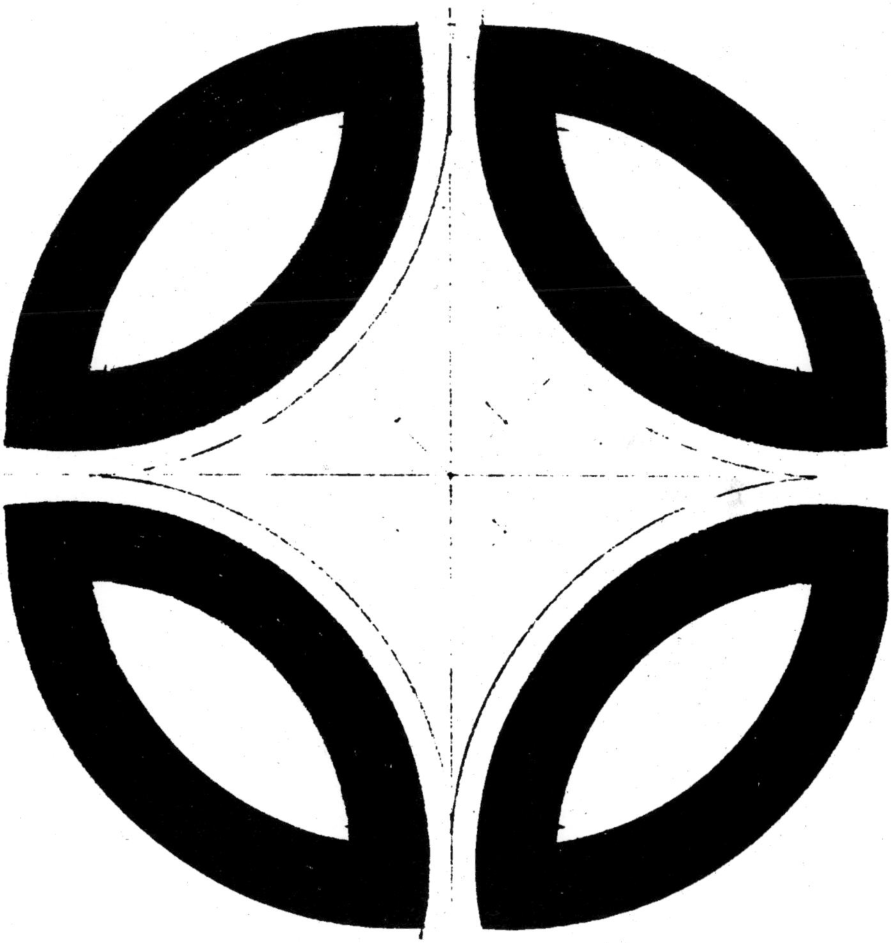

MOCA

denis masi

Distortion, 1973
A framework/concept of distortion (i.e., deform, distort, contort, warp, gnarl): to mar the appearance or nature of something as if by twisting. Deform, carries a slighter implication of twisting, but the suggestion of pulling out of shape is usually present. Distort and contort, clearly imply a twisting or wresting from that which is natural, normal, or true, but contort suggests a more involved twisting, and, usually, a more grotesque or painful effect than distort. Warp, which literally suggests a drying and shrinking out of shape, figuratively applies to that which has been given a bias, a wrong slant, an abnormal direction. Gnarl, used both literally and figuratively, suggests contortions induced by old age, weather, heavy work, misfortune, etc.
The central interest is DISTORTION; personal distortion manifested through the body and motivated by physical contact. It is important that this distortion should be operative both in form and content; it could also be extended to areas directly related to the personal, outside of cultural traditions (such as art), but not to the exclusion of an evident ethos.

The use of the body seems to be a very simple and logical decision; usually first consciousness is inherently associated with one's own body both in phenomenal and intellectual or intuitional experience.
My interest is, as well, in the aesthetic possibilities of a particular type of restricted and structured body psychology; maybe a celebration of the body; possibly an intrinsically symbolic usage of the body to reflect intentional inconsistencies.
It is important to consider that the content is consistent—distortion of the body (use of my own body or parts of it and/or the use of one or two other persons in similar or tableau situations). The distortion innate in the form is also consistent in that the end piece or object is always distorted through manipulation of technique. *Lip Smear,* for instance, was originally a videotape, but the two final objects of presentation are a 16 mm film (of the videotape) and a series of 40 selected b/w photographs & corresponding colour slides, thus in both cases allowing or even anticipating a definite degree of distortion through the breakdown in detail, etc. and the incorporation of chance happenings via transference from one technique to another or even a third, the resulting work seeming to be similar to the original but in fact very different.

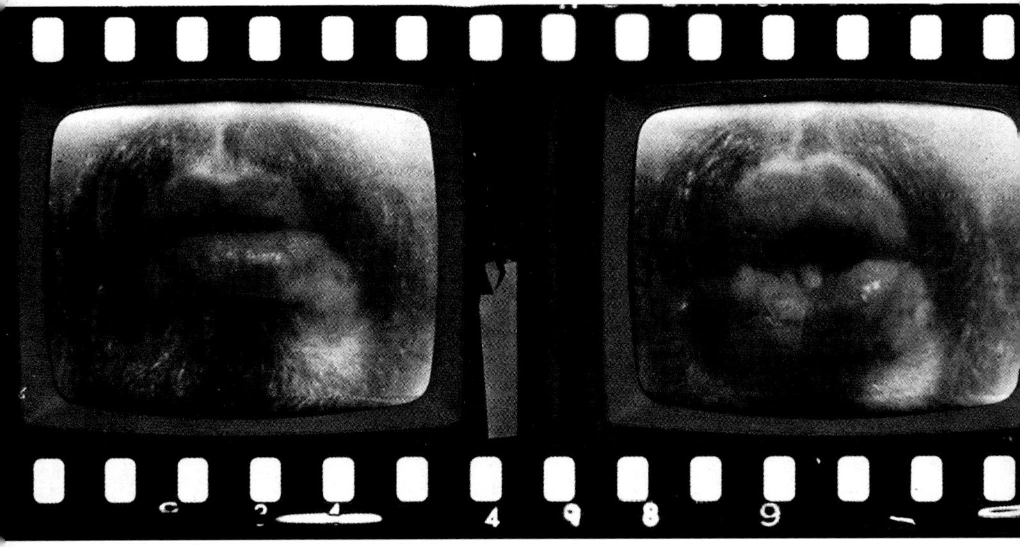

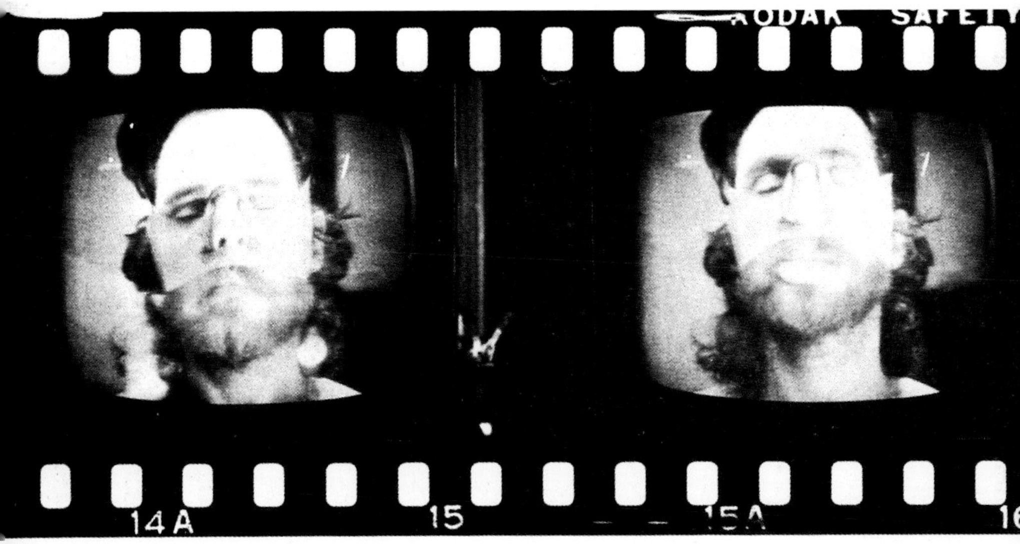

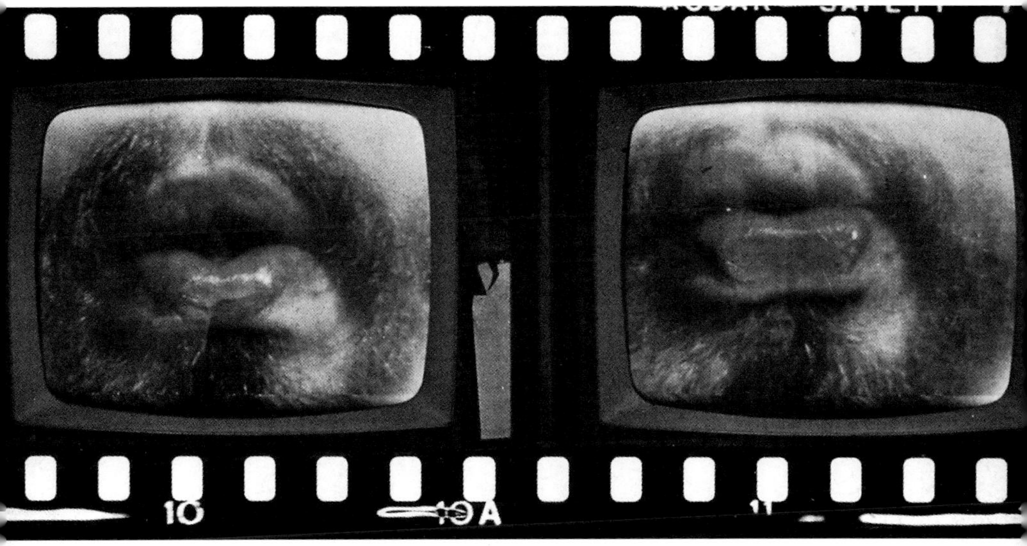
10
10A

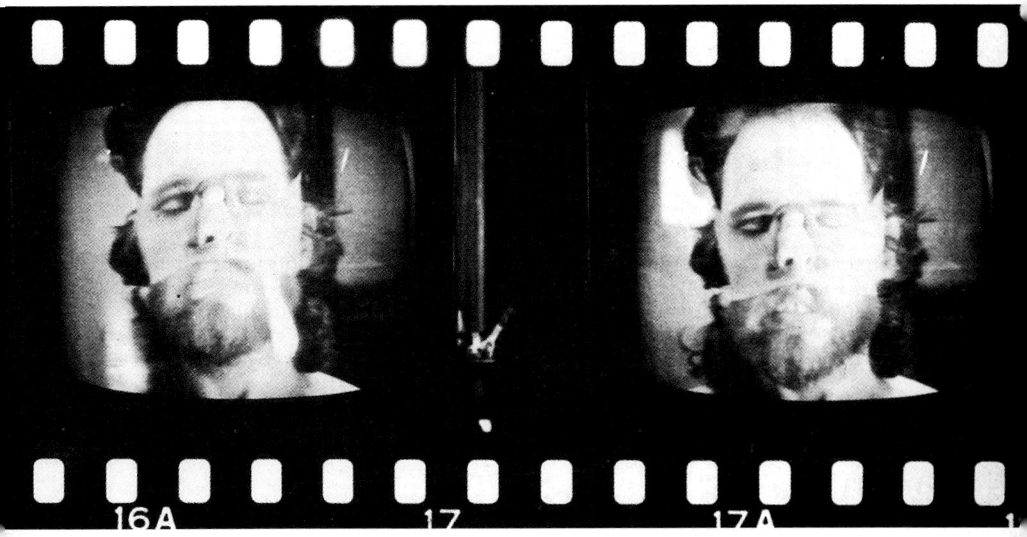
16A
17
17A

eliseo mattiacci

Remake Oneself, 1973
The artist covers his face with mud, seated at a table with a chair molded of cast aluminum.

To Think the Thought, 1973
A plaster bandage binds the eyes, the mouth and the ears of the artist seated at a table with a chair molded of cast aluminum, in front of a copper plate on which one can write with a metal point.

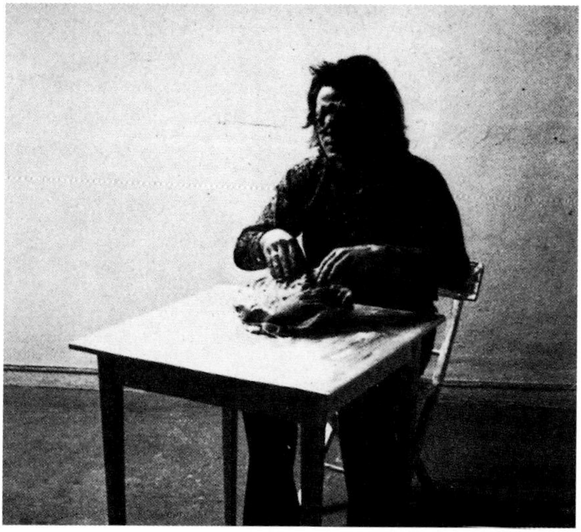

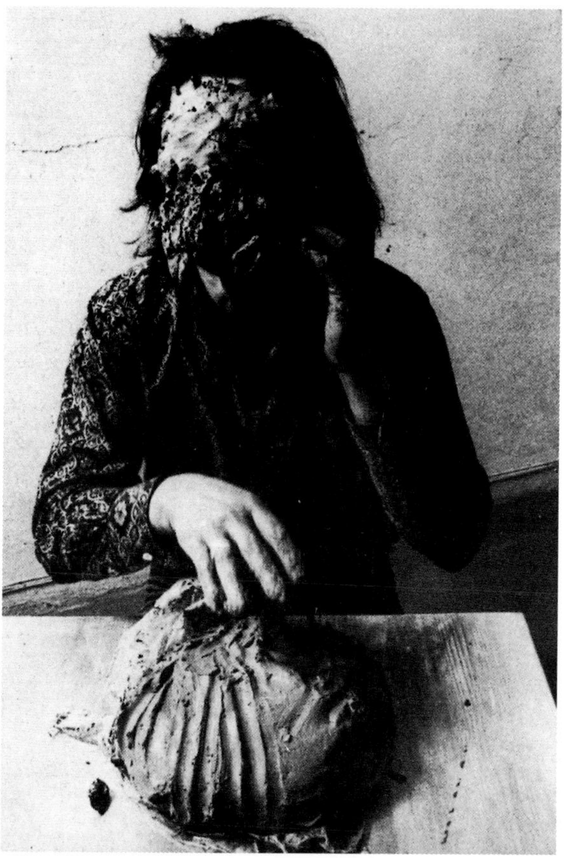

Remake Oneself, 1973

To Think the Thought, 1973

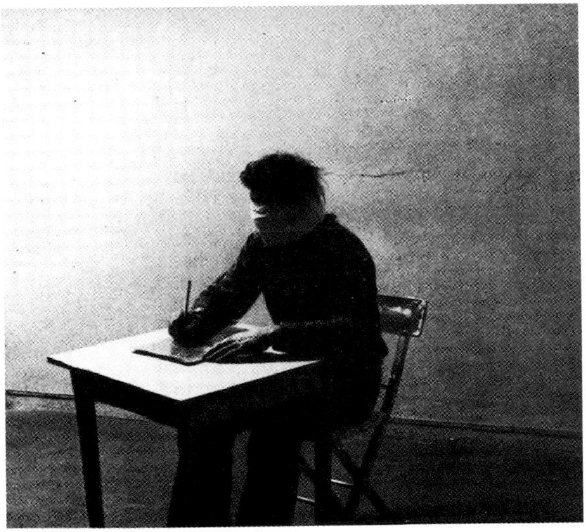

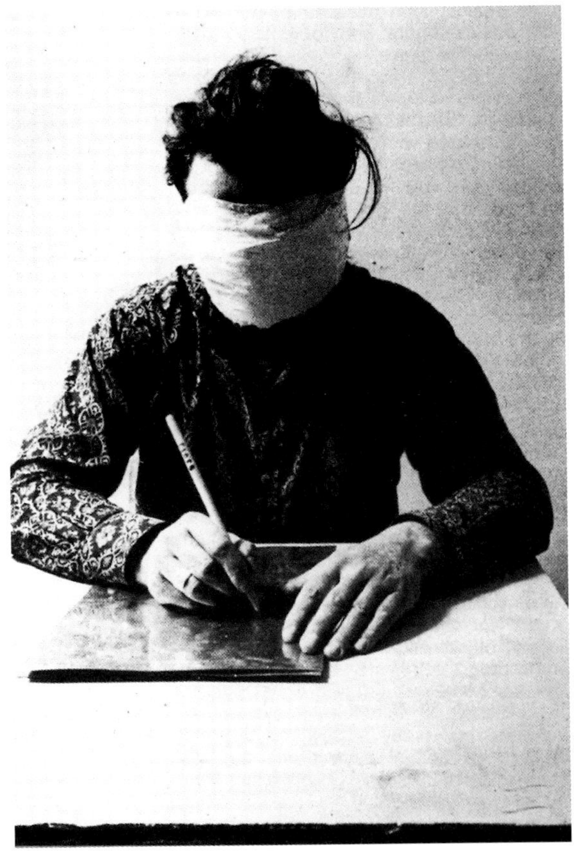

Ebrea, 1972
The girl cuts her own hair, forms the star of David on the mirror of the medicine cabinet
Ebrea may be a debt paid off today to a time which is now closed. It might be. A time—1945—when I too found myself in front of an intellectual operation based on a worked out system of "falsehoods." Anyway I saw racialism being presented again with variations which had already caused evil to an extent that had rarely been so pure.
In *Ebrea* anti-Jewish racialism represents the anti-black racialism and any other species or subspecies of racialism. This law, finally, can be summarized as follows: "discrimination exists because of a lack of values. Or, equally, because of values." And discrimination is the contrary of judgement. It is a sentence executed against man not because of his individual features but on the basis of infinitely repeated traits, objective traits, external and collective signs.
In Europe, from the thirties to the forties, racialism had a scientific origin: it stated that races exist, and that some of them are superior. These are two ideas which I recognized as being wrong, although the former is still largely accepted.

Not all has been lamented or enjoyed as it should have been.
In *Ebrea* it is the first case.
I had little time to examine the substance of that reality thoroughly. A disease closed my eyes at once, confiscating the whole postwar period. Somewhere an unexpressed lament remains. I am not a Jew, nor am I a son of a Jew. I have wished I could be a Jew. I feel I am a Jew whenever possible, and I suffer discrimination, an unfair discrimination. Concerning oneself with this question means completing the cry, for a benefit of poetic nature and, maybe, for one's psychological health. Nobody can prevent me from curing myself as I want.
In *Ebrea* the operation is cold. And tactlessly cultural. Patiently I repeat with my hands the experience of the shameful one. I explore his mental possibilities. By extending his action I invent new objects made up of new men. Incidentally I hinder the self-confidence of contemporary design with its faith in progress. I behave as if that historic reality had not had its final condemnation, but as if it were still adding up data today. Elsewhere, we may suspect, in different ways, the operation is still going on.

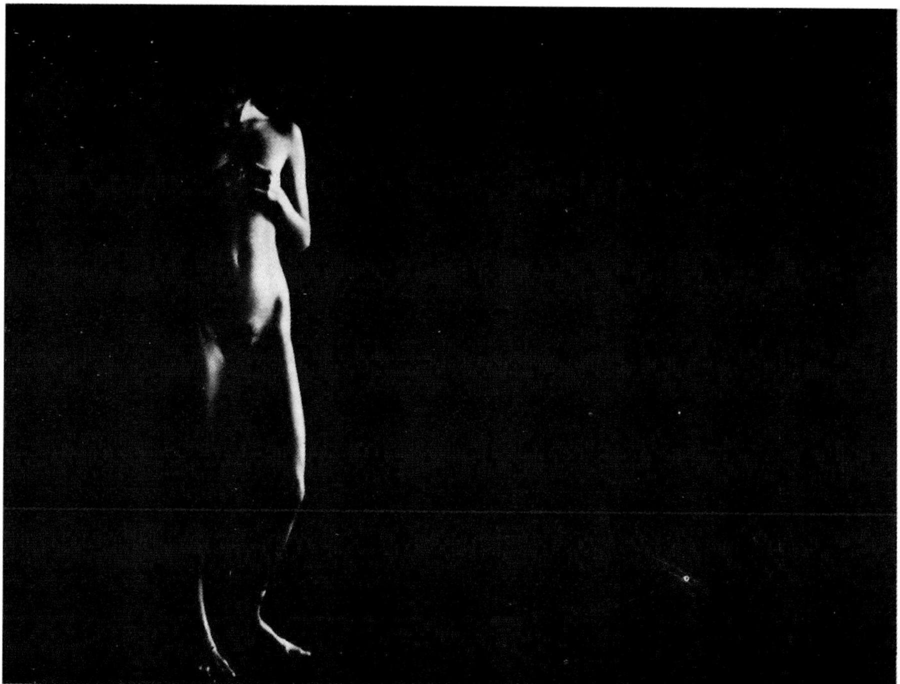

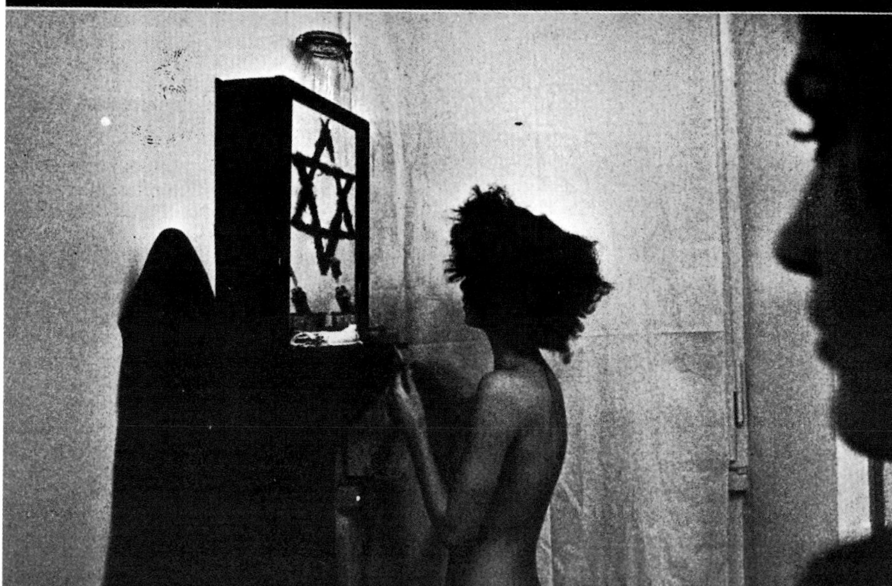

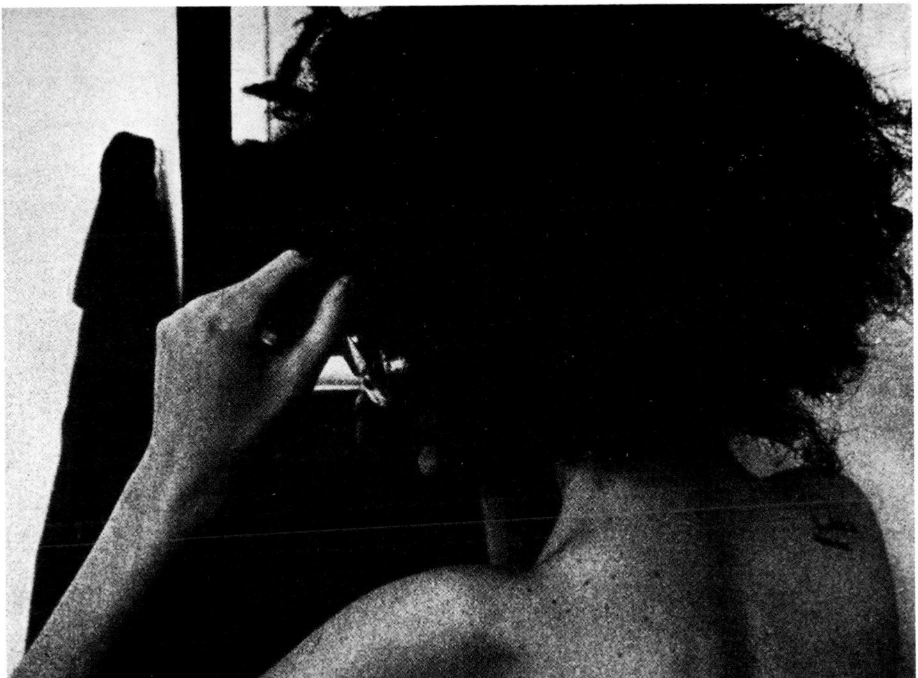

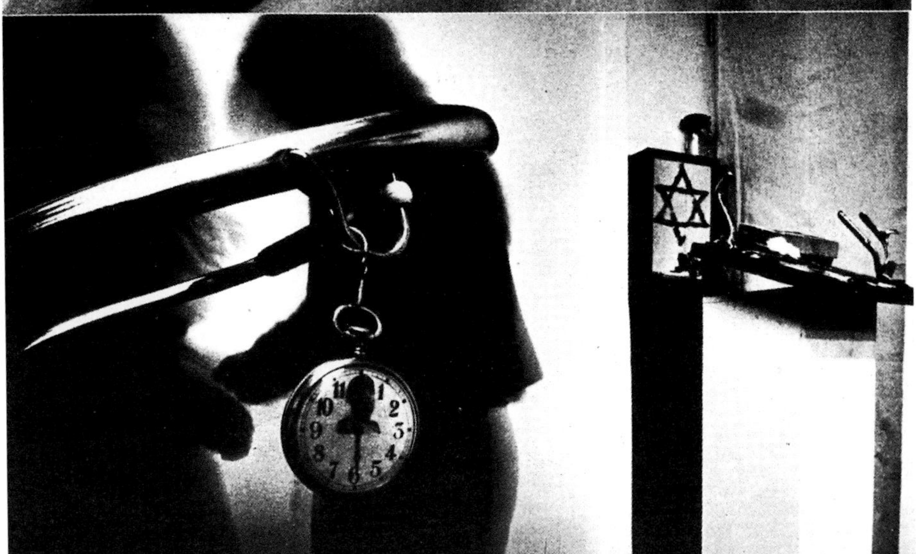

annette messager

Album-Collection no. 11, 1972
Men-Women and Women-Men
I love to observe men and women walking together. Not knowing them personally, I am better able so see to what extent the characters of the man-man and the real woman often seem inverted, but each one preserves the role which he or she is supposed to represent.

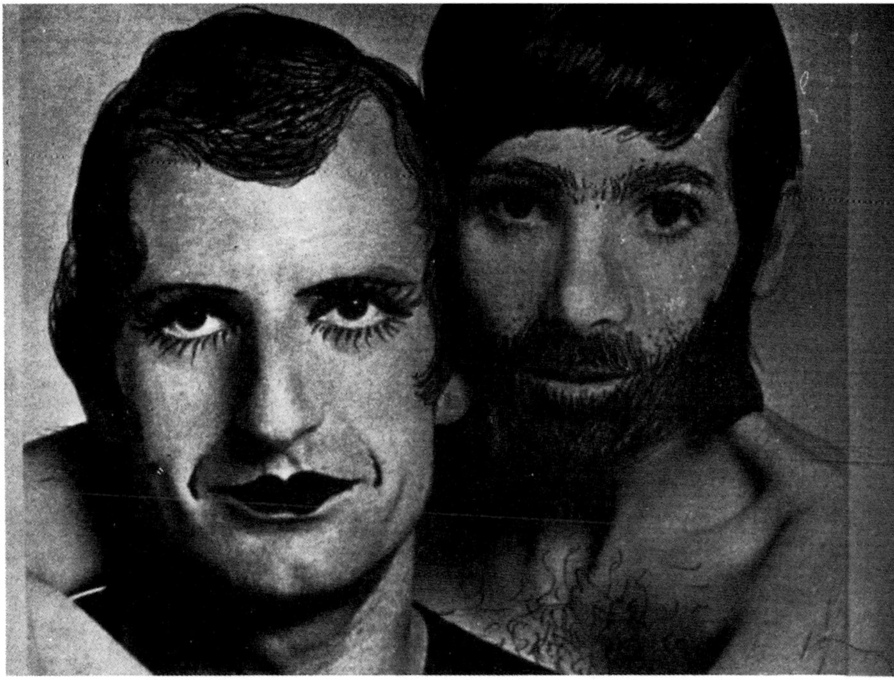

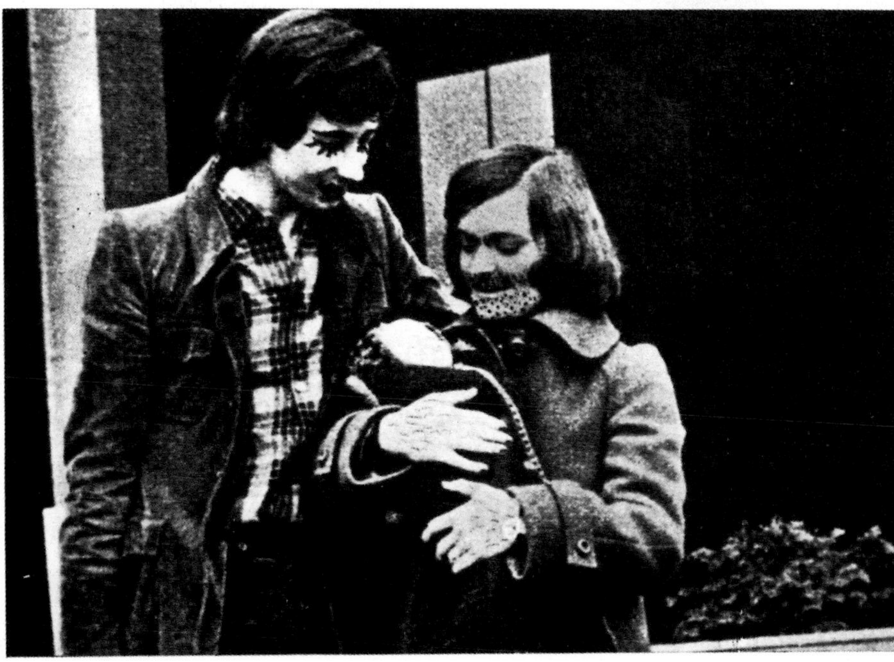

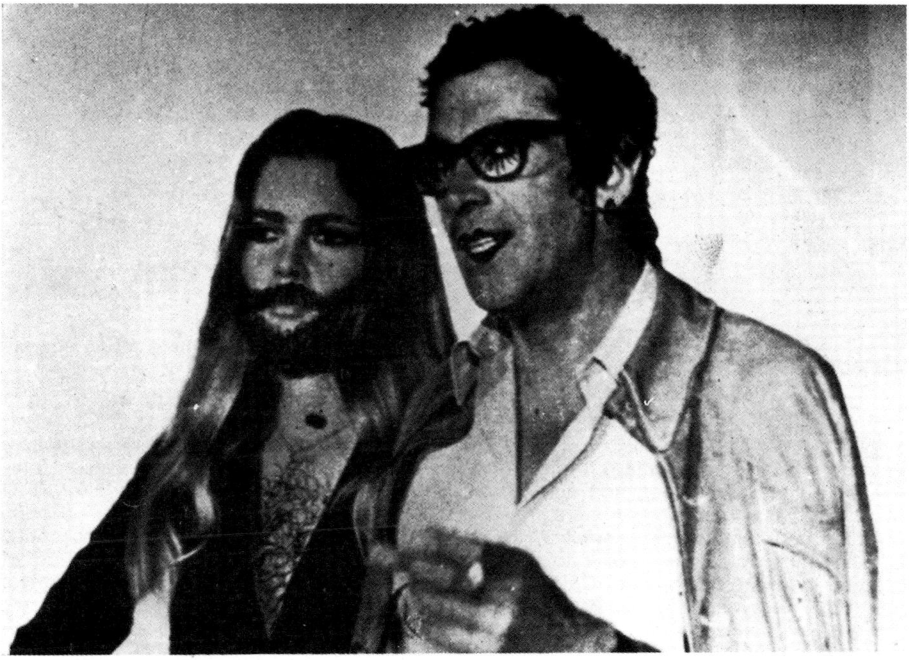

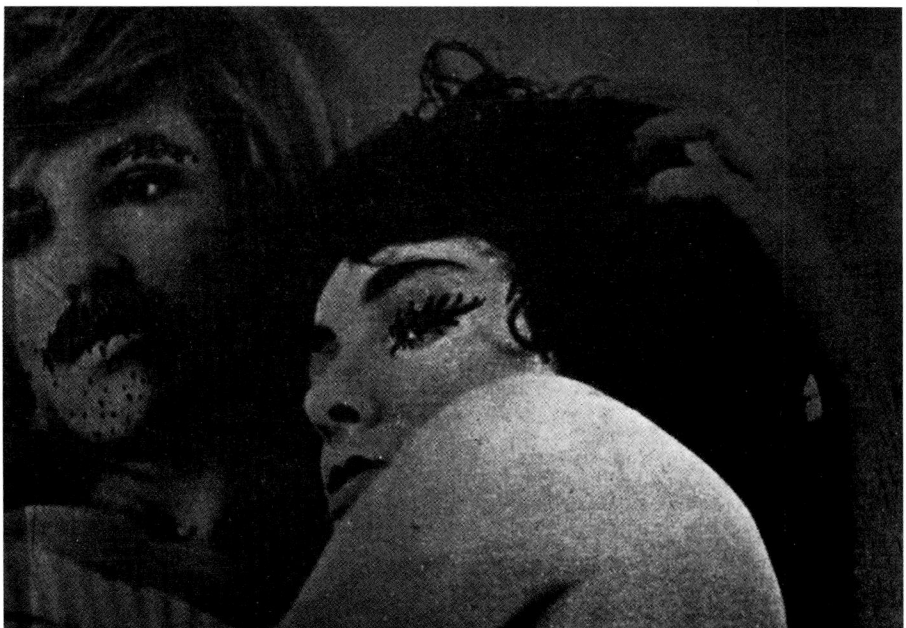

otto muehl

Metamorphosis with Jam, 1965
Action with Body and Food, Irritarte exhibition, 1969
My work is represented painting, it is self-therapy made visible. With food and edible material. It acts as a psychosis determined by the mixture of human bodies, objects, materials. Everything is planned. Everything may be used as material and matter. Color not as colorant but as crayon, liquid, powder; egg not as egg but as viscous matter. Associations are used which link themselves to determinate materials either because of their form or for their meaning or normal use. Real facts are imitated and mixed with materials; real facts which can be mixed with artificial facts. In the same way, time and places can be exchanged. A symphony orchestra plays, naked, in a swimming pool which, little by little, is filled with jam, for example. The representation of a melodrama is sprayed with colors and covered with food: the singers have the job of carrying on to the very end.

Mixture, exchanges, and metamorphoses can be employed even during official ceremonies, parades, marches and other demonstrations of the kind. Real events are imitated such as auto accidents, floods, fires and are mixed with various materials. Mixtures and combinations are carried out according to the dream method. In this way, events of a profound meaning result. Jam, dead bodies, road building equipment. Events will be formed, materials penetrate reality, common value no longer has sense, the jam becomes blood, everything becomes a symbol for some other event. The associativeness then has a large space within the possibilities which we have been given. If the audience cooperates, they become either actors or materials.
To impede interruptions during the action, the handling will be similar to that of a gym lesson.
(Manifesto of 1965, Vienna)

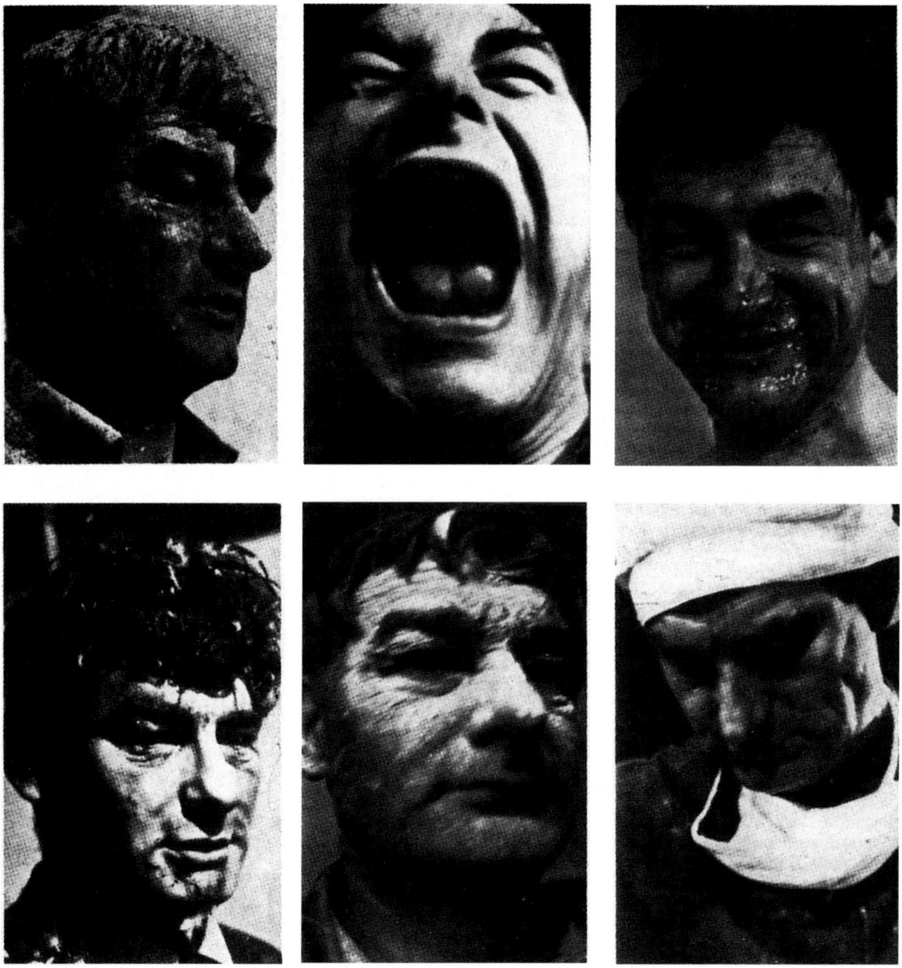

Metamorphosis with Jam, 1965

Action with Body and Food, 1969

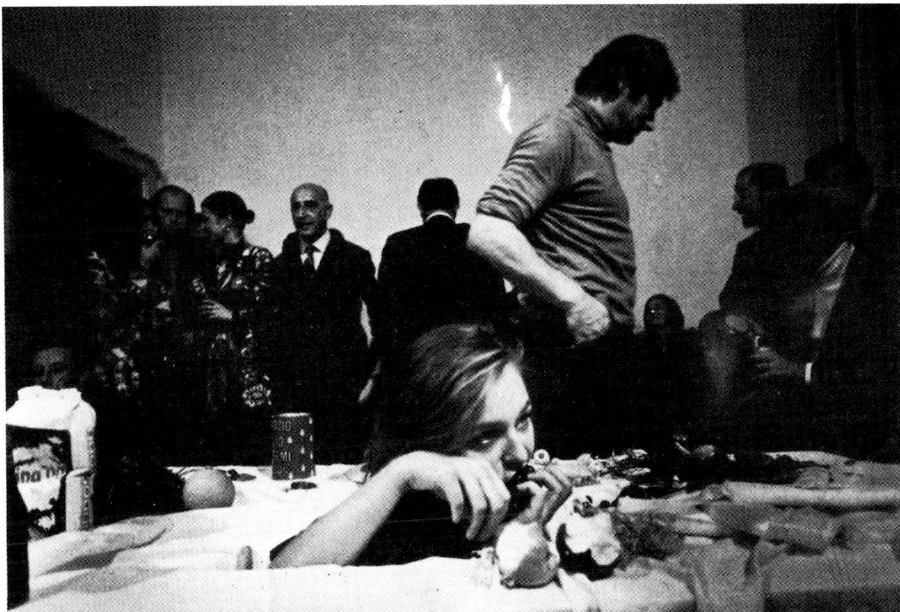

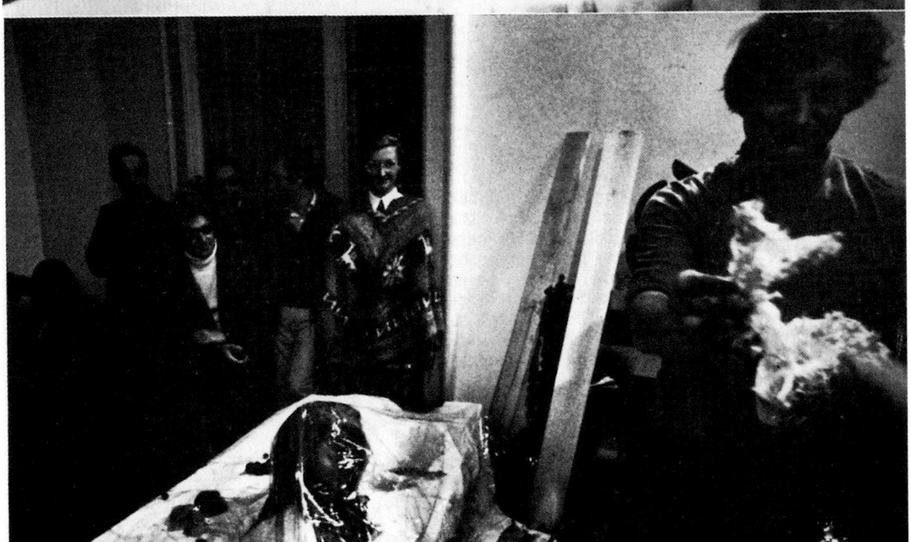

hidetoshi nagasawa

Without Title, 1972

To recover the memory of a hardly touched entity has been the subject of my work for the past few years. For the present work I have chosen the body because my hand had to be involved with a live substance. Thus, I begin by very slowly touching a naked woman on those points in which I am especially interested, almost the whole front side. At a certain moment the woman disappears, she is no longer in front of me. I find myself facing the cloth which was previously the background for the woman; my hand dirty with charcoal, I touch this cloth at the same points where I was touching the body, I repeat the same gestures; in the end, an image emerges on the cloth (the woman has disappeared only for the spectator, but actually she has remained behind the cloth, and only I know she is there).

I am interested in verifying to what extent it is possible to remember what one has seen, through touch. I think I can remember more through my hand than through my eye.

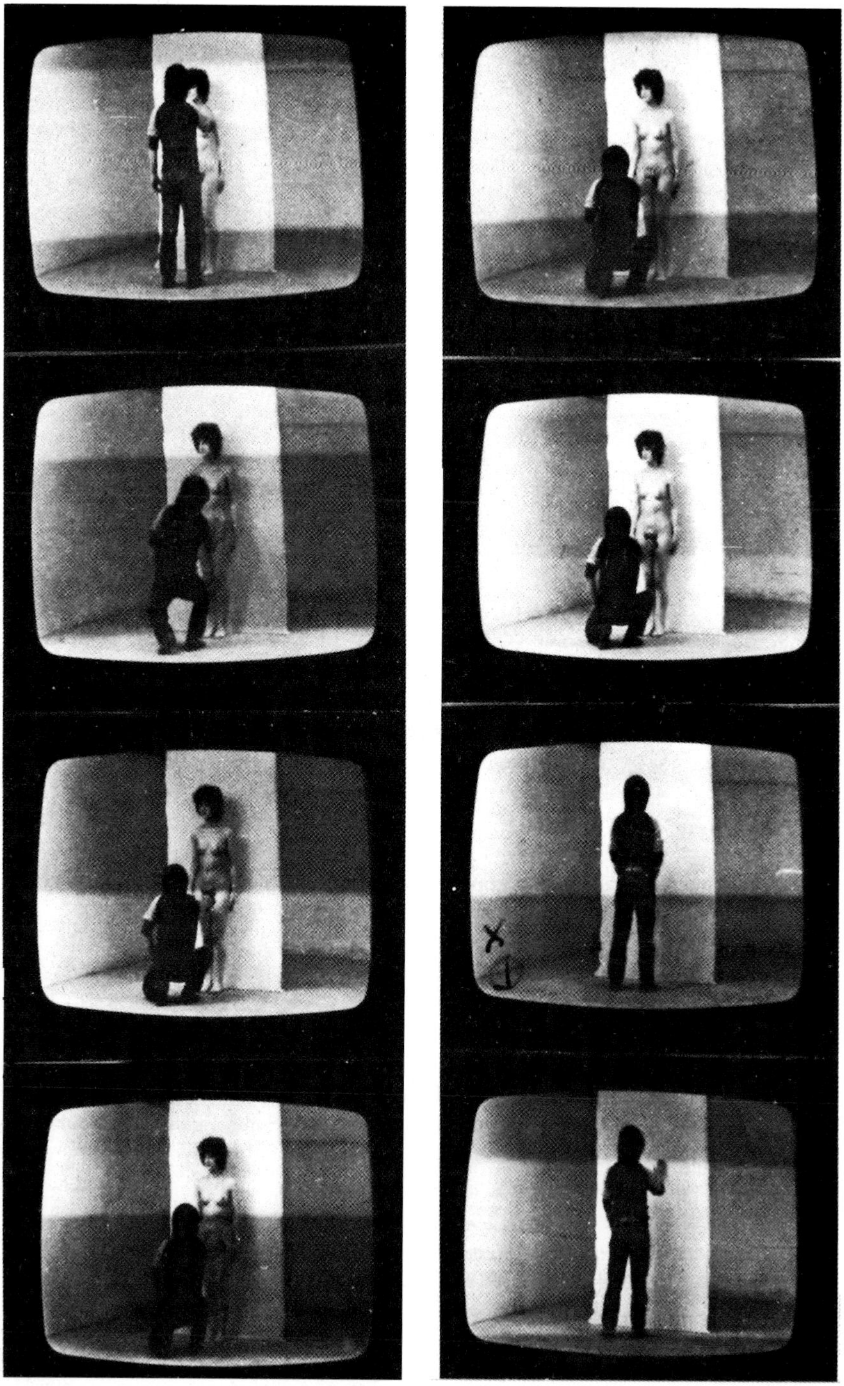

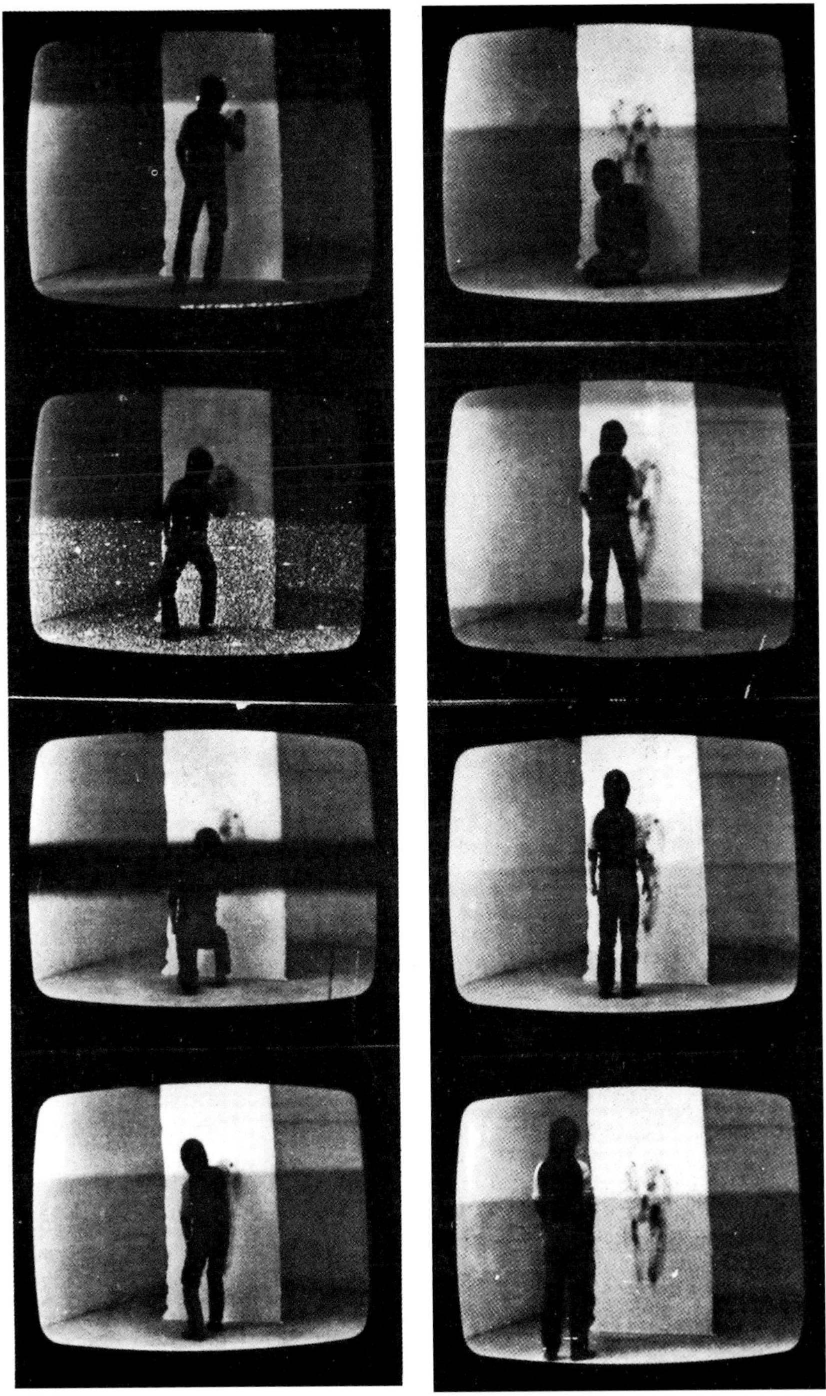

ugo nespolo

Cheeks Ablaze, 1967

"Les joues en feu", cheeks ablaze; after all, they are just cheeks, things that change, and nothing else.

The body is the static support of the ironic and everchanging game; a slightly (but not very) grown Radiguet in the "day of collecting ostrich feathers, bunches of curly waves, a fan of Venus."

Changes never cease: the altered use of a rhythmically quickened motion, and a parallel use of color, obtained instead through continuous reversals of the camera, as well as through repeated multiple exposures, give the film its "poetic soft focus."

And there are more than a hundred items of clothing coming and going in a continuous vortex of attitudes.

The key for access, then, is clearly thinking and saying (paraphrasing):

We have come to see the boy
who having, it seems, taken after
Cinderella, can direct
the cotillon
for six uninterrupted minutes.

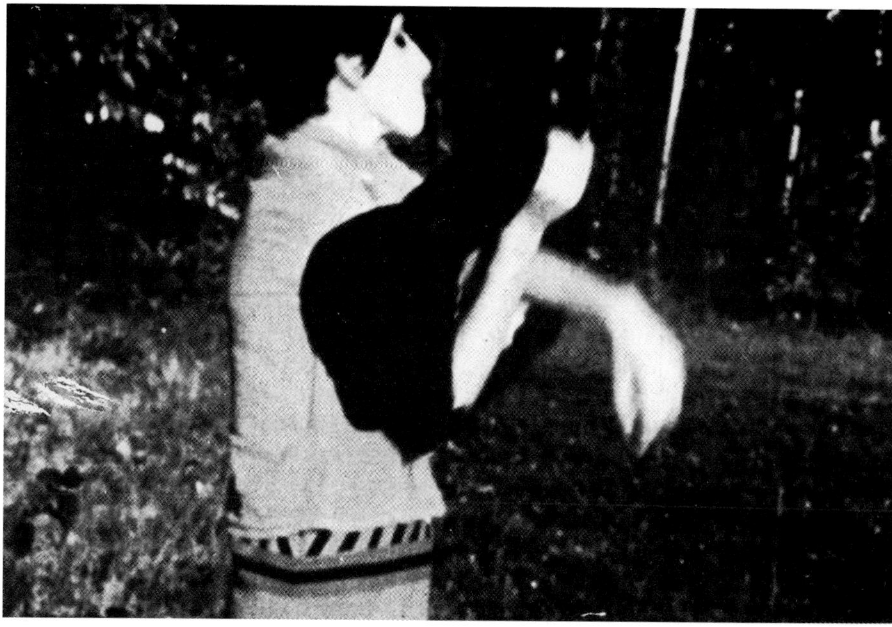

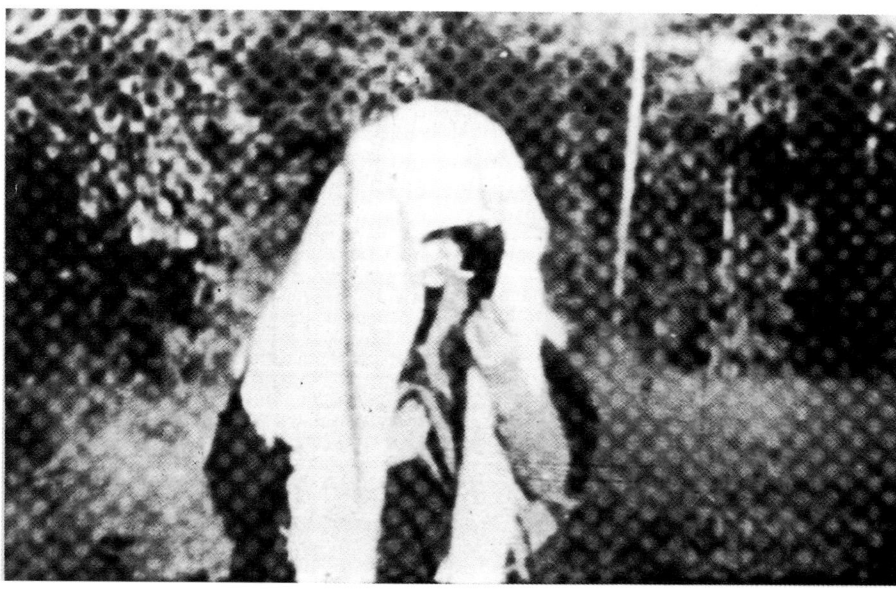

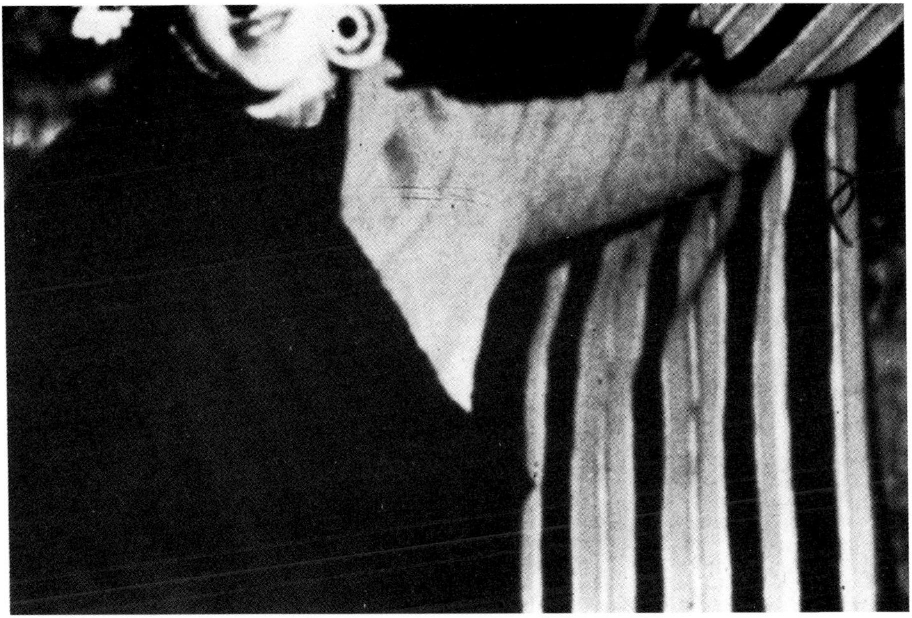

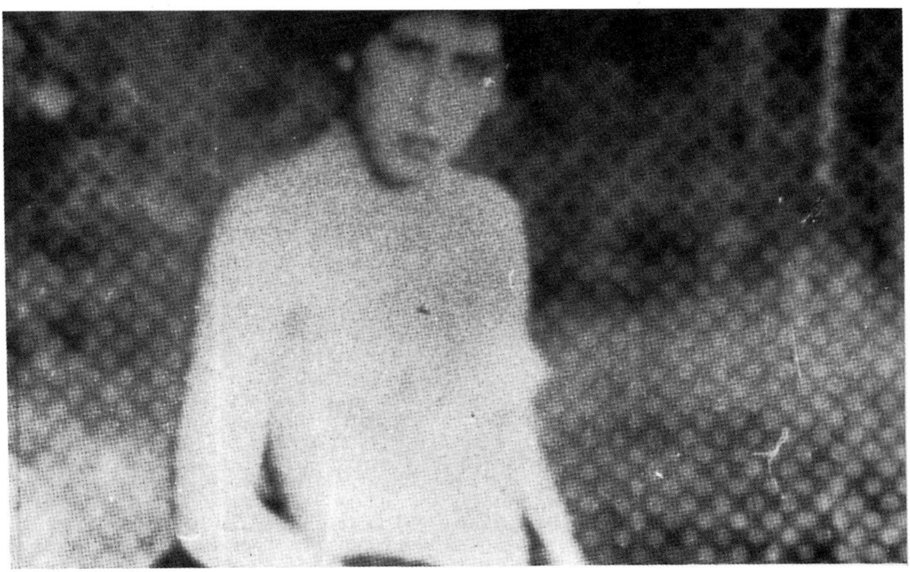

hermann nitsch

Performance, 1965

We are ever more attracted by our own existence. Every work of art is nothing but the mystique of the being. The aesthetics which pushes us until horror. The aesthetics of horror. This synesthetic attribute composed of
tactile sensations
taste sensations
olfactory sensations
acoustic recordings (sound colors)
and visual recordings (light colors)
exalts our orgiastic senses. This growing activity of the whole sensorial apparatus can be compared to psychoanalytic analysis. Instead of associations, we find actions having the task of recording the sensorial activities up to the final point of orgiastic reaction. (The sado-aggressive sensations, at an elementary level, which are obtained by tearing apart flesh, quartering the carcass of an animal and circling around the viscid mass of the intestines. The screams and noises of the action itself.) A long, exhausting crescendo of all the senses culminates in sadomasochistic excess. But it is just this excess, in its most complete representation, which provokes at the end, with an impressive lucidity, the real catharsis. This is the most dramatic moment of the action. A profound sense of repulsion pervades everywhere and at first charges the spectator negatively, but at the same time it acts subtly within the spectacle: the instincts are appeased, they sublimate themselves, they are dulled.

The events which actually happen on the stage of this "theater of orgies and mysteries"—contrary to the typical fiction used in the classic theater—are reflected in the soul of each spectator, favoring access in all its totality, of the lived existential mystique, this time, not individually but collectively.
Each gesture carries with it an enormous baggage of experience and a long series of profound meditations on existence itself. Instead of reacting, of denying, one accepts and visually sublimates every moment of the action, often helped by colored lights. Practically an aesthetic liturgy is born, which winds continually until the end.

FLESH
flesh
To dismember the flesh,
anal, sado-masochistically
(action of disenbowelment
and of laceration)
to better understand the
amorphous zones of the being.
Color does not appear immediately
as such, but intensifies only
the sensuous zones.

COLOR (light)
color
The sublimating action of quartering
sections the light and the
colors of the flesh.
Flesh = light.
Rainbow.
Lightbow
seed of light, circle of colors,
circle of light.
Matthias Grünewald.

The sadomasochistic abreaction sublimates itself during the action until it fully comprehends all colors.

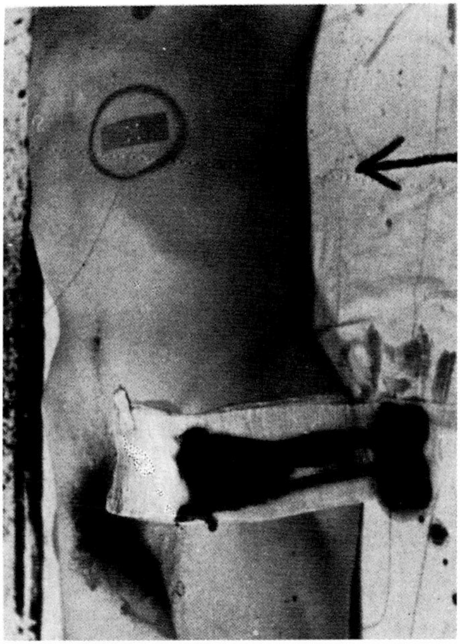

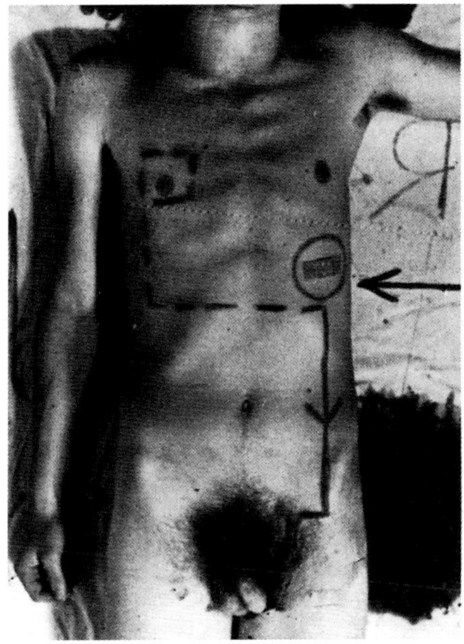

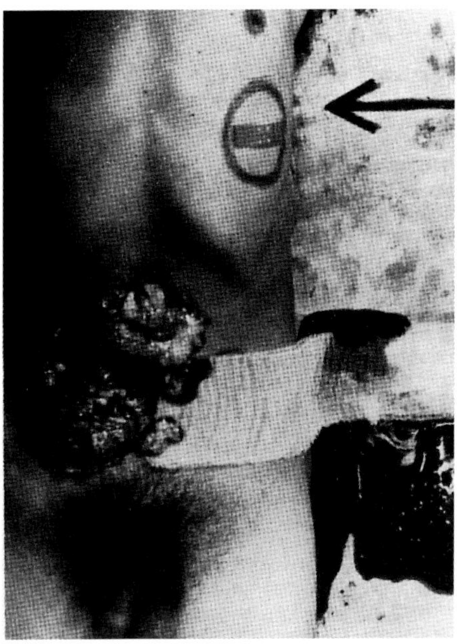

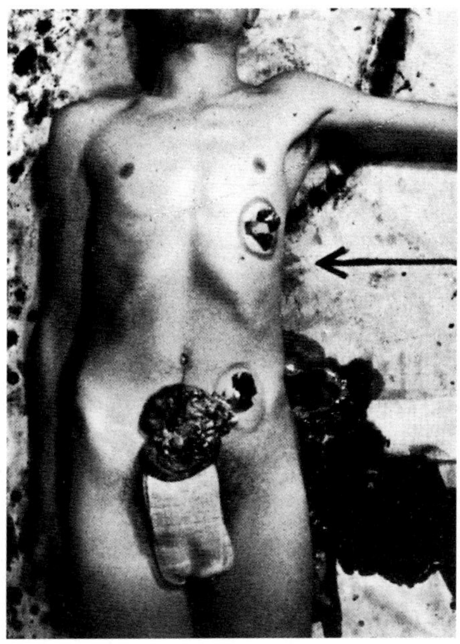

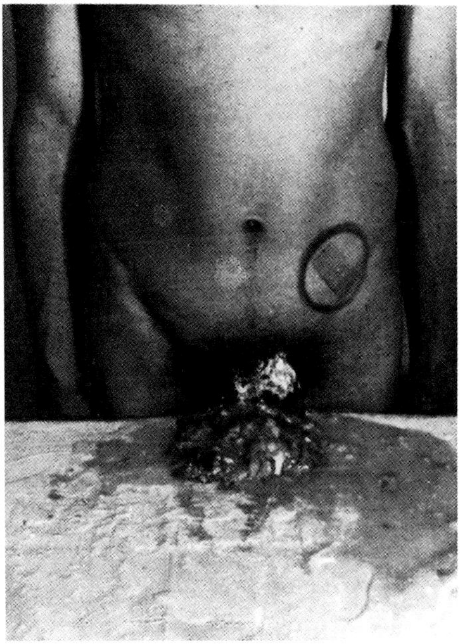

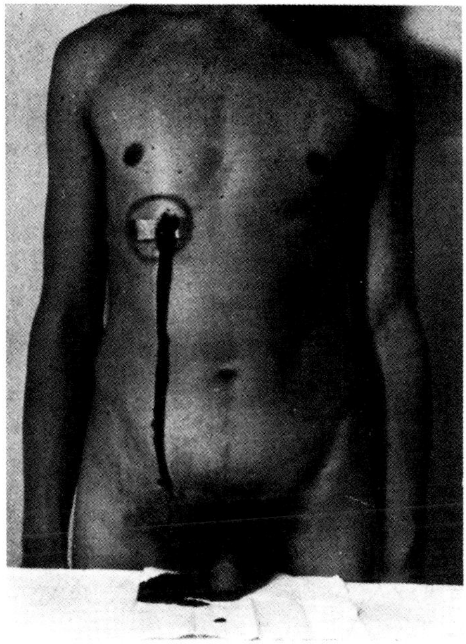

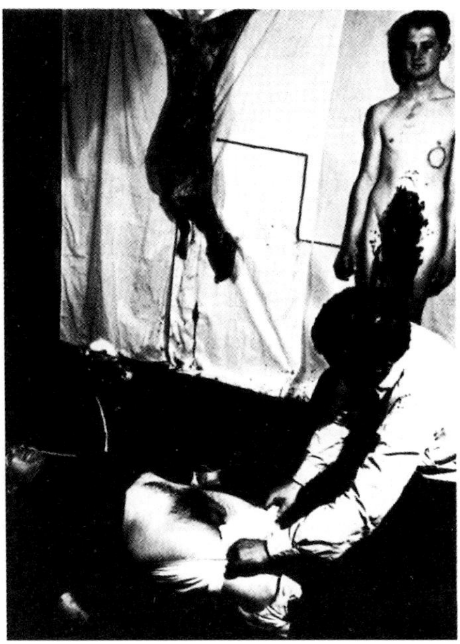

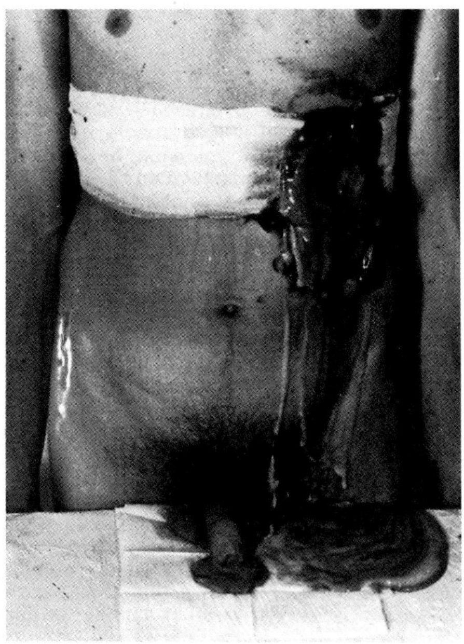

luigi ontani

Bacchino Poses, 1973

POSE = proposition of presence as possibility to outline the ideal self, probable freshness/intensity, by direct formulation or quotation, polyvalent rigorous accumulation = POSE = is a synthesis-moment as photographic expression and as a sample of behavior = Bacchino [Small Bacchus] is the quotation-case = is icon as revealing result = is conception/summary of the itinerary of knowledge = is the immediate sign of the meditated = is visualization of the postulated idea = is witness of the organic whole = is example/message of human thickness = is intrinsic deviation for the irregular = is pervasiveness in the vanity.

"the pretty statuettes" = is the sweetened hero of awareness = is radicalization of language = is the humor/lucidity as indigenous pre-eminence of life/culture = is condition of an effective connection for a further real = is concept/rainbow = refusal of separateness = is energy/present infinity = (and beyond) =

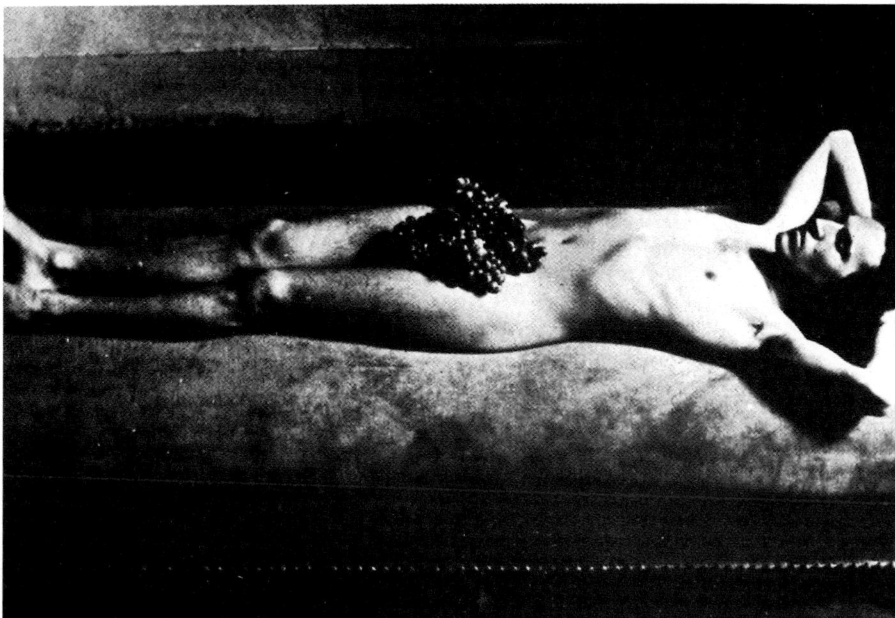

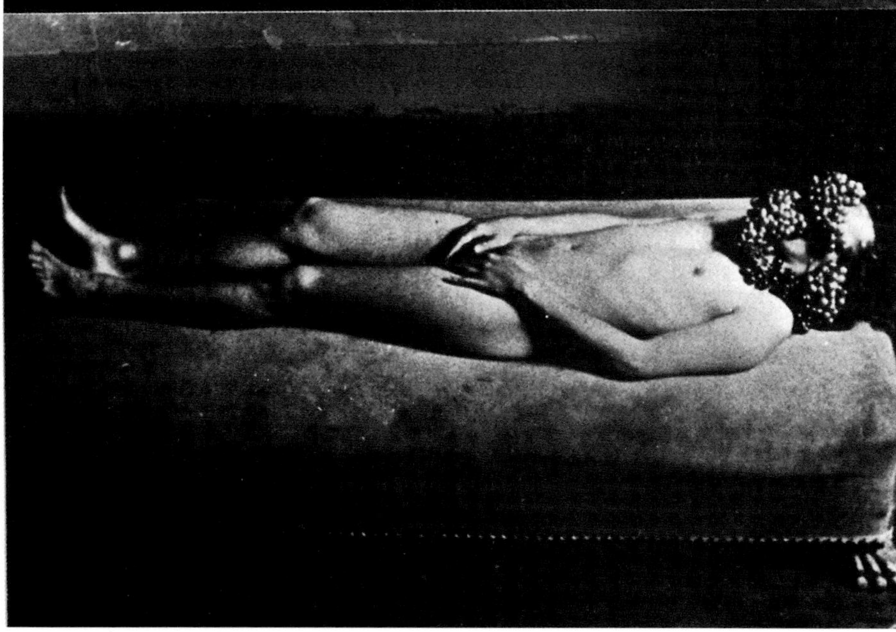

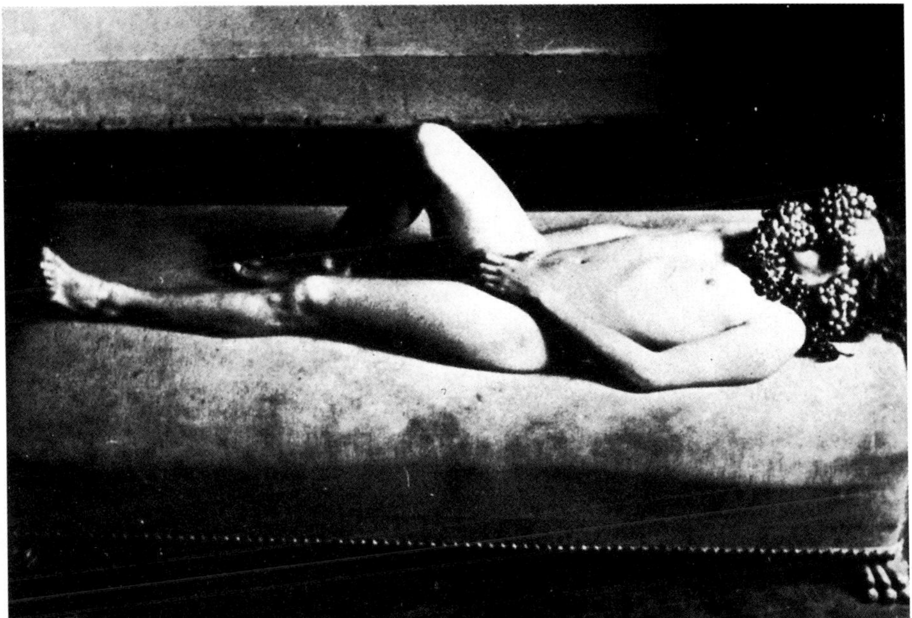

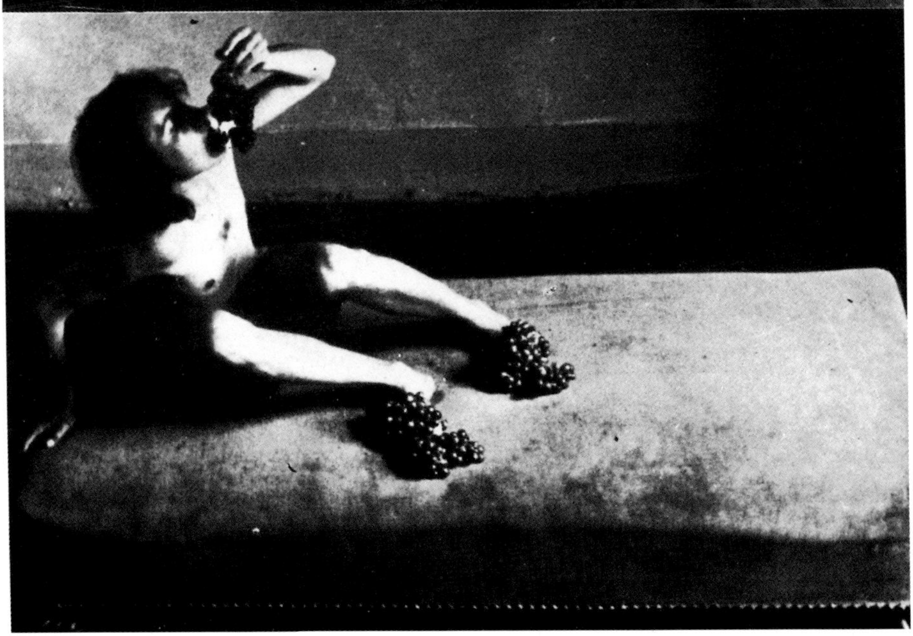

dennis oppenheim

Stills from Gingerbread Man, 1970–71
A project dealing with activation of digestive processes.
Situation created in which first... a symbolically human form is slowly broken down and subjected to the linearity of the intestinal tract... it is used to fill an internal space... and by emptying the stomach beforehand this material is allowed full occupancy... It takes over the space, forcing itself into a linear housing... where it is held captive to gastric processes, additional breakdown and depletion. Here the process of making (changes) is linked with that of a life sustaining interaction.

The residue (waste products) becomes the finished work
Micro-Projection-Feces
Gingerbread material consisting of: enriched flour, sugar, dried molasses, shortening with freshness preserver, leavening, salt, vegetable gum, spices, caramel color, was rolled into dough and shaped to resemble a human form. These figures were slowly eaten and digested. Later my intestinal tract was emptied. Ten samples of feces were placed on glass slides. These samples were viewed under a microscope at magnifications of × 280 to × 3000.

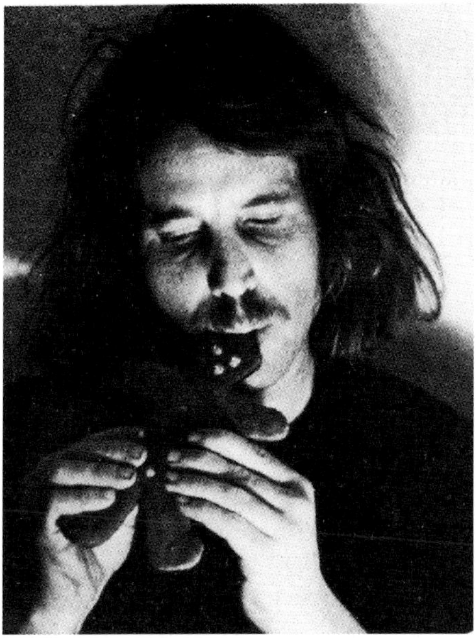

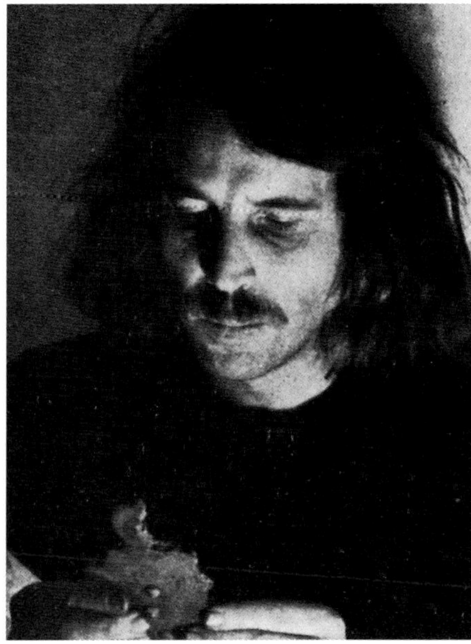

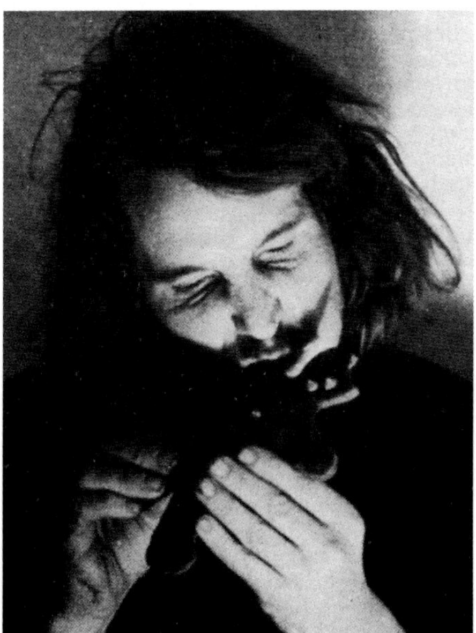

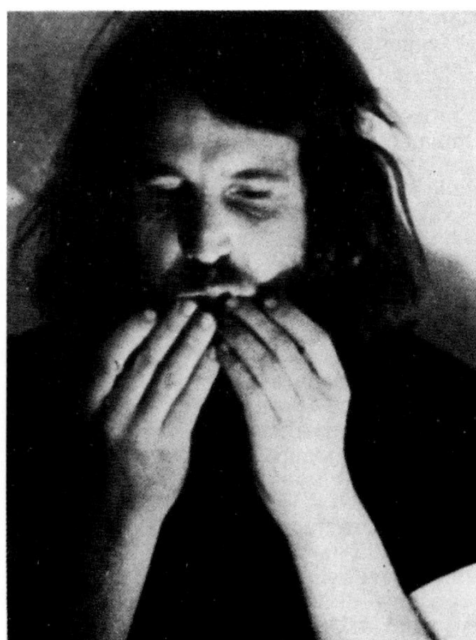

Stills from Gingerbread Man, 1970–71

Micro-Projection-Feces

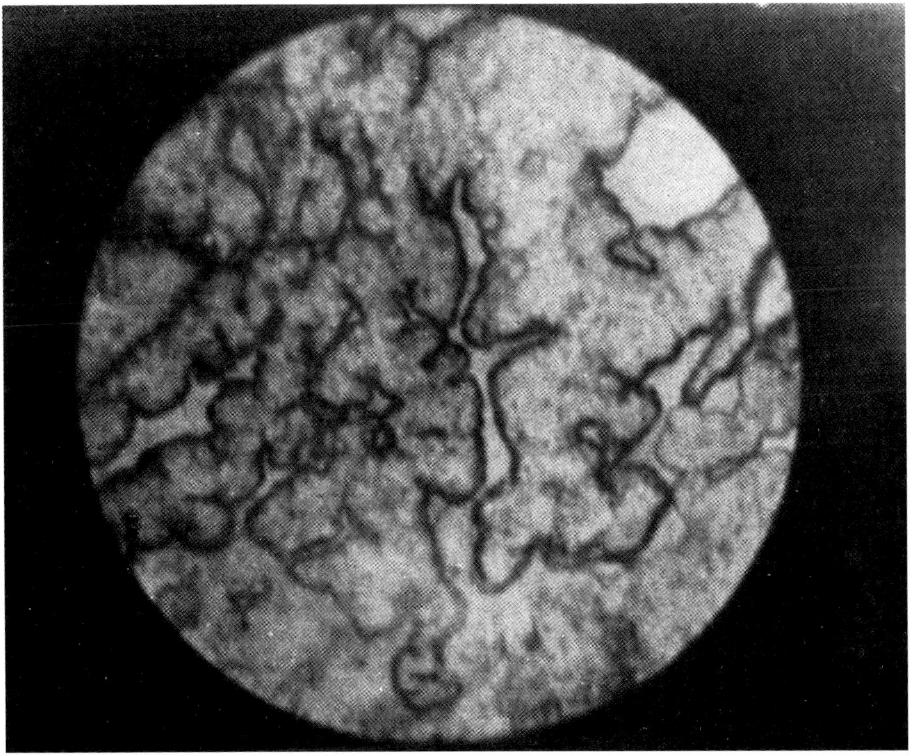

jean otth

TV Perturbations, 1971

The Limits. (Interrogation on "realities" of the image.)

The "limit" is a theme on which I have been working for the past two years. It is an extremely simple operation in which the primary gesture, consisting in the separation of two forms, is essential for me; at the origin, it is one of creation's first acts.

By breaking the dialogue into two surfaces, the "parasite" which I insert, signals or even signifies an image.

Being an element of a dialectics between an outline which isolates and a passage which "opens," the limit in itself is an exciting problem which was suffocated by a seeming banality.

To fix a limit graphically in the actions and the videotapes belonging to this series becomes, paradoxically, a pretext for an interrogation on the modalities of the "realities" of an image. In a strip like

Limit A, I intervene on the image of my shadow, with white chalk on a blackboard.
The interest of this experience rests on the level of magnetoscopic documentation, on the simultaneous presentation of three types of reality: my shadow, its graphic fixing, and the back of my image. Curiously enough, the highest degree of reality moves incessantly from one to the other modality of the subject. These are different readings of the very video image which will give rise to the problems of "reality." Pursuing this work, I made a certain number of magnetoscopic actions, in which I no longer intervene on my shadow but on my own image, both diapositive and cinematographic.
This ambiguous dialectic, by disturbing our perception habits, should incite us to an interrogation on the various statutes of iconic "reality."

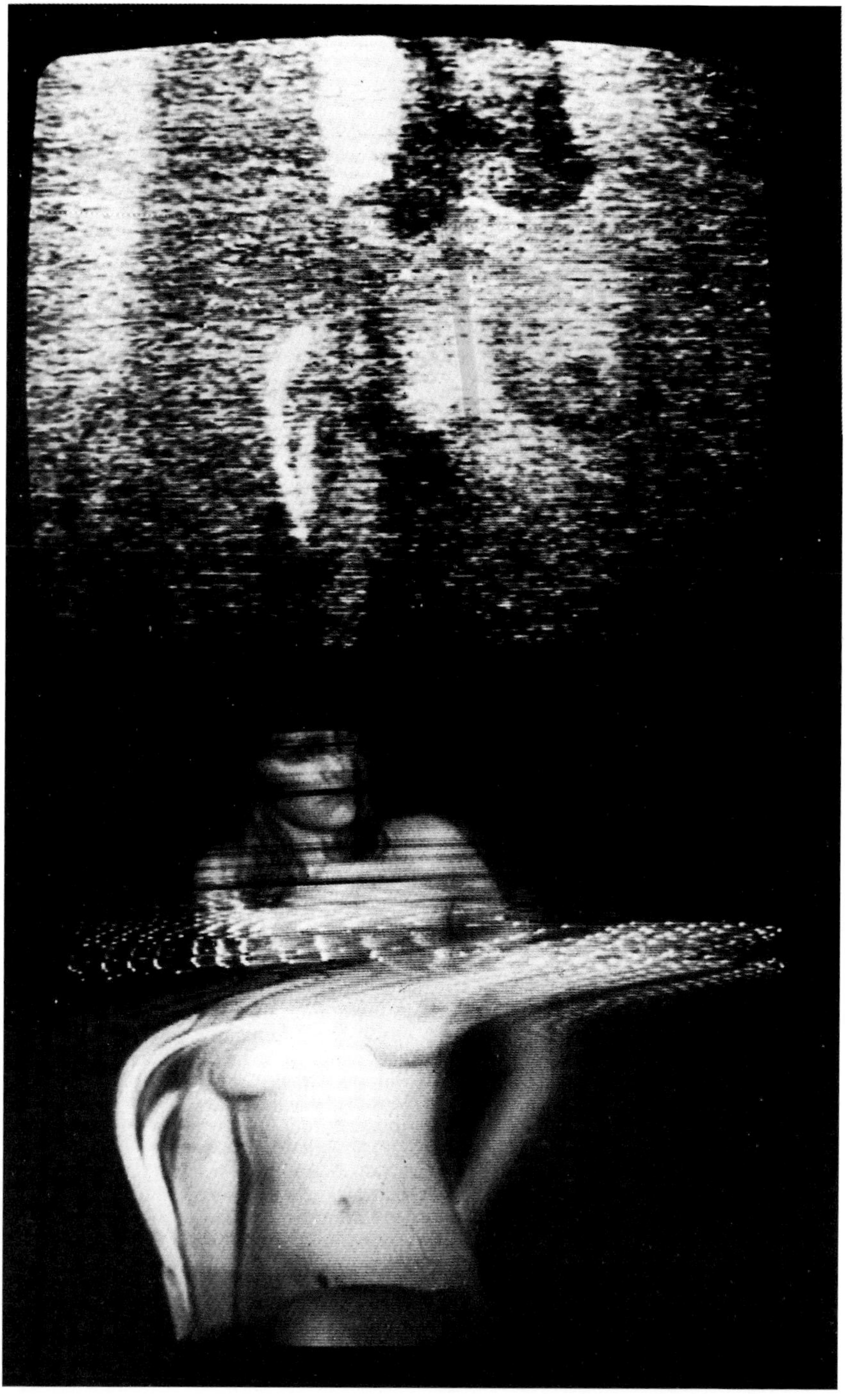

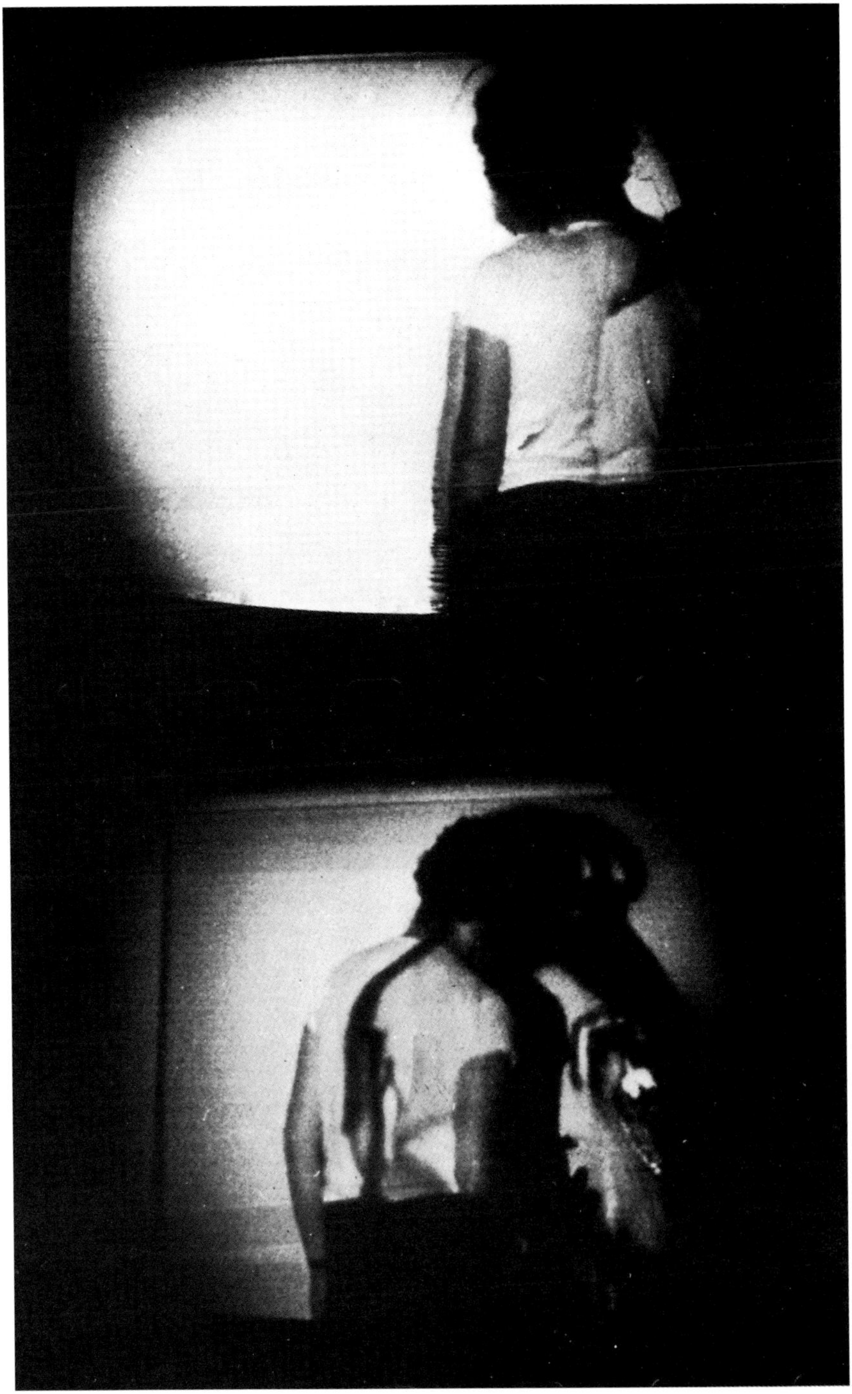

stanislao pacus

The Conquered Conscience, 1973

Actors: Lolly Santini, Stanislao Pacus. Material: book, quail, armchair, posters with the inscriptions "Selvatico" (Wild), "La coscienza conquistata" (The Conquered Conscience), string.

With this videotape I wanted to make evident the reconquest of his conscience by the artist, bewildered by his love for a woman, symbol of wildness. Woman nullifies creativeness, she is the dualistic model of love-hate in which the artist loses himself and from which, with intellectual effort, he escapes. To reconquer his professional conscience the artist derides the loved-hated woman's nakedness. The string that goes from the man's hand to the book (symbol of artistic construction), to the quail (symbol of the conquered conscience), makes evident the rediscovered condition, this slow resumption of the artist's conscience. The idea for this videotape was suggested to me by these lines by Leopardi, "Lovely as you were, you were / in the season which is conducive to sweet dreams," which, since childhood, impressed on me how great a man's love for a woman can be. I am very envious of the poet's imagination, liberated through his love for a woman.

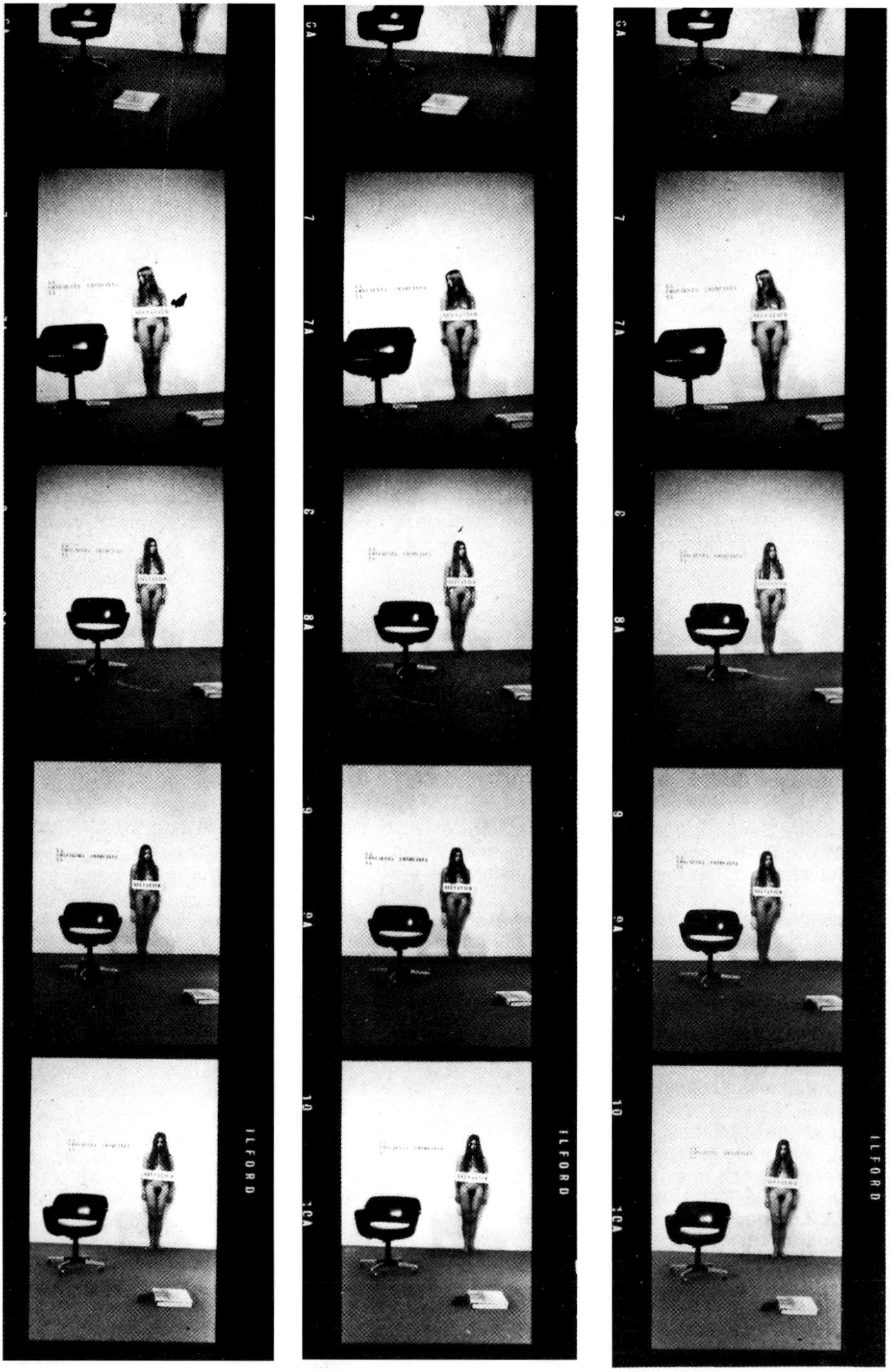
ILFORD
ILFORD
ILFORD

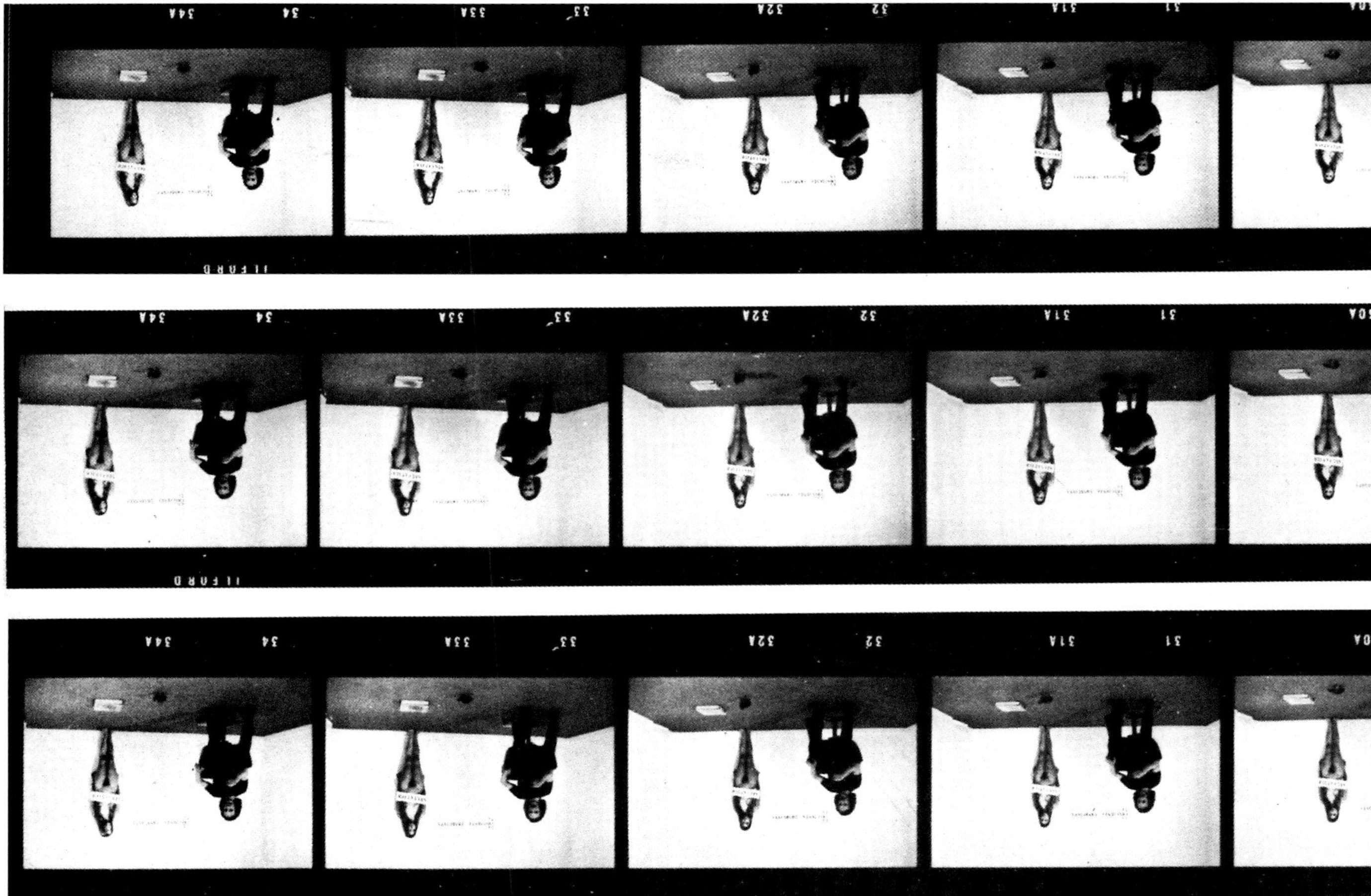

gina pane

The body and its support image for a non-linguistic communication
The body, which is at the same time project, material, and performer of an artistic practice, finds its logical support within the image, through the photographic medium.
Photography is a "sociological" object which allows us to grasp reality; therefore, it can grasp the heart of that dialectic through which behavior becomes significant by making itself communicable for a community.
Many types of black and white and color images exist:
a: a single fixed image: photography / transparency.
b: a series of contiguous images: photographs.
c: a sequence of temporal images: cinematographic film / videotape / transparencies.
d: an image along with other elements: verbal (the word) / non-verbal (music, noise, intonation).
e: a scripto-visual image (along with a caption).
A single image contains the "zero" degree of significance.
The caption is used in order to bring the excess of significance back to a single meaning.
The creation of series of contiguous or sequence images representing the same theme replaces the caption and enables us to neutralize the multiplicity of contradictory information.
The reading of an image, or a series, or a sequence establishes itself on two levels: on the one hand, on what is shown and on the other, on what it means.

The first is the statement of a reality to which the images refer, as they do not contain any arbitrary or unmotivated sign, the second consists in identifying and deciphering the semantic message.
One is tied to the semeiology of the optical image, and inversely, and the other is tied to the significance, that is, to the denotative structures.
The visual communication remains of the universal type because it reintroduces the fundamental social relationships.
N.B. - The objects presented in this artistic practice are not still-lifes, but the accessories of an action or the attributes of one or more persons. Therefore, they can keep their original context or that which refers to their reality through the support of images.

Sentimental Action, 1974
Projection of an "intra" space in which the relationship between two women is intercalated by the magic mother/child rapport, which death symbolizes.
This "intra" space is stated by an exchange/mirror closed circuit: the Woman/Women relationship, identifying itself in the primary emotive phenomenon—mother/child, a symbiotic relationship which can discover different emotional solutions to one's own conflicts of introjection.
My body is a conducting substance in a motion of "going to the return," coming back to its starting point through a deconstruction of the primary image (mental puzzle): the red rose, mystic flower, erotic flower, transformed into a vagina by a reconstitution in its most present state, the painful one.
It is through a rigorous use of form: mental/biological space, cadences, images, metaphors, that is, of the modality of my attitude, that I can reach my essence. The content is tied to the particular use of a language corresponding to the psychological process and to the sense of the action(s).

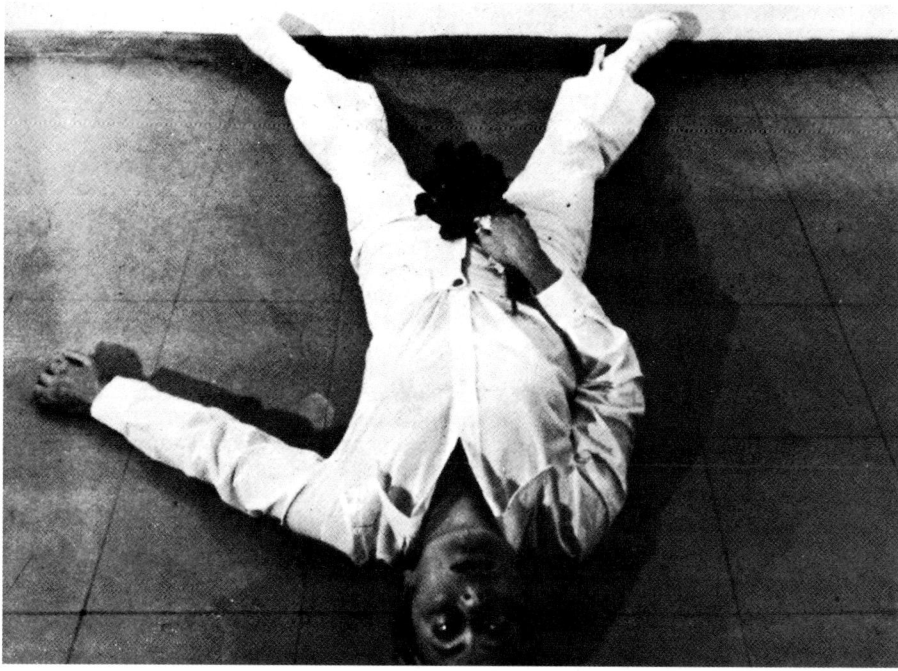

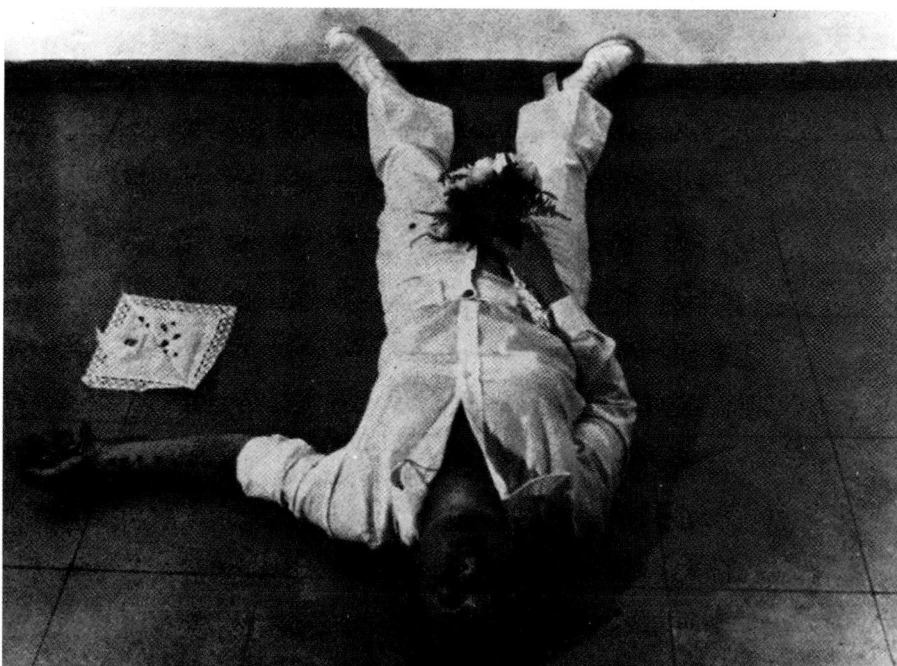

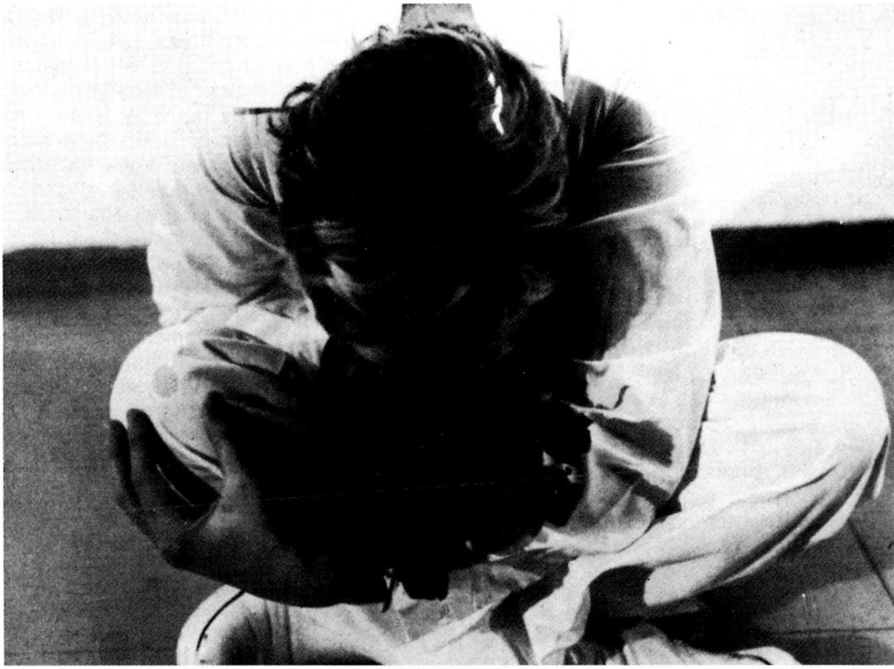

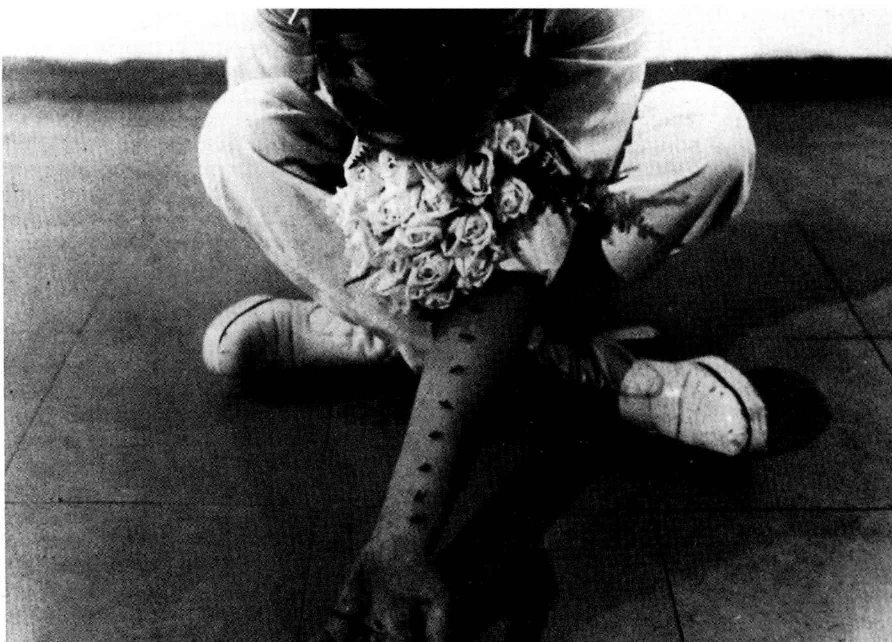

luca patella

Lu' capa tella
Film, 16 mm, 1h 30 min., color and b/w, ideas, photography, editing, texts by (and on) Luca Patella; sound Alvin Curran.
"Materials", instead, "psycho data" of '67 to '73
even if, not Freud-like, I believe in socio-formation.
Fades [the following fades are nontranslatable Italian puns]:
c'è er vello nel filmcervello (there is the fleece in the filmbrain)
o stile men tale, o se si vo' (the style less as such, or if one wants)
ostile mentale ossessivo (hostile mental obsessive)
noia (boredom) / gioia (joy)
ogni viaggio a ritroso (every trip backward)
vi aggio a ritroso (I have you backward)
with: Carlo Cecchi, Marino Masé, Luca Patella
dialectic between ideas, and "actions" by:
SAL = character, structure and totalizing creative behavior,
which trespasses into rationalizing obsessive passivity;
TIG = oneiric-optimistic, pragmatic and superficial;
MARS = extra neo to the preceding neurosis.
topi (mice) & tropi (tropes): Ronna = the place of History, of Swindle, etc.; Montefollonico = the place of Culture and Abstract Creation
Ronna, La Sgurgola, Montefolle '73–'74.

Here you are, as usual (with Luca), in front of complex ideas, which negate univocal simplicity, incapable of grasping and transforming the dialectic totality of the world, concretely made by man: from History, to Action! A re-penetration of filmic

dimension, which during the last 3–4 years Luca had looked at with a certain bias because of the excess of the sensitive image. His work, in effect, unfolded itself in books (*I am Here / Adventure & Culture*; *The Special Atlas of Luca Patella*; *Official Journals by L.P.*)
as well as "actual projective analysis" (public demonstrations and involvements: linguistic, psycho-sociological and political).
Substantially, the film is a theorizing analysis in progress,
even when the spoken text is off-camera. It is constructed in a pressing and disengaged way according to a series of successive total penetrations (by feed-backs more than by flash-backs).
Even more openly ideologic aspects are then reserved for
the other means mentioned.
"L.P. / L.C.T." is performance, documentation, critical analysis, trip by multi-significant transformative symbols, and creation!
Data concerning the takes:
1. Fade-in: Luca Patella / Lu' capa tella / lui sceglie telline (he chooses cockles) / patelle (limpets) / perle (pearls) / per le (for the) / creations & documentations by / Luca Patella...
2. Luca converses during a projective analysis in progress, '72 (in reverse-shot, or in his own shot: the others).
3. SAL and TIG (his travelling life-critic and biographer in progress) breathe, walk and converse in a field: "... that time you caught me on a holiday in the extra-Pluto asteroids"... (voices fade, buzzing).
4. A window at Montefollonico. Sign and dream. In the morning, on the grey stone windowsill, there is steaming coffee and fruit, evicted in the afternoon, by transformational transformative fades, by the tempos of trial diasynchronies. The light gust of wind turns your pages, in the evening, and color temperature rises inside, toward warm sentiments, while it comes down in the open, toward the rational blue and a purplish cold, or pitch dark. a squirt soon jumps on the black.
5. Totogrammi [a play on the word "fotogrammi" which means frames] of strolls in sprawling Ronna; a glance from bottom to top.
6. Sst! te llà, ròsa (star, rose); we two suns shining in the night, no:you [night is "notte", no:you is "no:te"] are in it even if you're not present: because what counts up to three: up to thee, is human relationship, from History to the Action. History of relationships.
History as relationships.
We two: Luca / affixes himself there / as signature of the "id e azione" [meaning both ideation and "id and action"].
Then, walking into society, toward the: End...

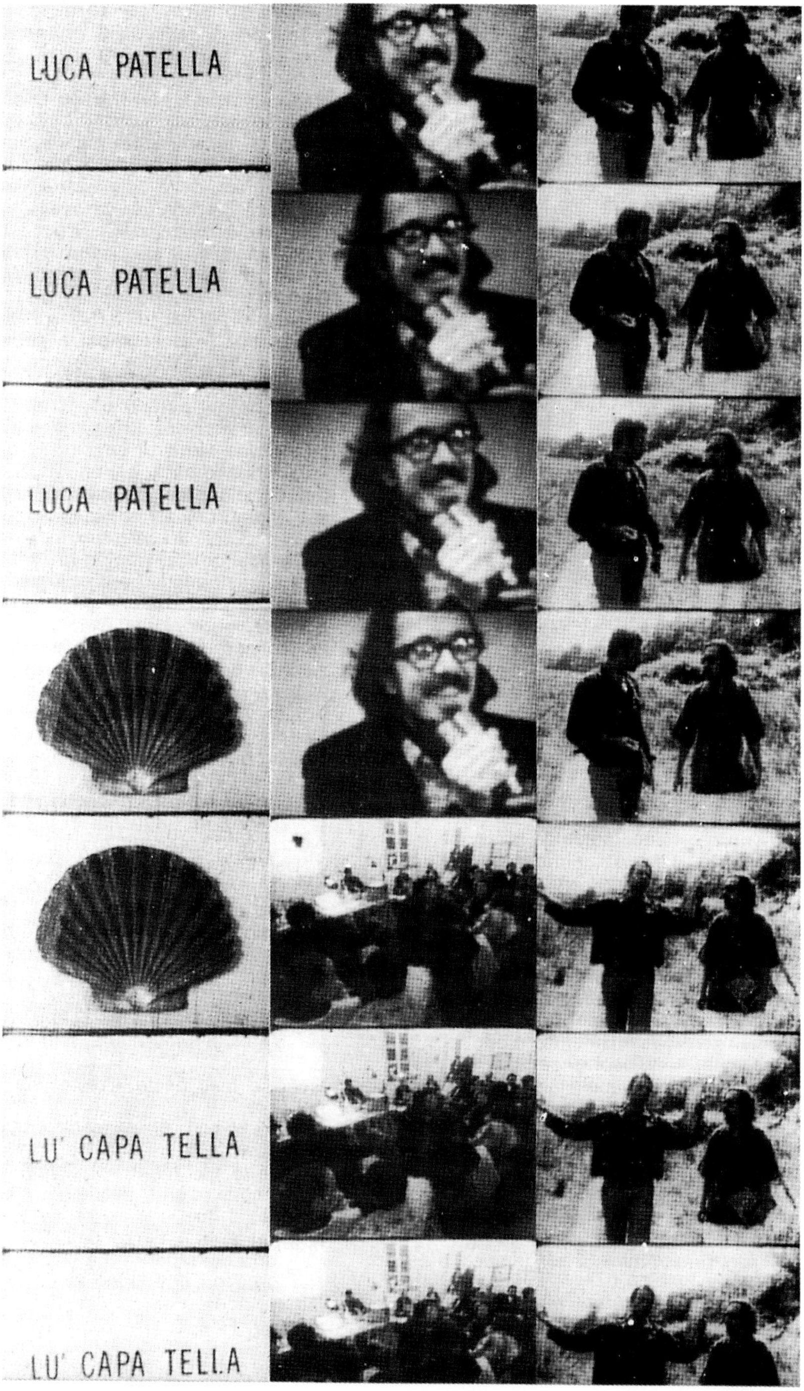
LUCA PATELLA
LUCA PATELLA
LUCA PATELLA
LU' CAPA TELLA
LU' CAPA TELLA

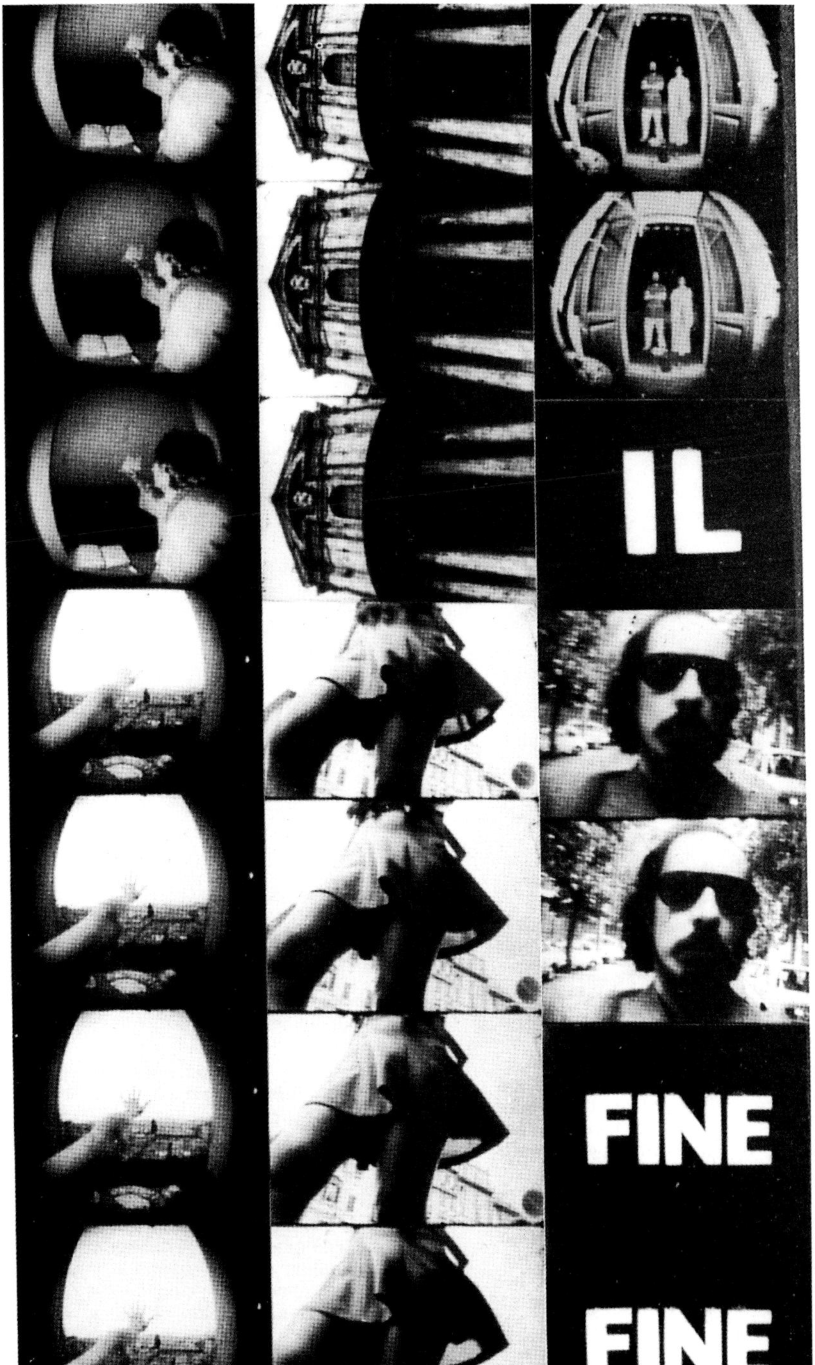
IL
FINE
FINE

giuseppe penone

The Hair, like the Nail, and the Skin Occupies Space, 1973
Plaster mold of my right foot—inside part and projection of a slide.
The mold of my foot preserves an element of my reality: the hair. During the forming of the mold some hairs are torn away from their roots and reappear on the plaster mold in the very same pore of the skin from which they were torn.
Therefore, technically, this work is a sum of the elements which reproduce a reality (plaster mold and slide) and of real elements (the hair). The photo, taken at a time following the molding of the plaster and projected on it, completes the preceding reality of the image of my actual foot.

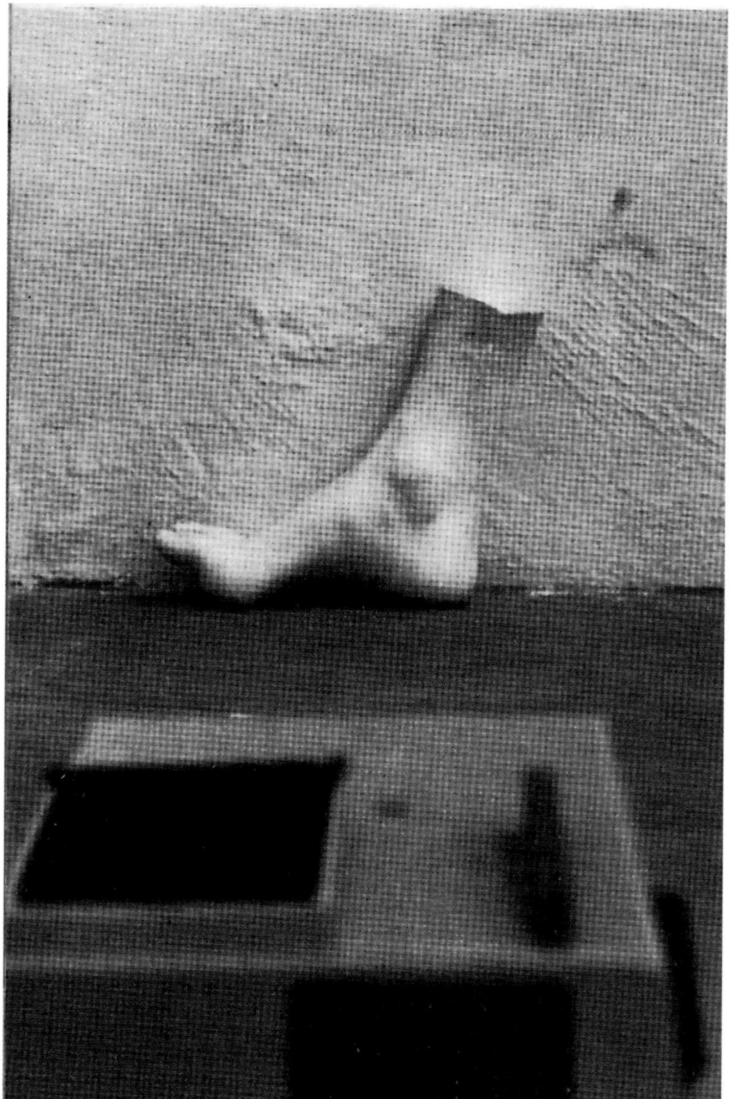

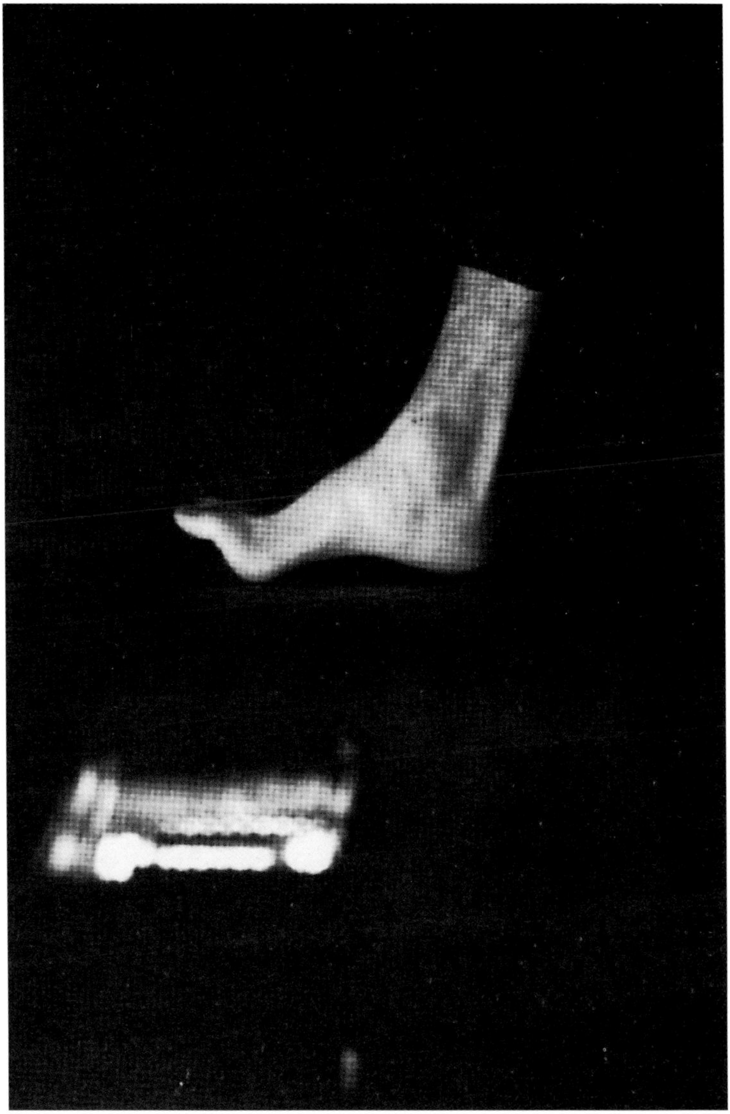

gianni pisani

Each Morning Before Going Out..., 1973
Every morning, after a shower, I rewind the umbilical cord on my abdomen (it is not made of plastic, it is taken from the intestine of a cow, it is that kind of tubular velum used by butchers to make sausages; I tied it at one end and then I inflated it with a bicycle pump). I arrange this skein under my shirt; as I am buttoning it, I completely conceal the "inconvenience." I hide it from the others with my bourgeois clothes which make me similar to them; I compress it under my everyday appearance and go among people. The idea of the umbilical cord is tied to my preceding work, from the representation of my suicide to guns, from my old paintings or more recent drawings to the rocking chair or to the destruction of my coffin. So, I do not know whether it is possible to speak of an idea. The idea is a thought and these things cannot be thought, they are felt. Perhaps the story of the umbilical cord is a return toward life, it is like a need to attach oneself to something, it is the searching for a father-mother-son tie... the others stay away from us, but these are the fundamental ties...

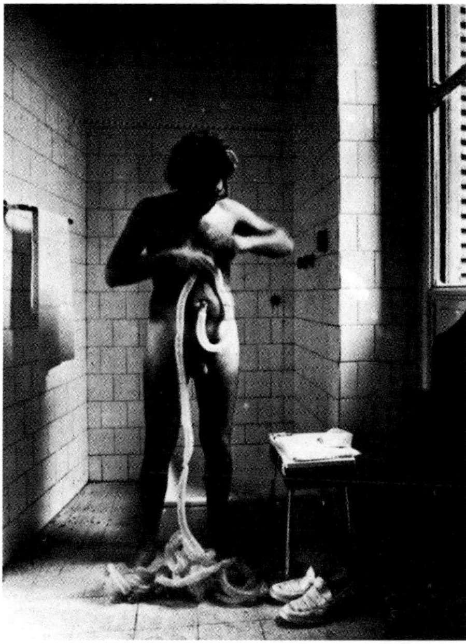

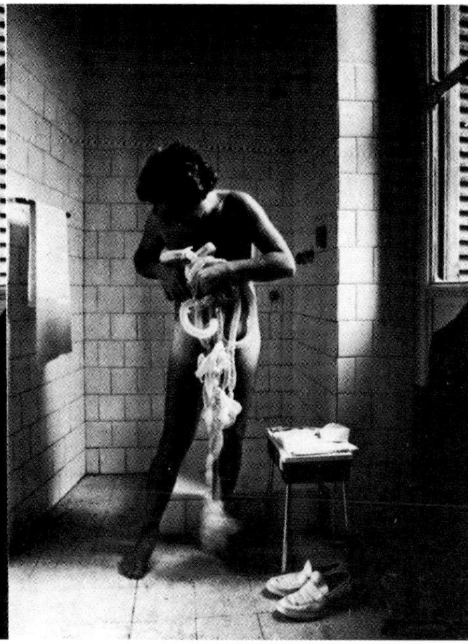

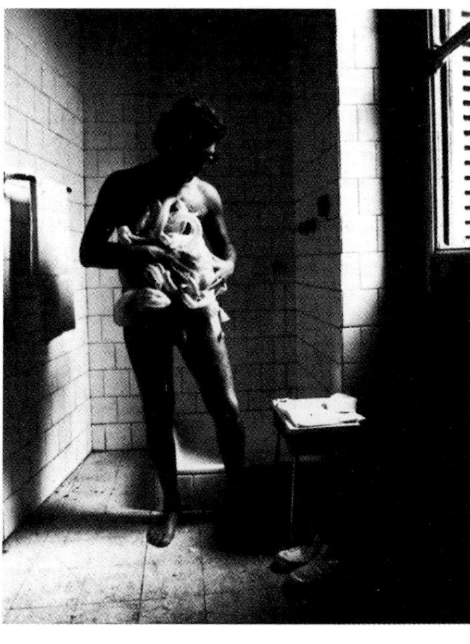

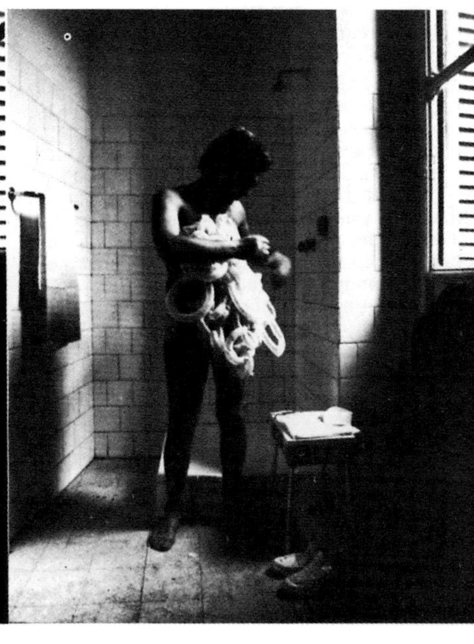

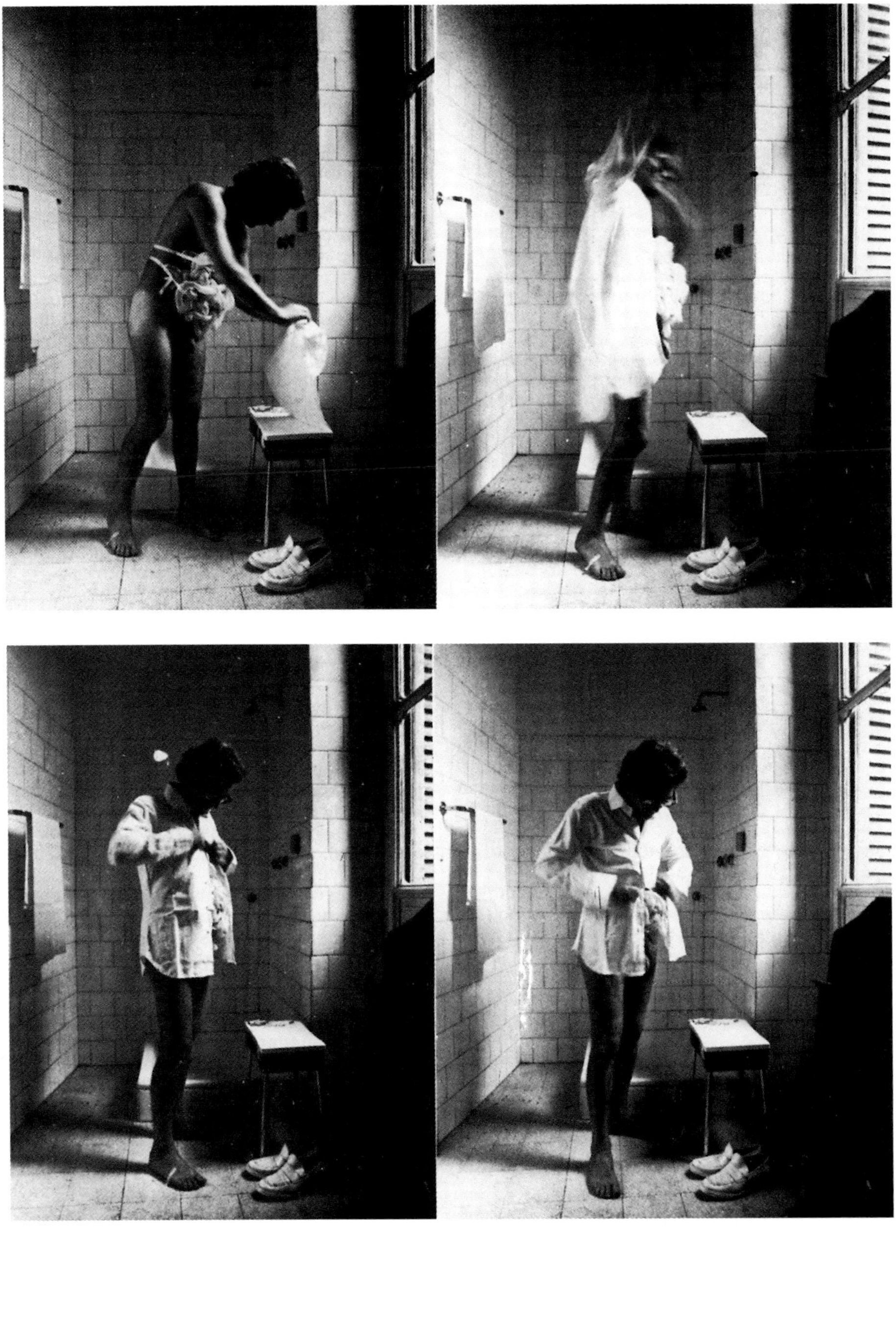

vettor pisani

Nature Does Not Love Nature, action lasting 5 days, 1973
Durand, on the trails of Jung, Frazer, and Mircea Eliade, organizes the imagination and its figurative space in a vast division between two regimes of symbolism: one diurnal and the other nocturnal; one founded on the time before the fall, on the rituals of elevation and purification, the other on the time after the fall and its astrobiological dramas.
Following the archetypal routes of imagination, Vettor Pisani recreates, experience after experience, the motions, antitheses, dualisms, and the circularity of imagination itself. Thus, the references and quotations lying at the base of the critical aim of the comment, of the ideological negations, turn out to be necessary.
That part of his work which converges on the figure of the Hero can be ascribed to the diurnal regime of imagination.
This is the Hero who limits his monarchic space, the Hero who manages nature, thought, and ideology, the Hero who crosses the border of reality in order to fuse himself with the Absolute.
In contrast with the figure of the Hero there is that of the victim (the woman). The woman (nocturnal regime) plays the terrifying role of darkness, of castration, and of death.

In the work *Nature Does Not Love Nature*, the woman is sitting on an iron table in a room swarming with rats.
Here, Vettor Pisani contrasts nature with nature and matter with matter, gathering the conflicting solutions.
Rats are the swarming and obscene sign of chaos, their accelerated animation seems to be an assimilating projection of anguish.
Bachelard in his *Alchemical Bestiary* suggested a "dental" sadism in animals with sharp teeth ready to bite and to swallow.
The woman is a nyctomorphous symbol, like the animal, darkness, noise, deep and black water.
The woman on the table tries to differentiate herself from the natural world. She carries an instrument—two brass cymbals, a weapon with which she annexes power, virility, and purifying force.
The instrument is as circular and golden as the sun: it sheds light and its sound resembles the rumble of thunder.
Bachelard analyzed this "complex of Atlas" as a scheme of the verticalizing and imperialistic effort which "Gulliverizes" the world.
The woman betrays her own nature and becomes a heroic figure who fights against darkness and belligerently seeks transcendence.
(Mimma for Vettor)

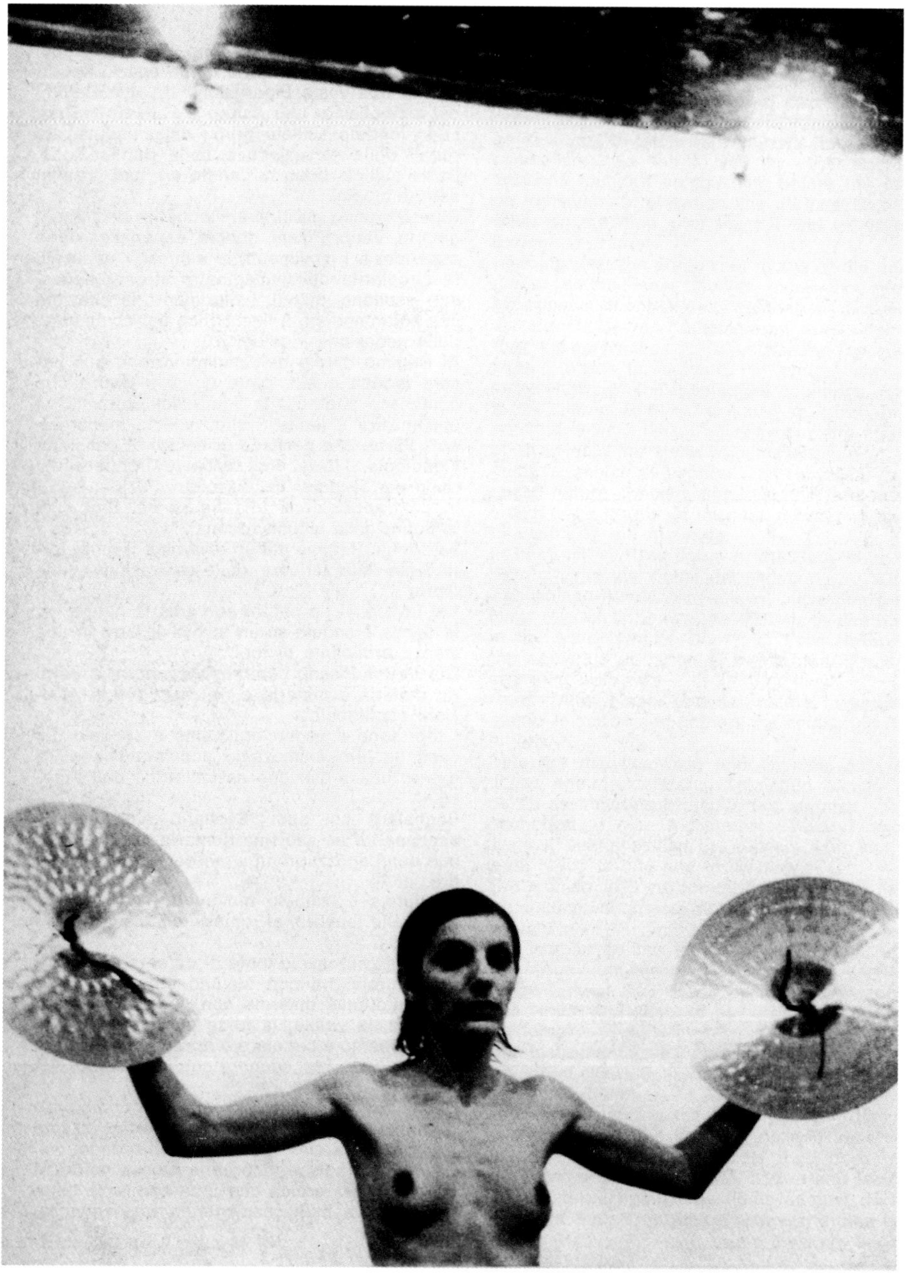

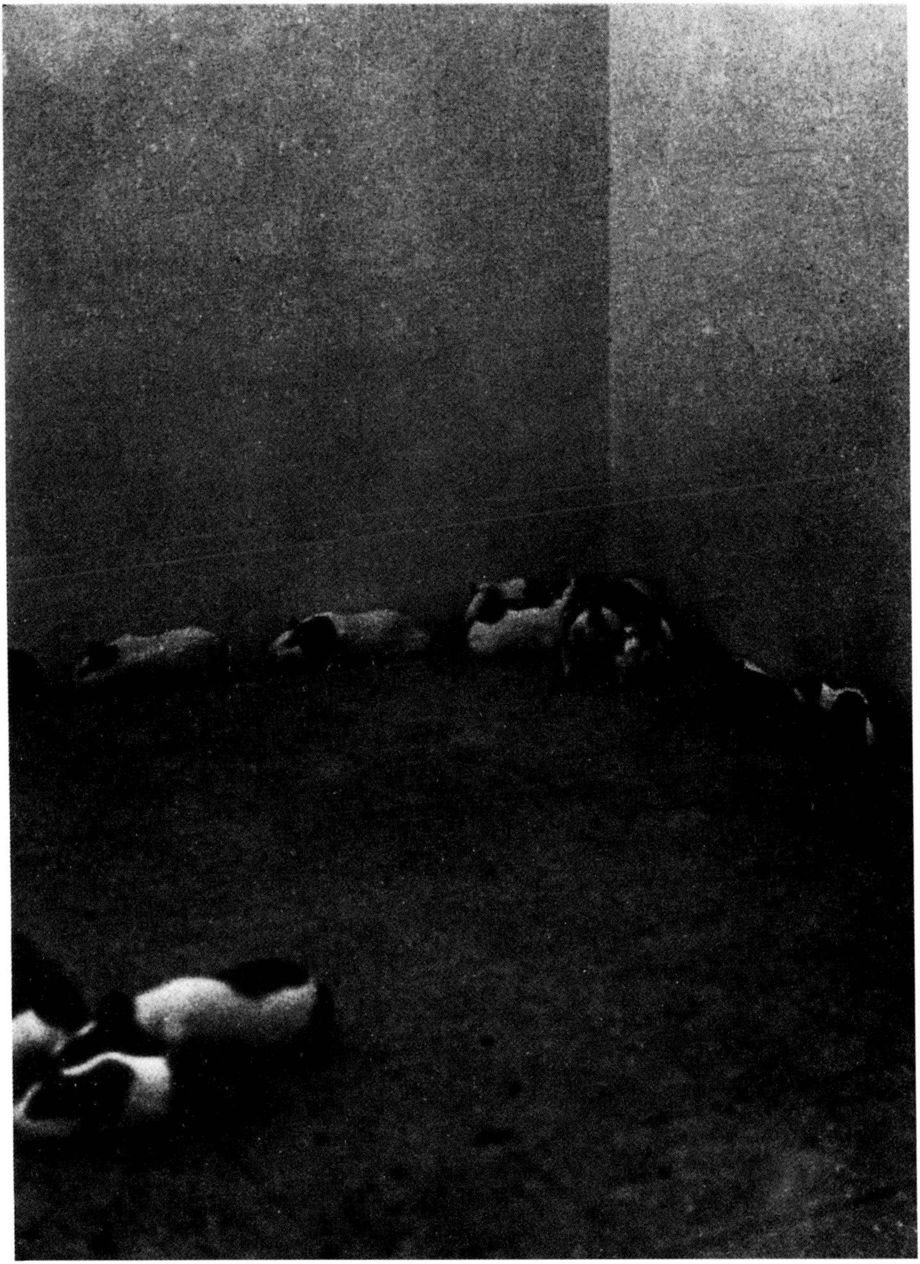

arnulf rainer

Face Farces, 1968

When I used to draw faces I got the habit of "defacing" them in various ways. Then in '68 the production of *Face Farces* started in an automatic photo booth located in Vienna's West railway station. Today, I still work in this way almost every week, with the help of a photographer or a movie cameraman.

I emphasize the selected photos or sequences with marks in order to make the facial dynamics and mimicry evident. Since then, I have been interested in all abnormal situations like ecstasy, spasm, psychoses, breakdowns, humiliations, etc.

But I do not consider these psychophysical reproductions as being just a mimic expression: in fact, they are the attempt toward a surmounting which every human being can afterwards extend. As artist I limit myself to fix them in part, and only on the paper.

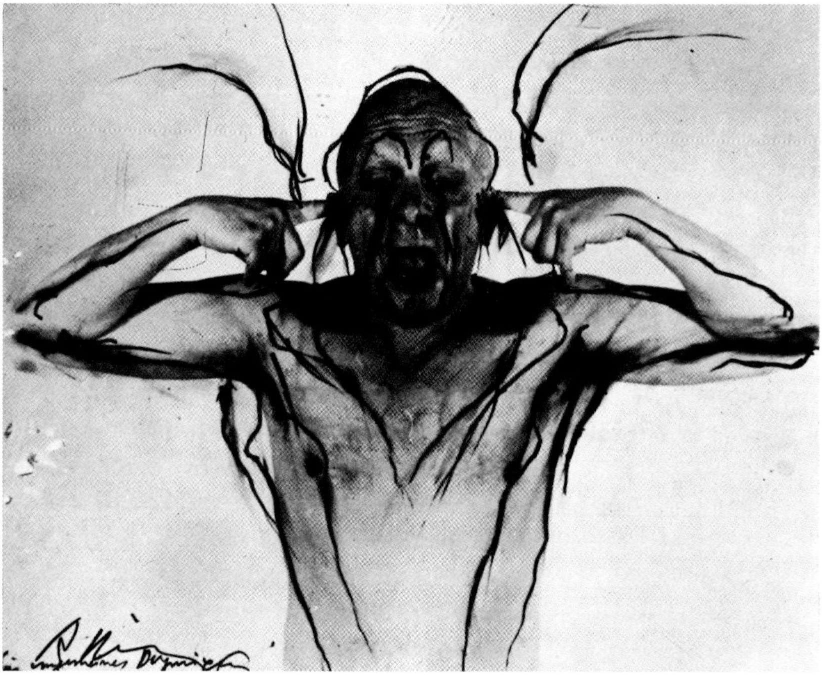

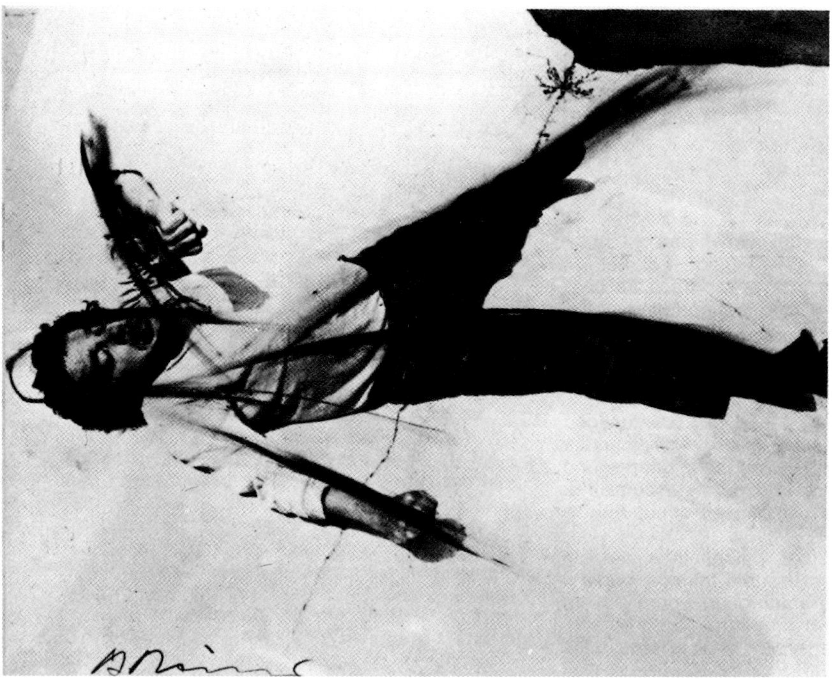

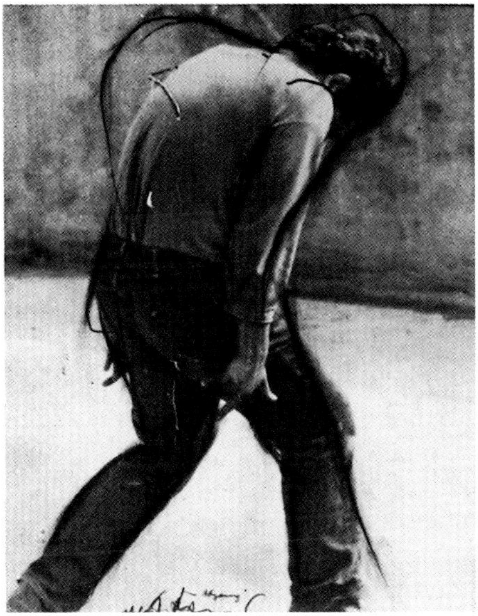

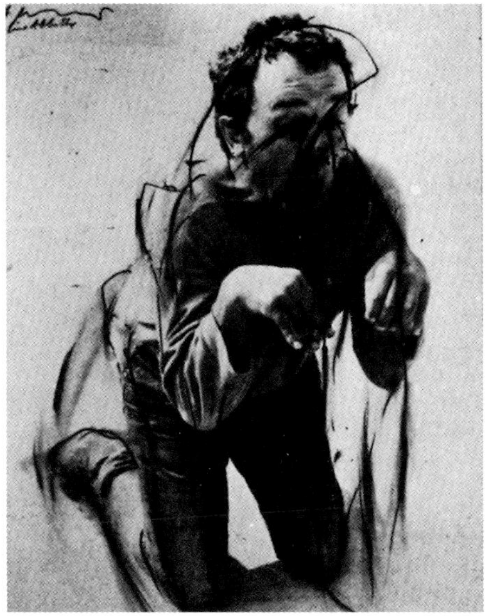

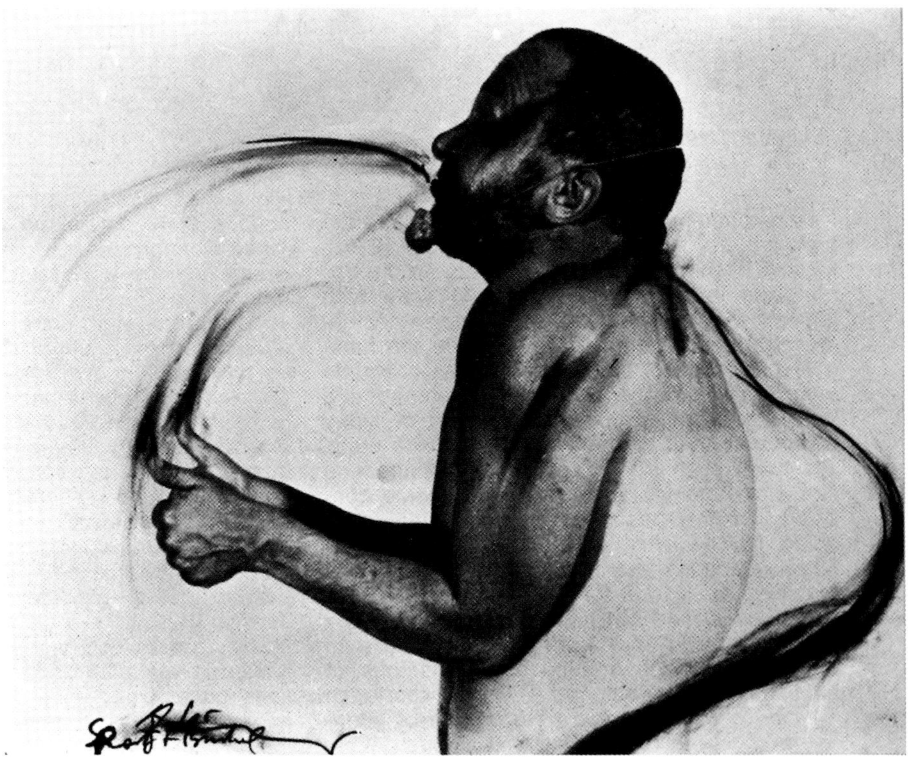

klaus rinke

Mutation, 1970
Wand, Boden, Raum, 1970
I am explaining that every person from where he may be or from whatever social background he is coming… should obtain the opportunity to know himself and to work with himself with the help of these elementary demonstrations of reality.
Most people are hampered because of their more or less complete integration into the battle for existence and they are attached to certain forms of living which take their course in them and with them.
The study of this book could signify something like a starting factor in order to become conscious of the basic structures of individual being… The artist should have the opportunity to place environmental situations in a way that they are useful for consciousness. These situations should not limit somebody but they should help to free activities. For instance people should be continuously conscious of time in their environment.
By this experience everybody could measure the degree of intensity or dullness of the life he is living.

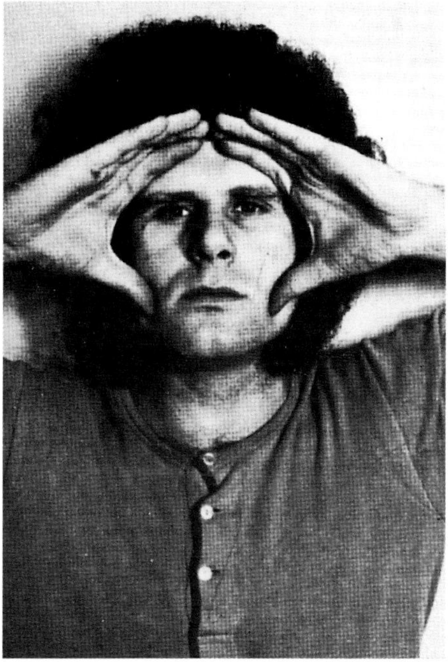

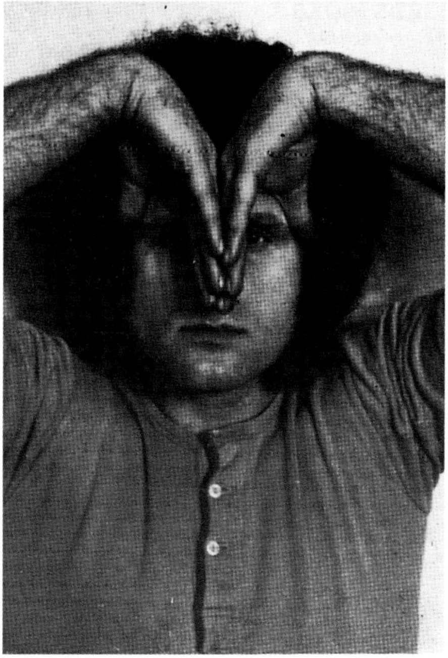

Mutation, 1970

Wand, Boden, Raum, 1970

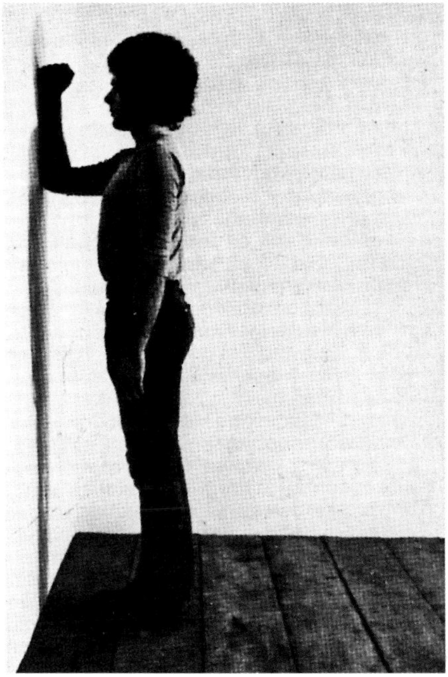

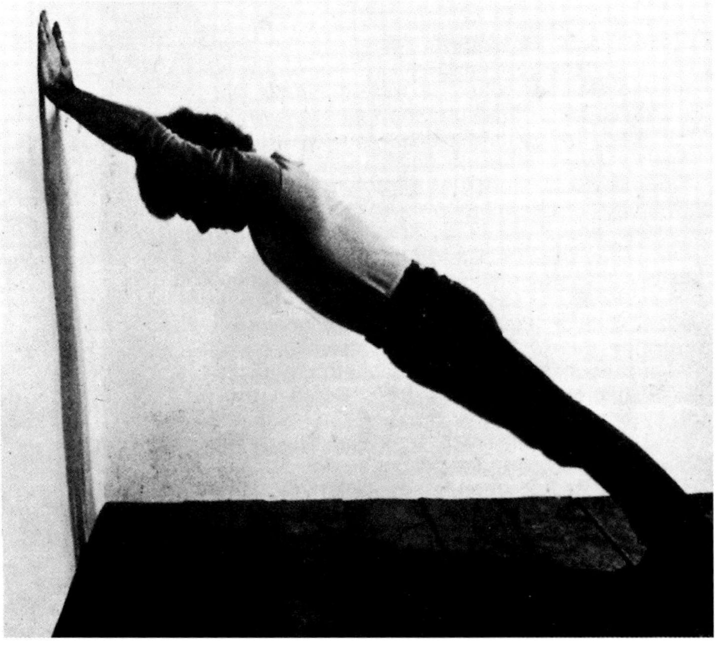

allen ruppersberg

A Lecture on Houdini, 1973
Good morning. Today's talk concerns a man whose name has been a household word for almost three quarters of a century. However, it will not dwell on the details of an incredible life, most of which are readily available to any diligent student, but instead will direct itself to exploration of the heroic belief which carried and sustained him for almost forty years. We will see the strength of this belief not only throughout his own mortal life but probably also (to use his words) from the world of the beyond. The man: Harry Houdini. The idea: To establish physical contact with the world of the spirit. Is life continuous? Can one reach back from the reaches of the beyond? The determination, energy and emotion behind the ideas of this man are indeed of legendary proportions and have continued to expand since his death in Detroit, Michigan, on Halloween, 1926. His thoughts and research into the activities of a professional magician, and escape artist are still among the finest of today but the promises he saw from the beyond have yet to be fulfilled or surpassed.

Houdini was working as always as the complete madman. The fateful chain of events started October 10th. He was in Albany preparing to be lowered into the water torture cell to close the act. Something snapped in his ankle. "I've a show to finish" was his reply. Later it was confirmed as a fractured ankle. He continued with the show, traveling for two weeks. He arrived in Montreal, Monday October 17th, with the ankle knitting but Houdini exhausted. One challenge which he continued in every town was a long standing dare to punch him in the midsection with no visible reaction due to his physical prowess.
A college boxer and friends approached him backstage at the Princess Theatre. "Could I try it right now?" asked the boy. "Sure" was the reply. As Houdini rose from the couch the boy smashed him in the stomach. Houdini gasped. He hadn't been ready. He was white but he set himself and the boy hit again to feel what seemed like an oak plank. Houdini's side bothered him. During the matinee he suffered pains in his right side but faithfully chose to ignore them. By evening it was worse and Bess wanted to call a doctor. "No" was the answer.

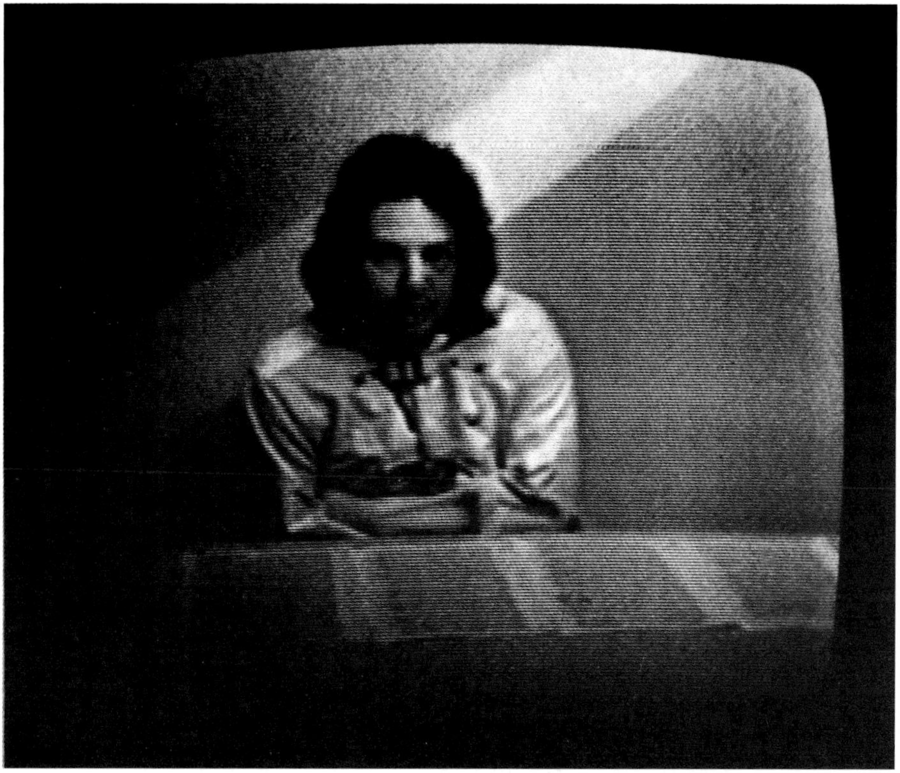

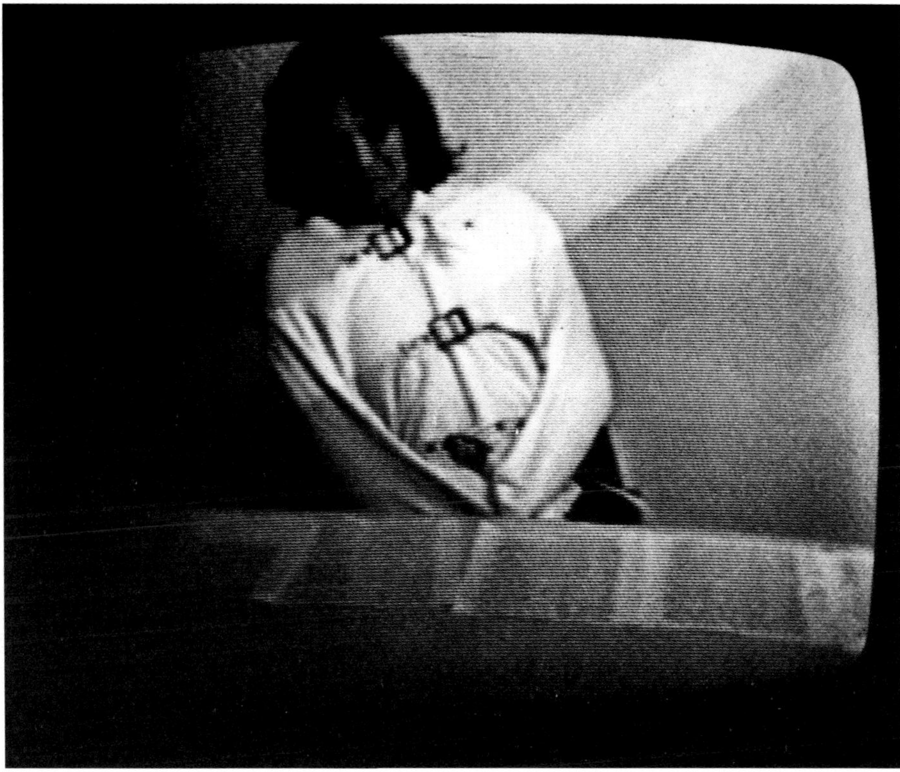

lucas samaras

Autopolaroid, 1971 and 1973

Other than being an autobiographic postulate of some of my present attitudes or a complicated gift to others, these photographs are a way of studying my polaroided self as an abstraction or translation of aesthetic speculation, psychological perspicacity, sensual subtlety and a warm embarrassment.

Or they are a method for declassifying hush-hushed feelings. Or they are a stylized pretension of emotion-acting. Or they are a reworking of the form of self-portrait. Or it was a matter of one thing leading to another and piling up into an elaborated accomplishment.

Also they are evidence of an enjoyment. Most of them were done late night or early morning. Uninterrupted times. I rediscovered a number of techniques already available to students of photography and had a funny feeling of re-experiencing history. It wasn't all regurgitation. I allowed satire of my art education to enter into the compositions.

Polaroid, nevertheless, has a feel, a look, a dialect of its own.
It is programmed to give you acceptable flesh colors, but it is possible to cross its normality with colored sheets of plastic either in front of the lens or in front of the lights. Moreover the speed with which a result is obtained without outside help and the complete privacy afforded me an opportunity of doing something impossible with regular photography. I could tone up or tone down my emotion. I could move a little to the left or shift this or that and be my own critic, my own exciter, my own director, my own audience.
I did these things between December 1969 and May 1971. I had wanted to photographically explore my body for years and was going to have a professional photographer do it. But I have never been able to work well with others, and I was not going to go to a photography school and learn photography. Polaroid came in handily.

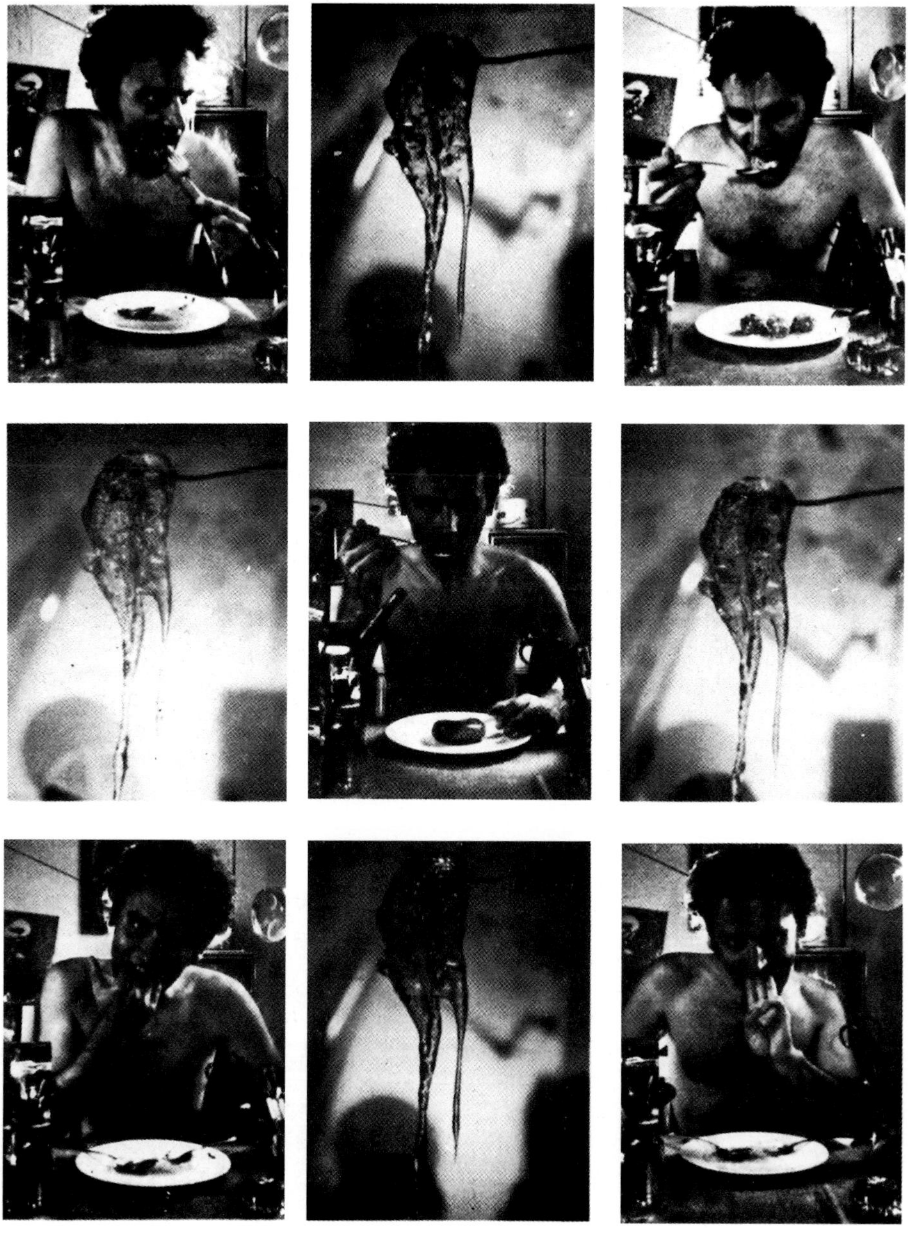

Autopolaroids, 1971

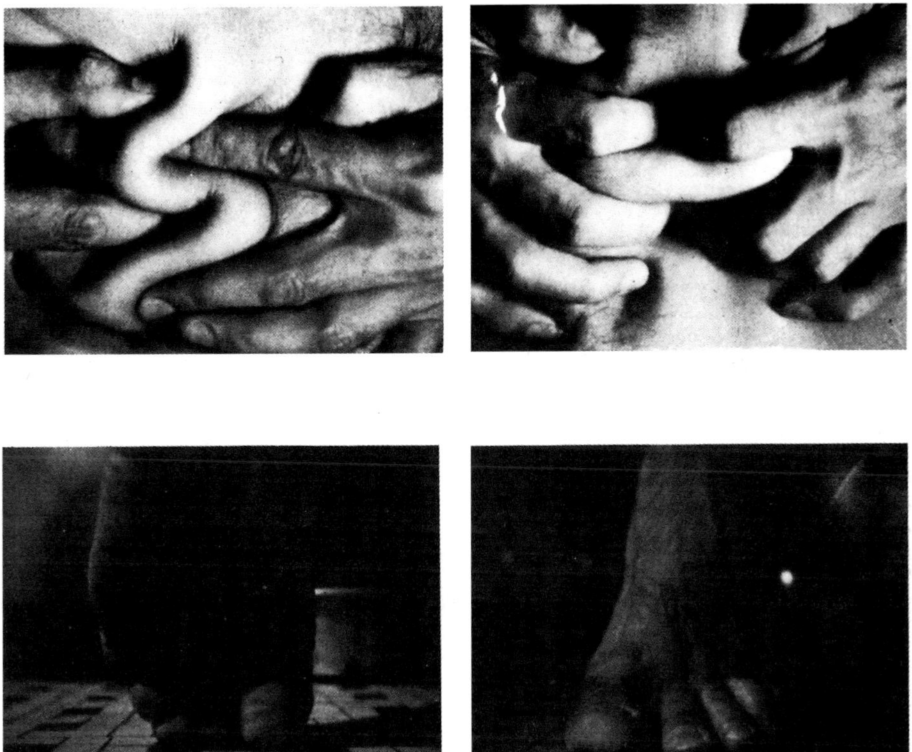

Autopolaroid, 1973

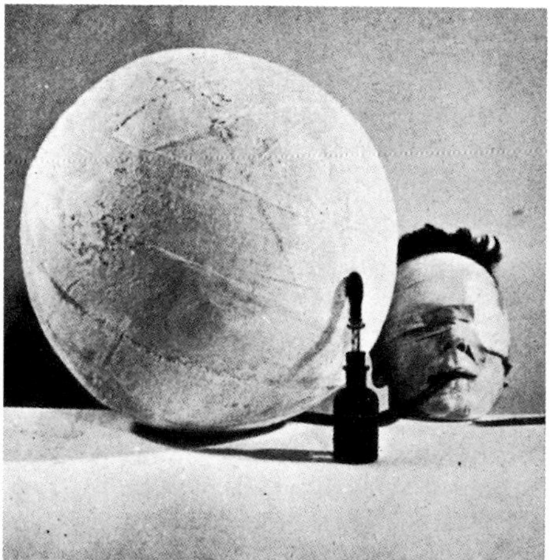

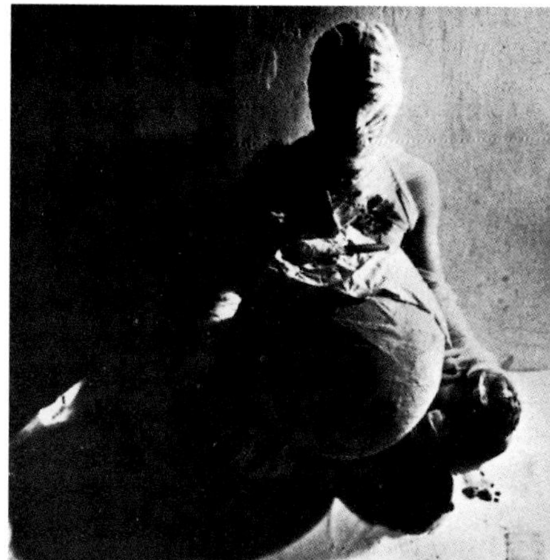

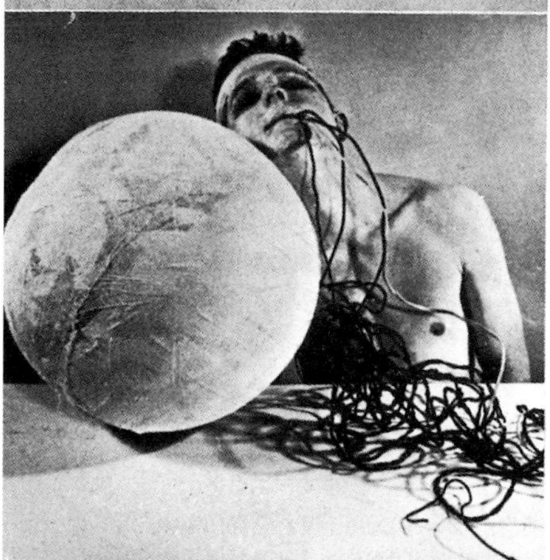

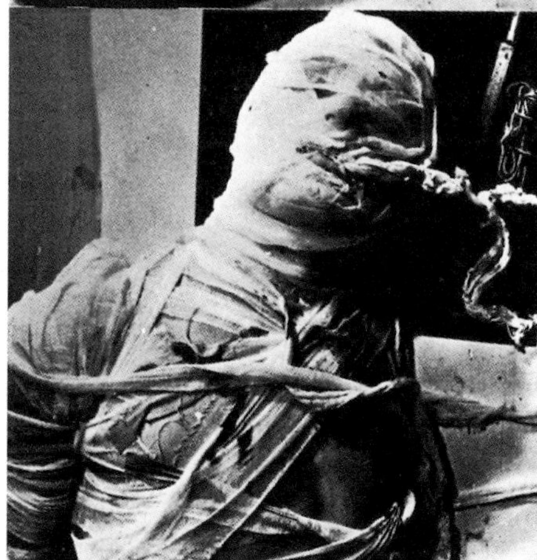

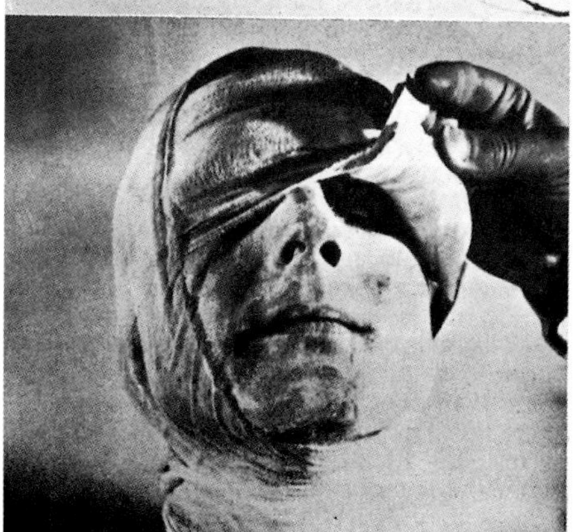

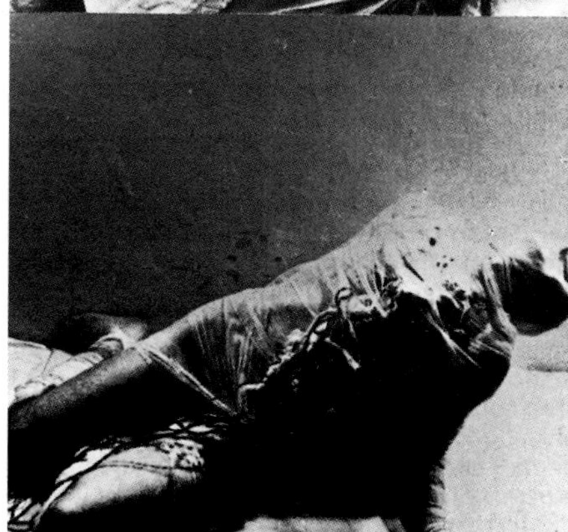

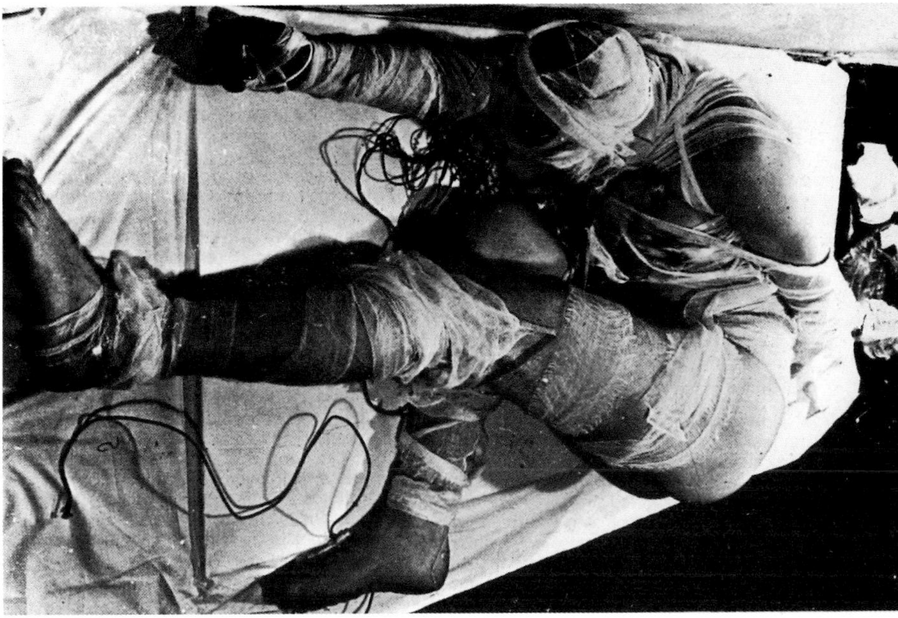

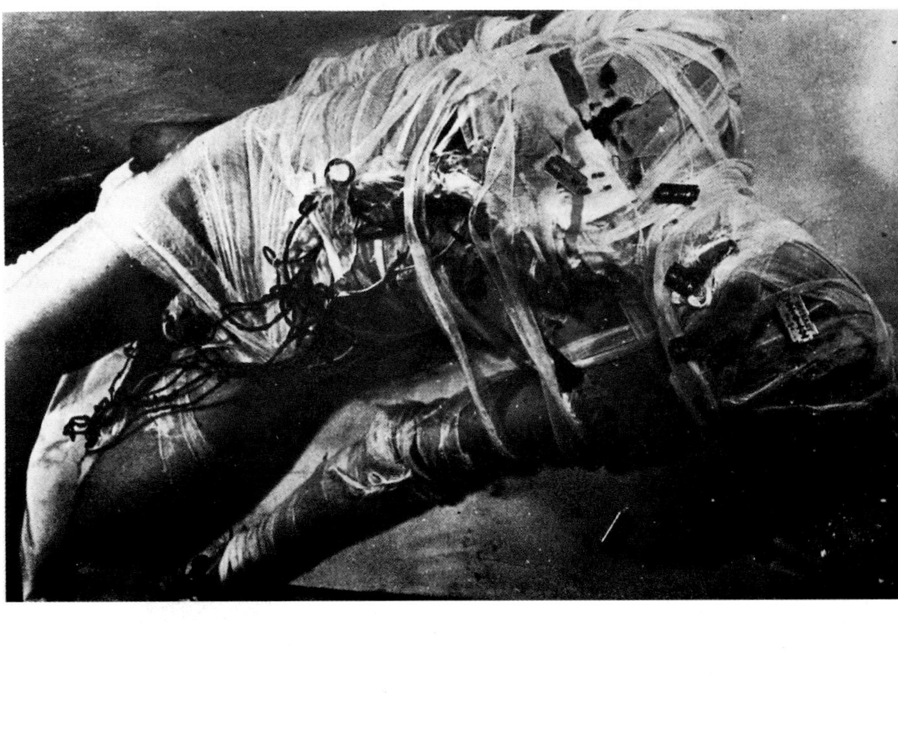

richard serra

Frame, 1969
Color-aid, 1971
The works are described by a simple verb action performed on the material by the artist, available to the viewer as residue of an in-formation (the stage of the process described in applying the verb action to the material place where it is present) time. The viewer's time field is as much a part of the process (reading) as the artist's former relation to the same material and the material's process in the former time...
So if there is a time, it is hidden in the object itself and it allows itself to reveal itself as you try to deal with the false possibility of reducing it to sequences—kinesthesia in Serra's work (literally the work done to the material to inform the verb action) is linked to the visual perception—the visual field...
Spatial behavior and spatial perception are co-ordinate with each other in the process of time, guiding manipulation and use of tools, including the base tool—the hand locomotively directed by muscular action... Kinesthesia is actually part of a larger group of integrated stimulus-correlates for perception of oneself.

to roll / to crease / to fold / to store / to bend / to shorten / to twist / to twine / to dapple / to crumple / to shave / to tear / to chip / to split / to cut / to sever / to drop / to remove / to simplify / to differ / to disarrange / to shave / to open / to mix / to splash / to knot / to spill / to droop / to flow / to swirl / to rotate / to smear / to flood / to fire / to impress / to inlay / to lift / to curve / to support / to hook / to suspend / to spread / to hang / of tension / of gravity / of entropy / of nature / of grouping / of layering / of felting / to collect / to grasp / to tighten / to bundle / to head / to gather / to arrange / to repair / to discard / to pair / to distribute / to surfeit / to scatter / to complement / to enclose / to surround / to encircle / to hide / to cover /to wrap / to dig / to tie / to bind / to weave / to join / to match / to laminate / to bond / to hinge / to mark / to expand / to dilute / to light / to revise / to modulate / to distill / of waves / of electromagnetism / of inertia / of ionization / of oscillation / of polarization / of refraction / of simultaneity / of tides / of reflection / of equilibrium / of symmetry / of friction / to stretch / to bounce / to erase / to spray / to systematize / to refer / to force / of mapping / of location / of context / of time / to talk / of photosynthesis / of carbonization / to continue.

Frame, 1969

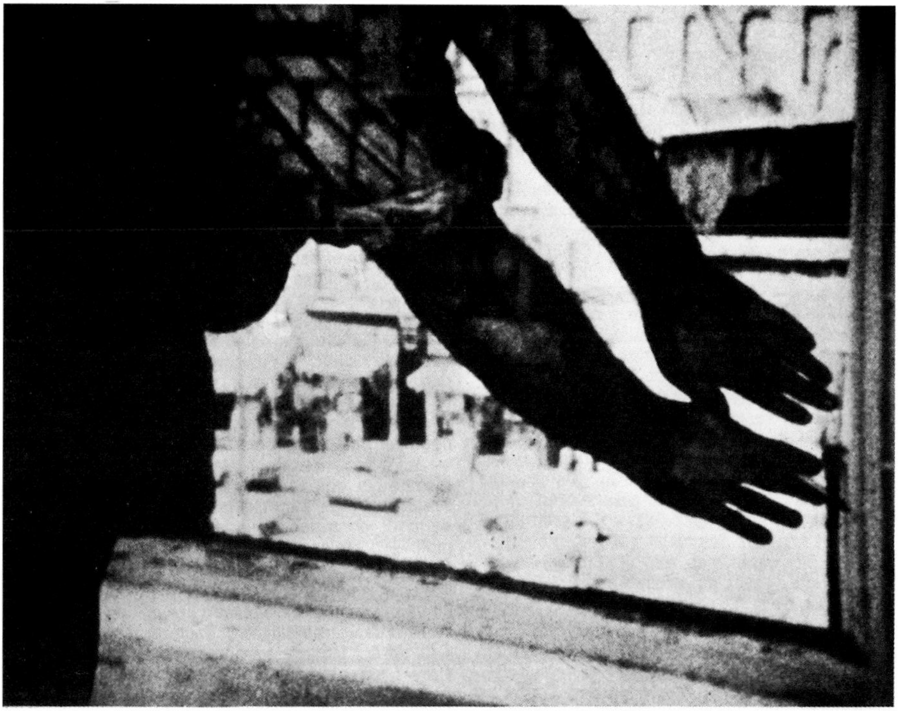

Color-aid, 1971

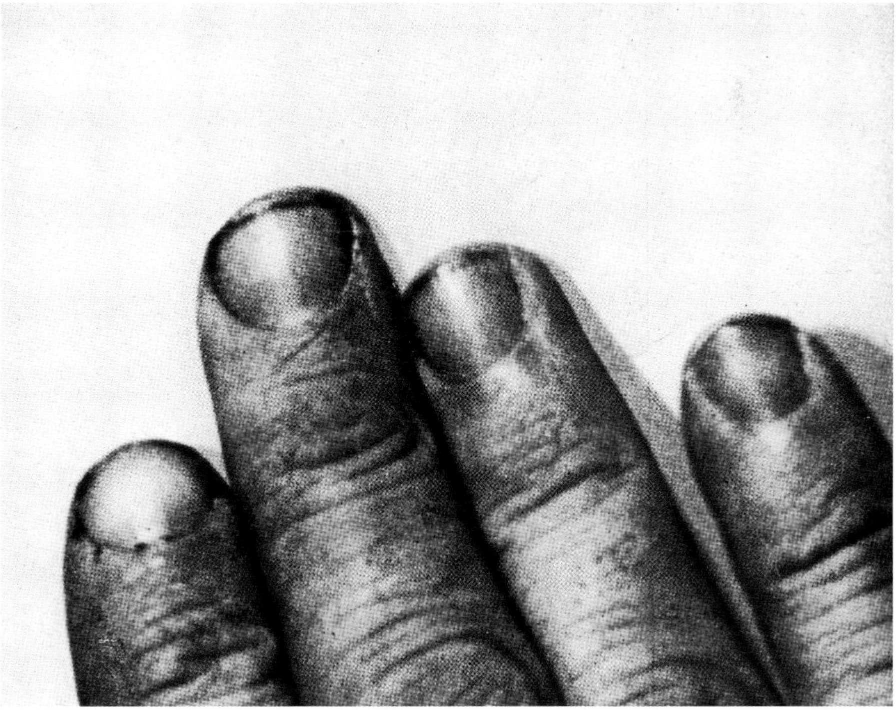

katharina sieverding

Selection of 148 Phases on the Same Situation "Untitled", 1973
My films and series of photographs are neither projections nor fictions they happen directly their realisation is the maximum of free communication i.e. an action of love possibility of totally living what they would like to be and what they are I can imagine making a film with anybody at all whenever this free communication is developing since people want to know who they are and even more to show who they are even children are stopped from this kind of experiment no voyeurism no demonstration rather a discovery no criticism no norm no solitude finally the interchange of identification becoming equivalent to the other calm self-awareness that enables you to go on this does not mean "to jump off a fast train" rather search out your own beauty exploitation of men material moral or ideologic deprives men of their legitimate claim to produce and reproduce themselves.

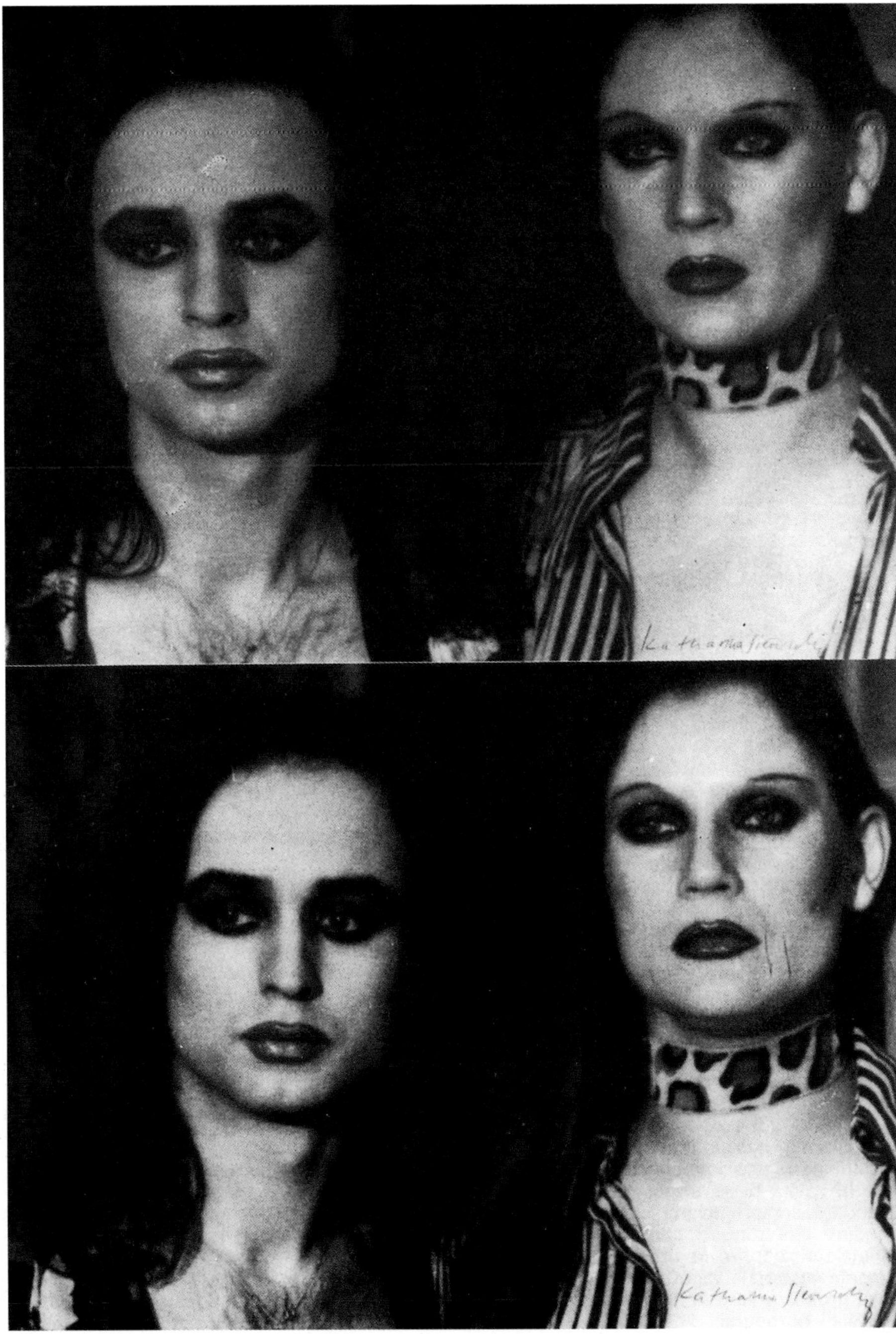

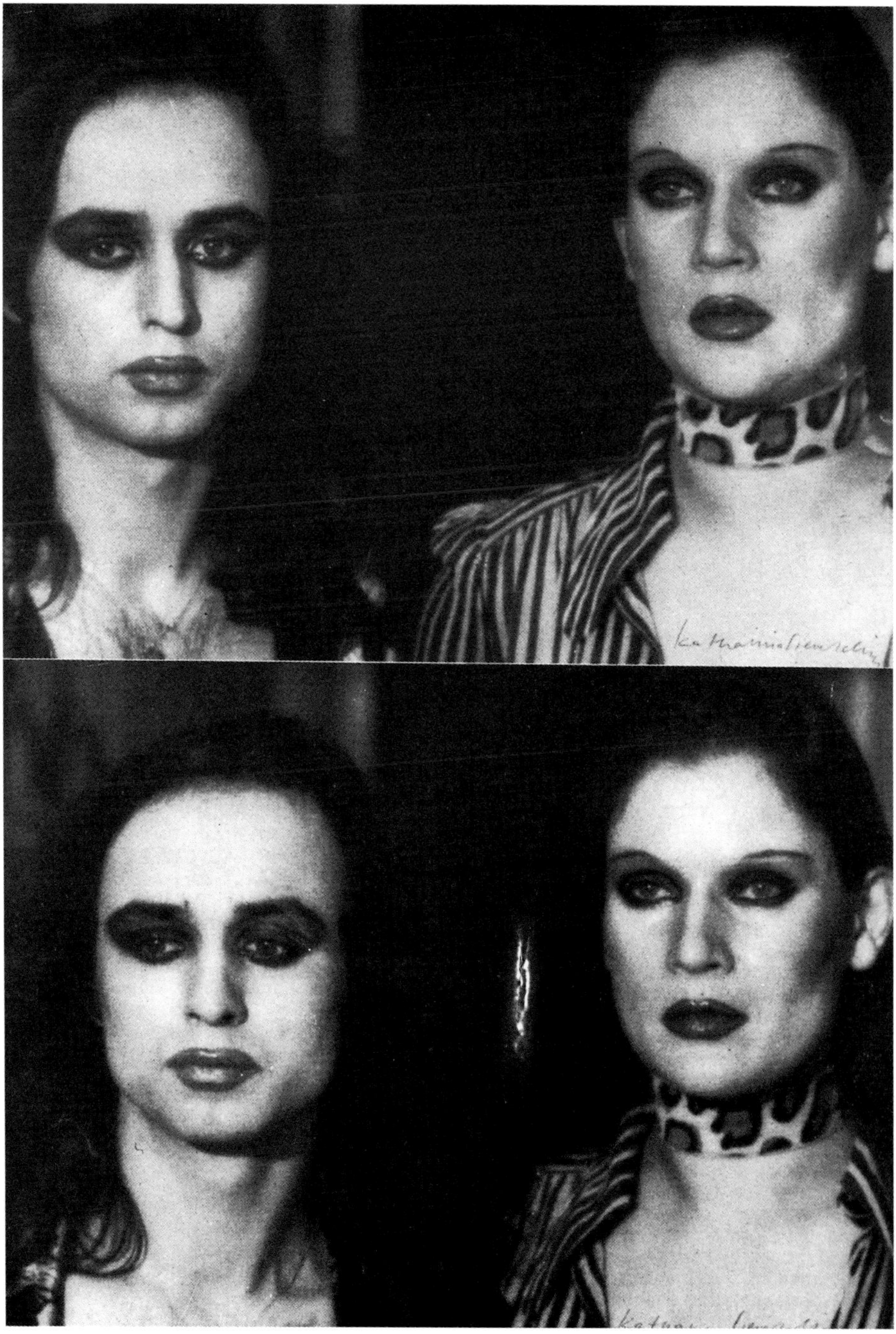

aldo tagliaferro

Identification, 1973
This analysis is a component of my MEMORY AND IDENTIFICATION AS SUPERIMPOSITION ON REALITY.
Memories of external things and memories of the ego—therefore, of identification.
In this work there are several aspects of memory and of identification. I wanted to give this specific analysis a negative sense, to create a model of depersonalization. For this reason I had twins pose for me, because in them (as external images) there is already a beginning of depersonalization. For the solution of my work I tried to create referential or substitutional poses, so that the subject could, in the end, assume the rhythm of an object.
This work has two stages of interpretation: one is the verification of the likeness between the single images represented; the other is the global reading, in which, because of the structure assumed by the image, a depersonalization of the representation ensues and such an image becomes an object or writing.

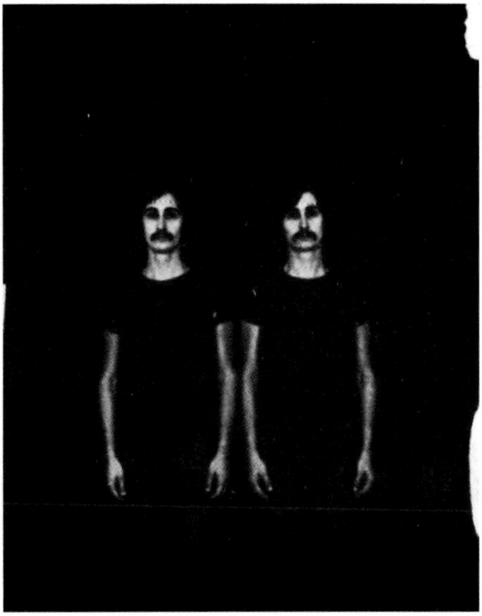

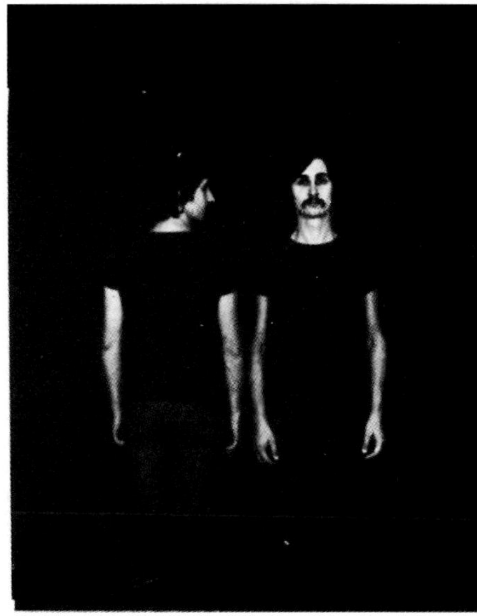

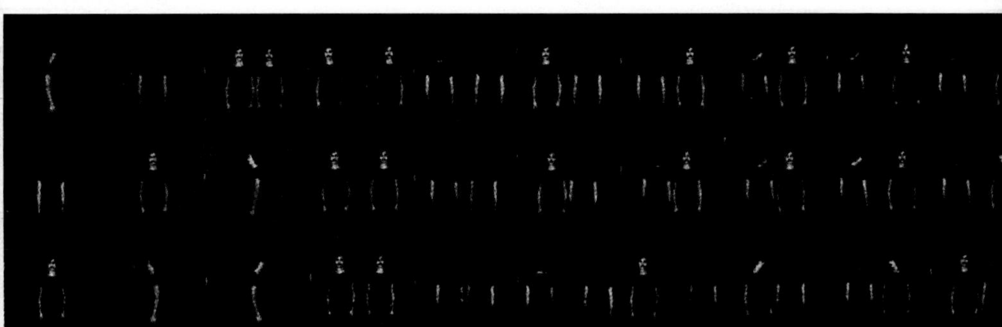

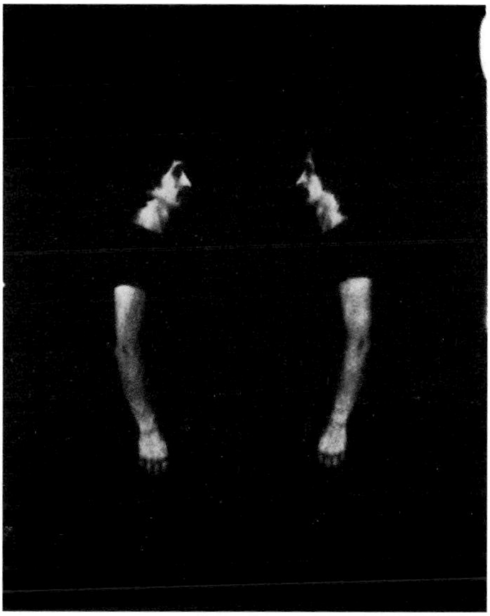

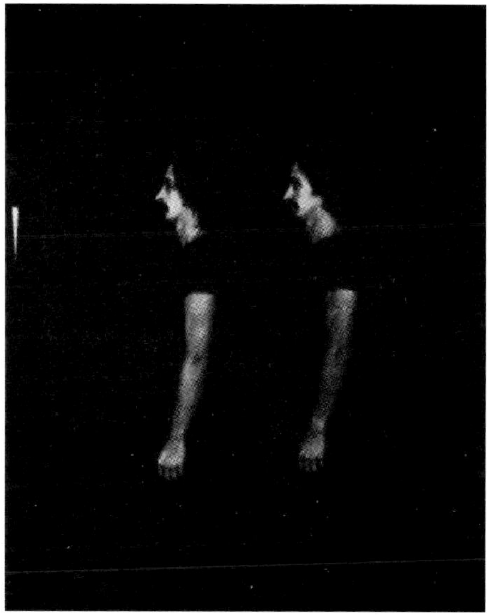

antonio trotta

The Space between Me and the Work, 1972

The space between me and the work starts to nullify itself at that moment when I can see all that surrounds me as if it were already painted or sculpted. (Painting, sculpture, literature, history, then, are the only materials that it is possible to paint, sculpt, etc.)

Going toward a state of petrifaction among things and feeling doubt about one's existence, is like observing the irreality of the outside by staying in the reality of the work, within which a photograph is true like an image in a mirror.

The feeling of space is born parallel to the wish to get out of one's own painted image.

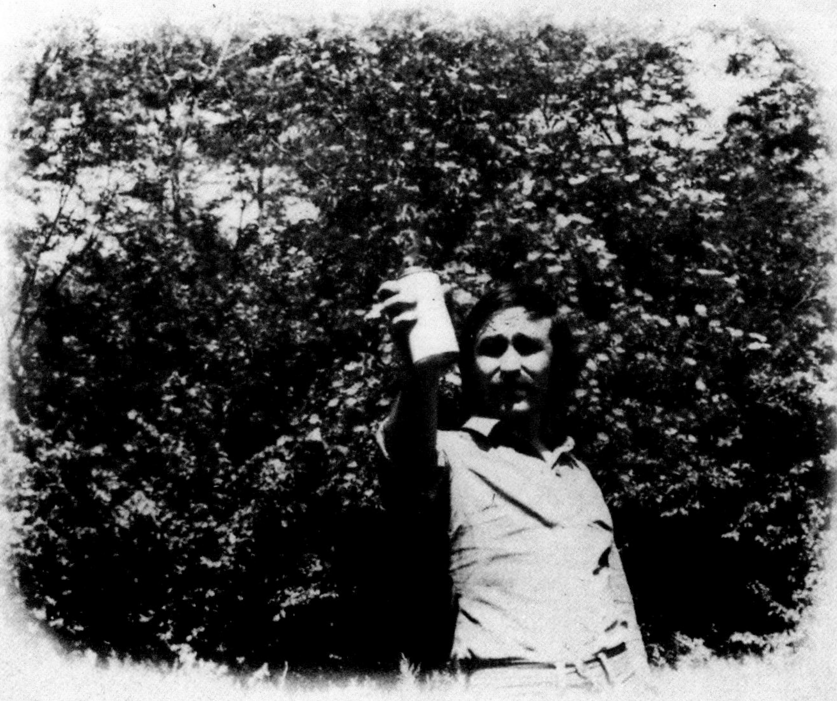

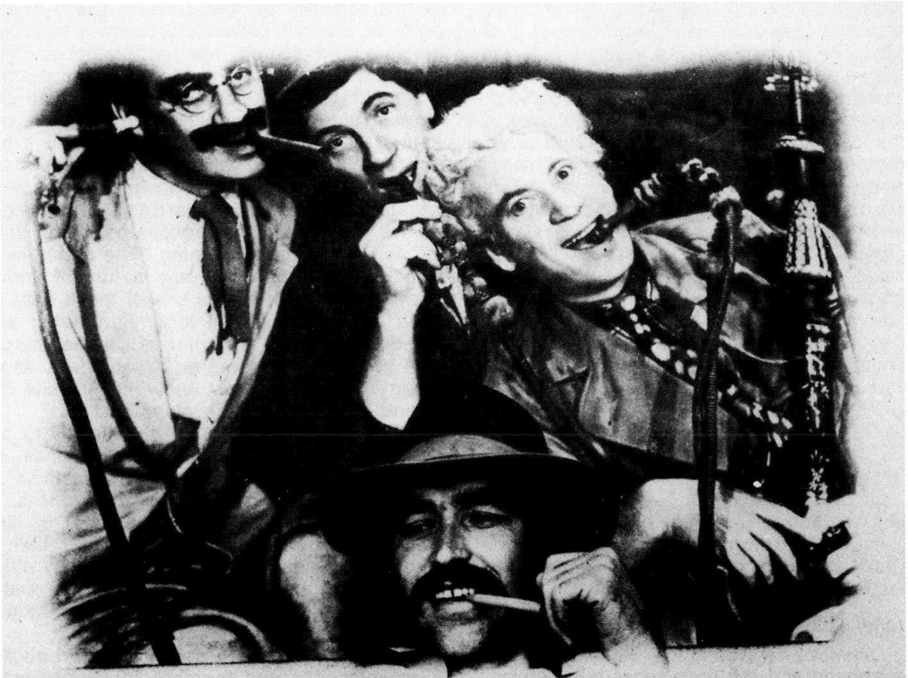

janos urban

Parallel Times, 1973

The left side of the screen, connected with the first TV camera, moves constantly, in depth and also laterally, according to the camera's zoom which goes forward and back, slowly, while focusing always on the same scene: some trees and bushes, at the beginning of that day's afternoon. The second camera, which determines the image on the right side of the screen, is focusing on another monitor where fragments, previously collected from current feature programs, mainly people in "transitory" spaces (i.e. stairways, corridors) are played. The process of mixing up goes on, the division of the screen is never the same, until the reserve of the collected material, a non-narrative miscellany, is exhausted.

The sound is replaced at the same time: collected acoustic fragments of other spaces and times, mainly situations acoustically analogous to the TV fragments, are played back and recorded on the Sony tape. The dialogues unite foreign languages, noises, and excerpts of music.

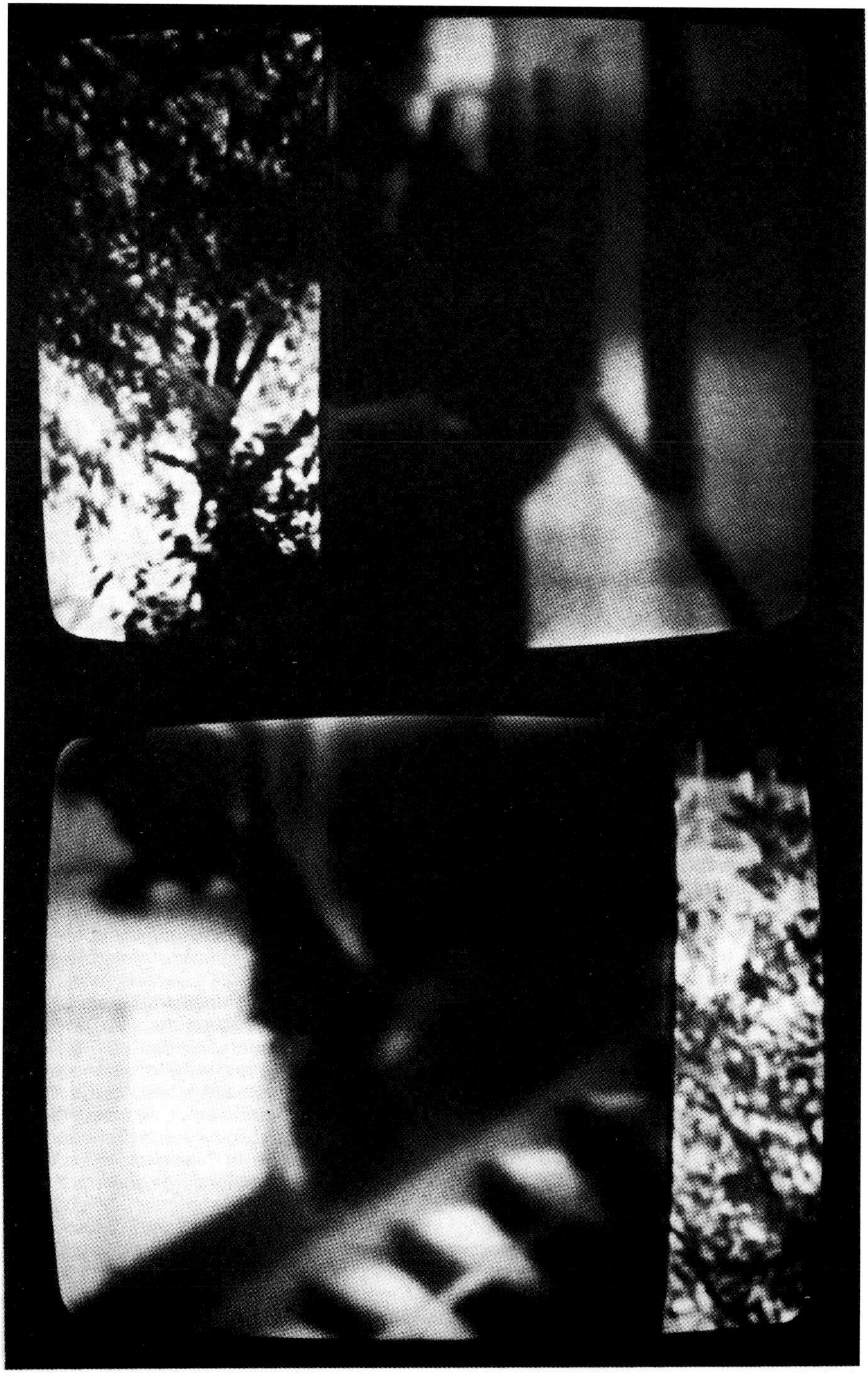

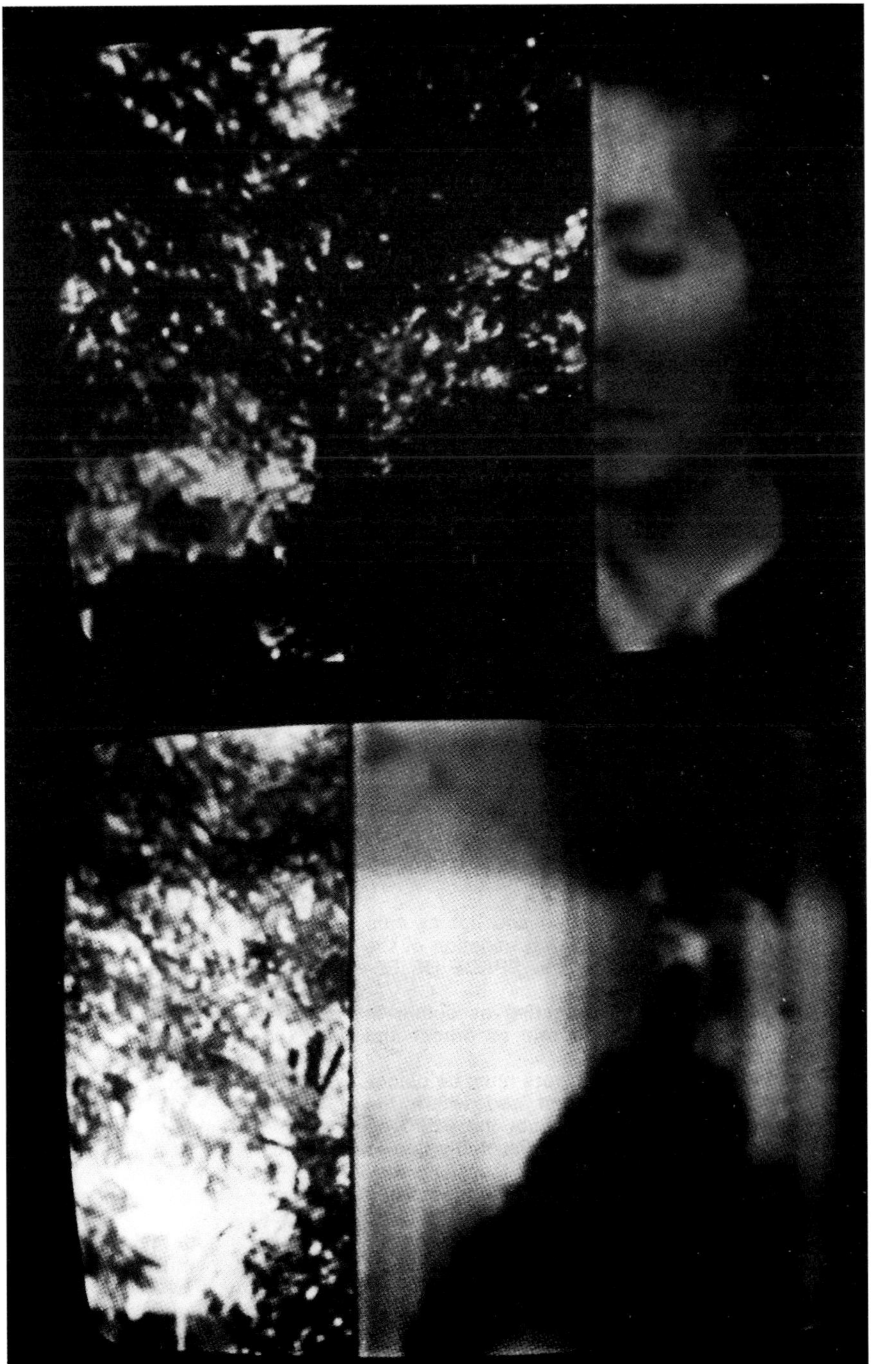

franco vaccari

Exhibition in Real Time, 1969
I had some hundred masks handed to people sitting in a hall. The masks reproduced the plain face of a common man. The hall was in darkness and I started walking about, holding a flashlight and a camera. From time to time I lit someone up and took a picture. Surprised and annoyed, all of them lifted their masks and hid their faces behind them as if the mask were a means of defence, a way to gain anonymity and avoid the clear individualization that photographs generally produce.

I use photography as action and not as contemplation and this involves a negation of the optical space in favor of the SPACE OF RELATIONS.
I want to disappear as artist in order to assume the new role as primer and director of processes.
The ambiences in which I work must be places where things really happen and where the AFTER is always different from the BEFORE. My operations prove to be indissolubly tied to the occasion which determined them; they affect the occasion itself and will afterwards be its unrepeatable witness. In other words, I am interested in rediscovering the risk, intended as rejection of every type of a priori guarantee; in fact, it is possible to state that artistic events become NICHES OF REASSURANCE where one is certain that absolutely nothing will happen.

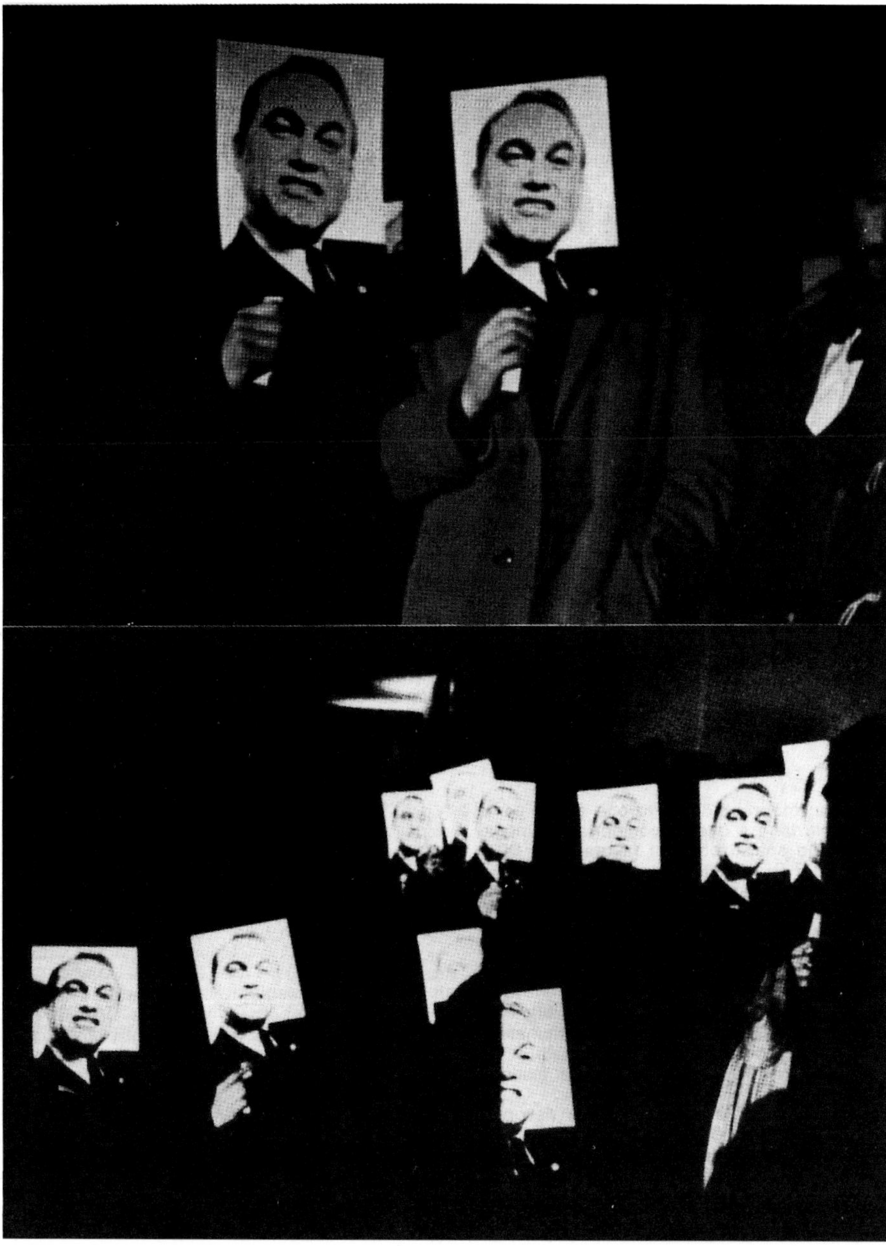

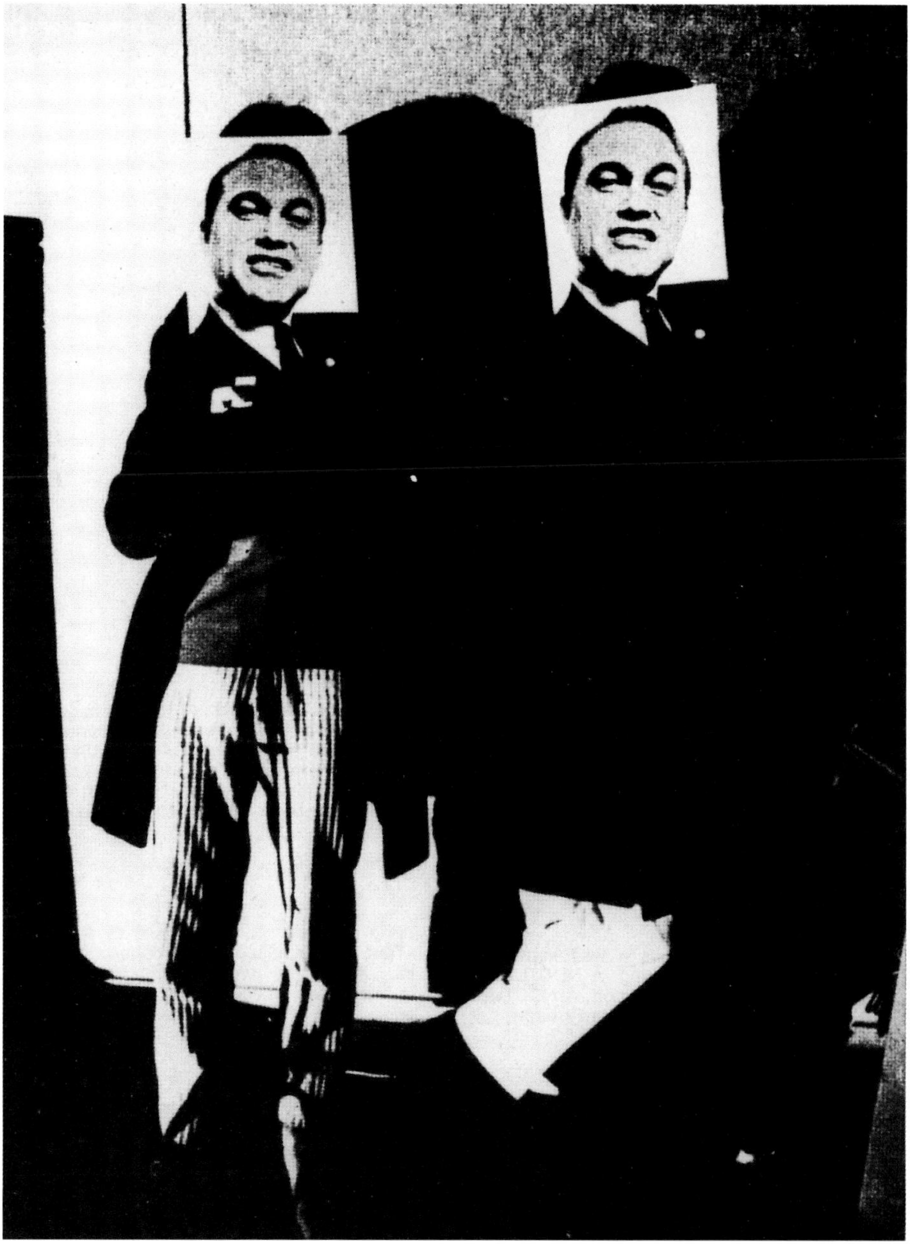

gruppo zaj

Mask, 1964–73
A man is behind another one a long/very long time. Both of them hold one another down with their arms around their waists. If need be the genitals of the one behind could press the buttocks of the one in front.

Nocturne, 1964–73
Luckily a NOCTURNE is a well known thing. The poor know its meaning. A NOCTURNE is not only a rich man's situation. A NOCTURNE is a poor cry in the middle of a starry night. KILL US!

A Camel Strip-tease, 1964–73
A man with 8 dignifying rings fixes a Camel cigarette, perforating it with a long hatpin from a woman's old hat. Then, with extreme care, he takes away the paper that wraps its nudity revealing its obscene tobacco.

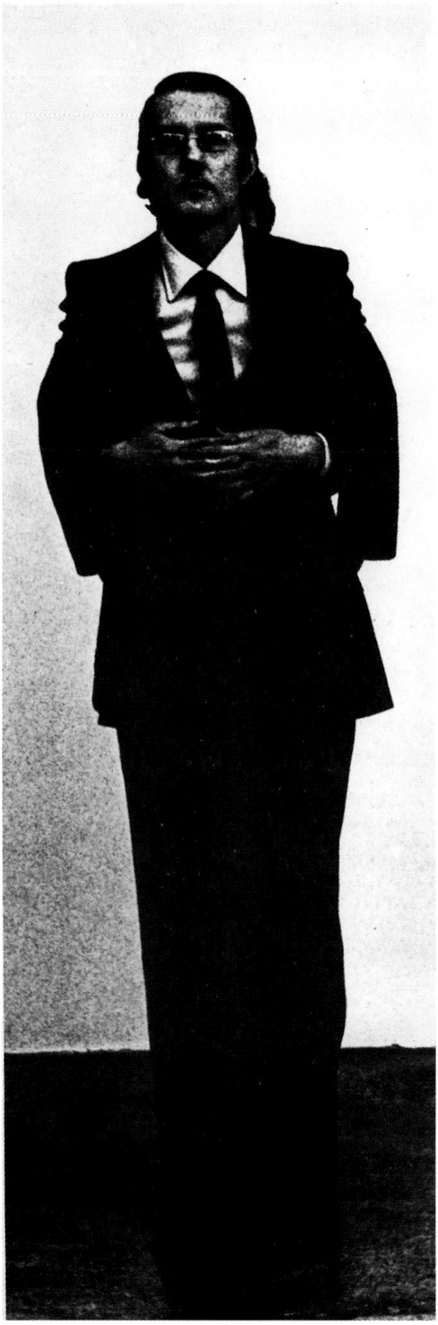

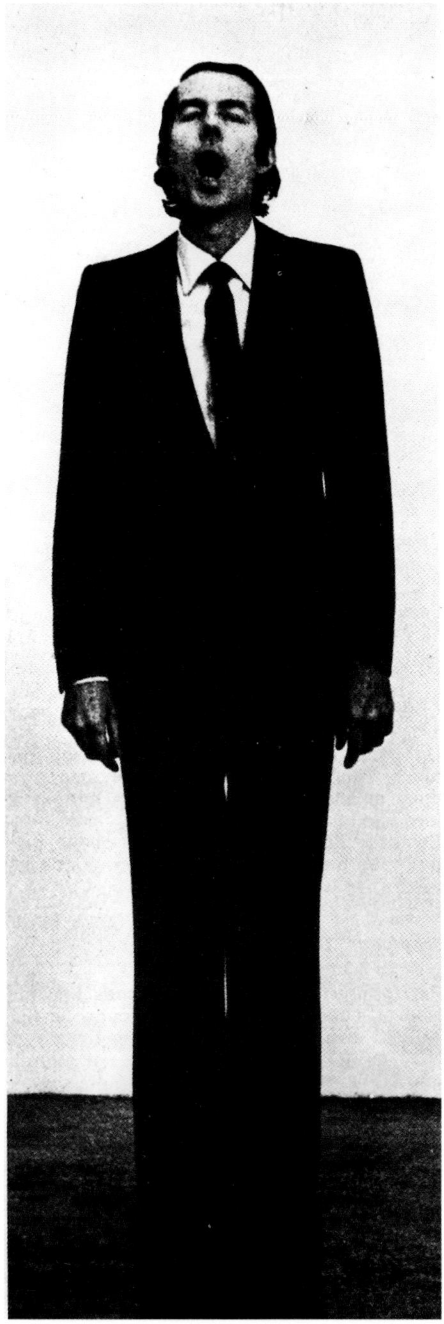

Mask, 1964–73

Nocturne, 1964–73

A Camel Strip-tease, 1964–73

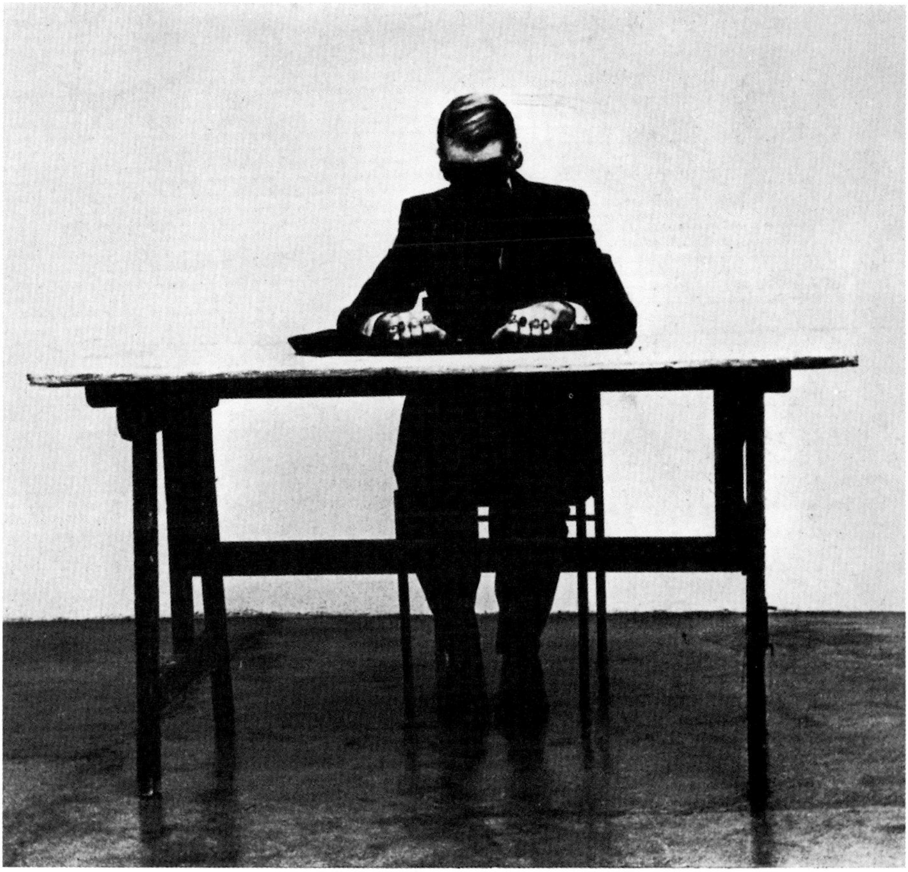

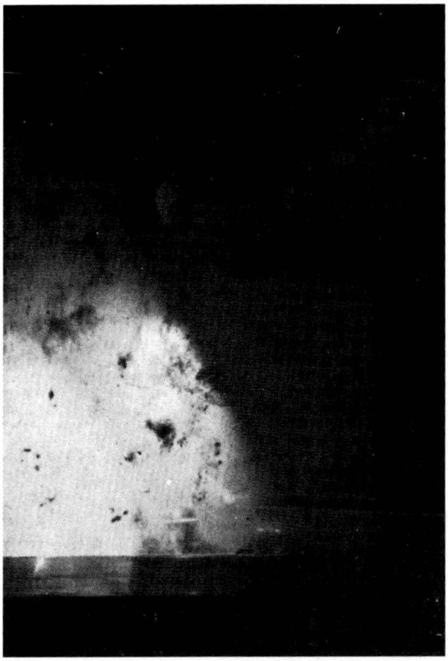

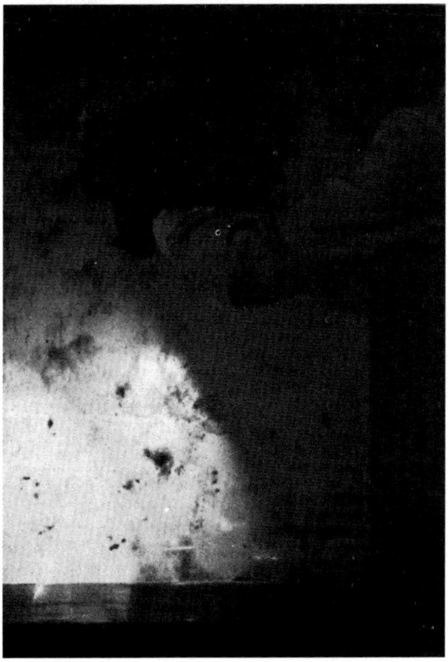

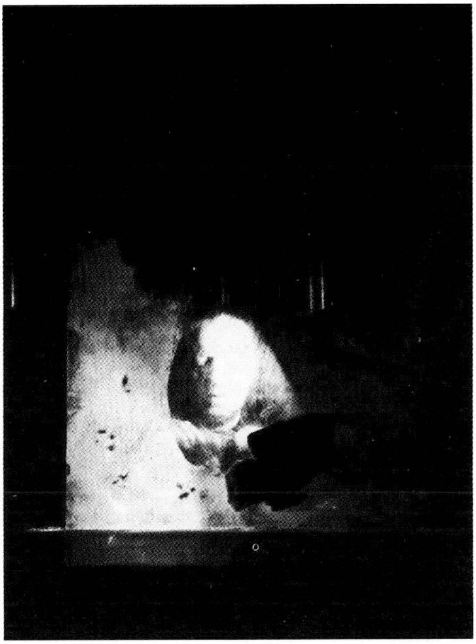

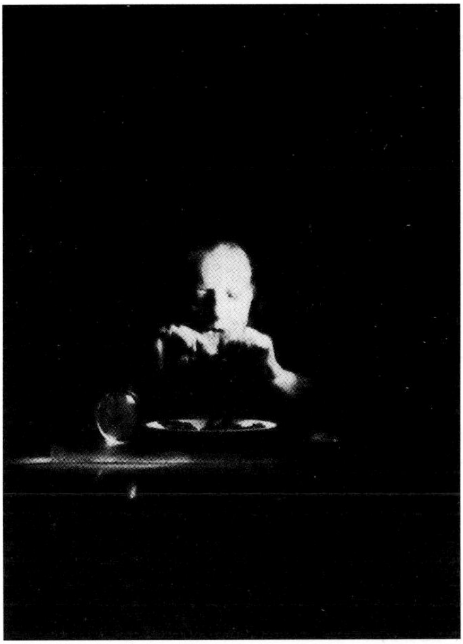

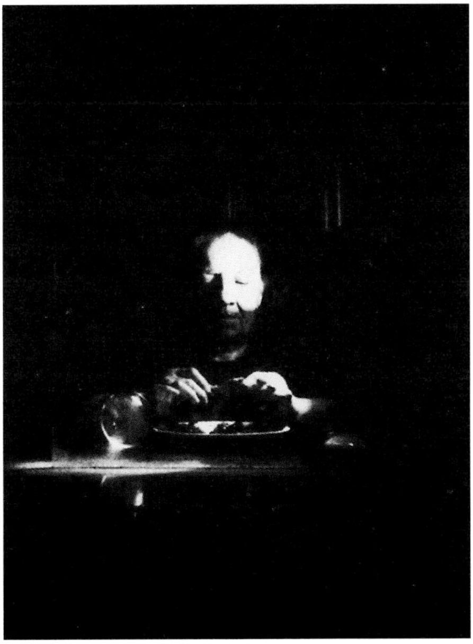

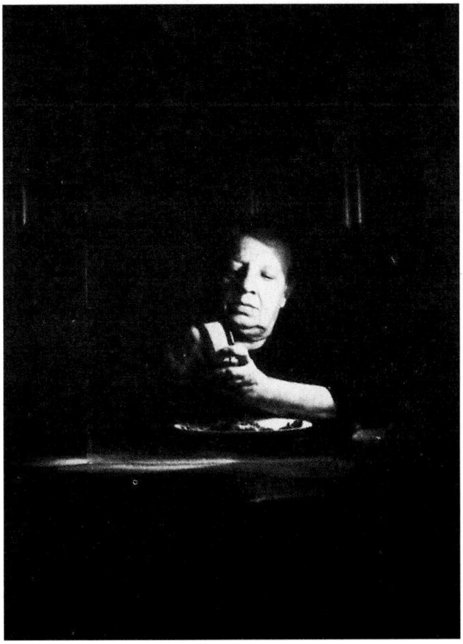

Diffused Body and Mystical Body

What's happened in the meanwhile? Well, by 1975 the American artists Chris Burden and Carolee Schneemann commanded an intensity that could counterbalance retreat from the fronts of polemic and sensationalism. The musicians Brian Eno, David Bowie and Mick Jagger turned their attentions entirely to the stage. And the Slavic artist Marina Abramović (first alone, then with Ulay, and today alone again) has assured herself a place as one of the most notable representatives of Body Art.

The use of the body as a language for art was gradually abandoned by the protagonists of what I then referred to as "like stories." That's to say that artists like Giovanni Anselmo, John Baldessari, Joseph Beuys, Pierpaolo Calzolari, Terry Fox, Eliseo Mattiacci, Vettor Pisani, Annette Messager, Hidetoshi Nagasawa, Dennis Oppenheim, Giuseppe Penone, Richard Serra and Antonio Trotta revealed such stories to have been a question of temporarily measuring themselves against the theme that the moment presented.

Some, like Ketty La Rocca and Michel Journiac, were to die quite shortly after the book's appearance. Others continued to pursue their work by way of a series of shifts and adjustments (actions were replaced by photos and drawings and at times by paintings) but without forsaking the themes of identity and self-concealment. I'm thinking here, for example, of Gilbert and George, Urs Lüthi, Katharina Sieverding, Joan Jonas and Rebecca Horn, no less than of Gina Pane and Fabio Mauri. Pane and Mauri demand discussion in more specific terms, because of their subsequent career.

Gina Pane—who unfortunately passed away in 1990—opted in as early as 1981 to present *partitions* instead of actions. "Partitions"

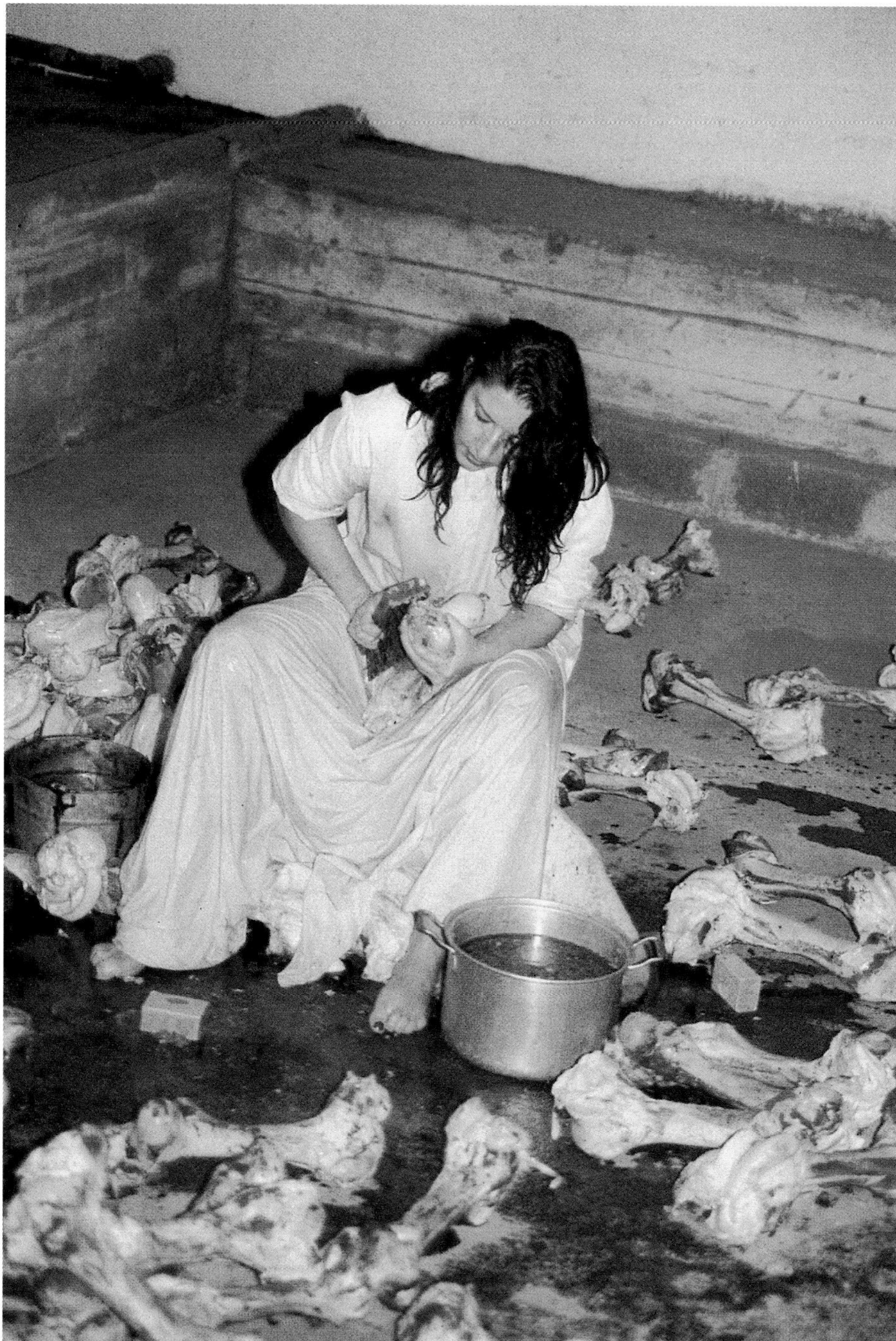

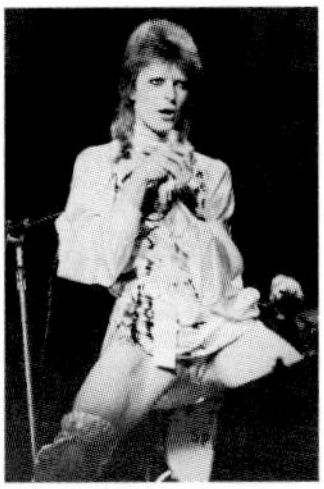
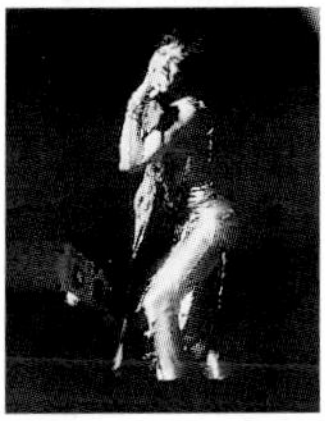
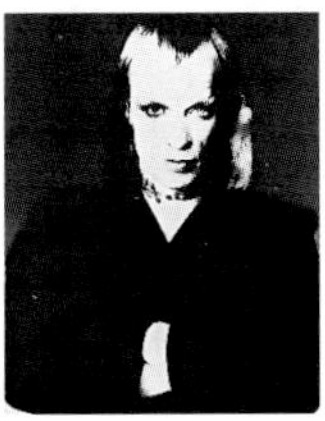

David Bowie, Mick Jagger and Brian Eno in three photographs of the early seventies

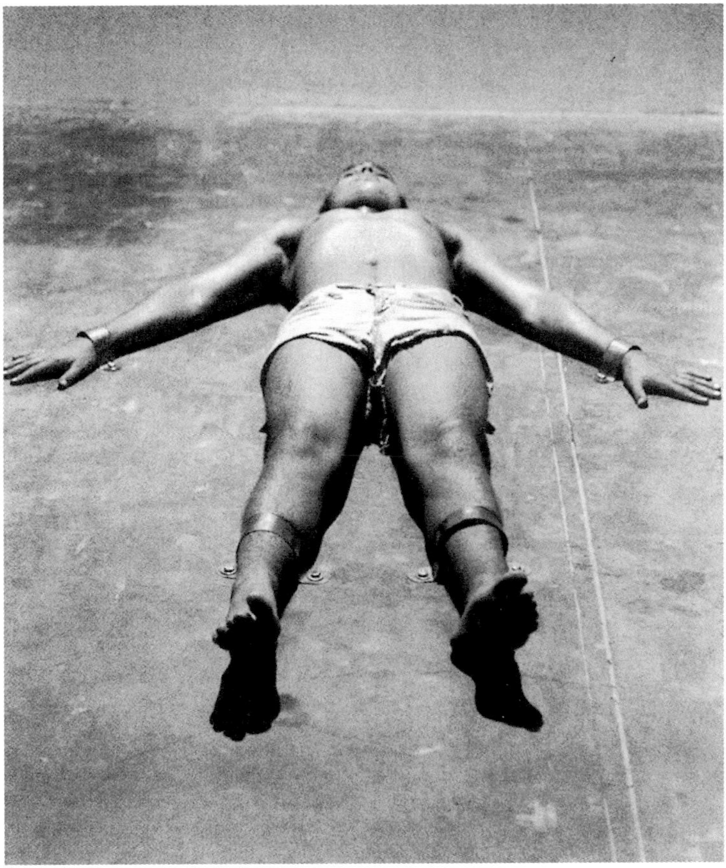

Left
Marina Abramović, *Cleaning the House*, New York, 1995

Top right
Chris Burden, *Prelude to 220, or 110*, September 1976

in the sense of dividing things up into constellations of forms, materials and sounds, but also in the sense of scores, as musical structures. She continued, essentially, to develop her discourse on the use of the body as a language, but chose to do so through different means. A further variation on the same theme: my body and yours. Walls—the screens on which life is projected—as well as the spaces before them were turned into sites that hosted drawings, photos of the particulars of former actions, toys, and other vestigial presences. The body is no longer there. There's the evocation of the body. Gina Pane removed herself from the scene, but in doing so expanded her body into the realm of the ethereal. The body as such has not disappeared, it's missing. We encounter new spaces where absence asserts itself. We look at the invisible; we look at the body's absence. In *Saint Georges*, for example, all that remains of the martyr's body are his footsteps. Or, better, the enigma of the body remains. Red plush, photos of blood, shards of glass and also the bow are there on the wall, but as well they are somewhere else.

Franko B., *I'm not your babe*, 1995

In *La prière des pauvres et les corps des Saints* (1989) we gaze at a great display, in nine vitrines, of objects symbolizing the bodies of saints. And we newly encounter the whole range of the interlocking themes which were characteristic of Gina Pane's actions: existence and demise, the whole and the fragmentary, harmony and dissonance. We likewise encounter that network of memories and analogies which always accompanied her inventions. Here in this room, as we view its vitrines—charged with signs that can also be read as relics—calm defeats anxiety, and we truly experience the *fine pointe de l'âme* of those ceremonies to which Pane referred as "actions." This, perhaps, is her most essential action. It finds its origin in the absence of all desire (or in liberation from desire), and in a kind of rhythmic presence that coincides with its material and pictorial substance. The prayers of the poor and the bodies of the saints become transmuted at one and the very same time into something both ethereal and marble-like. The paradox of art. Gina Pane seals things up, but sharp pulsations and quick presentiments find their way to the interior of these vitrines, evoking halos around them: assumptions and precipitations, impulses and energies. Gina Pane is found both *here* and *there*: in the realm of the body, and as well in a weightless otherwhere.

From *Ebrea* (1971) to *Via Tasso* (1993), Fabio Mauri has always constructed a theater of figures—with images that are also apparitions, and two- and three-fold scenic spaces—that directs its attention to the themes of oppression and injustice. A number of elements are common to almost all of his performances: the individual's condemnation to mortifying tasks; personal stories that open out into group scenes controlled by repeated gestures; complex superimpositions of times and spaces; the interpenetration of chorus and protagonist. Within an atmosphere that's always charged with cultivated references, Mauri conducts the spectator through a daedal of visions and hallucinations, and while doing so is always ready to dwell on minor episodes and to illuminate zones of obscurity, revealing all minor circumstances and calling attention to the frailest of indications. His actions are neither exclusively carnal nor exclusively theatrical, if not in the sense of finding their guide in the aspiration that defines and lies at the heart of theater: the lending of substance to shades. Mauri might perhaps be

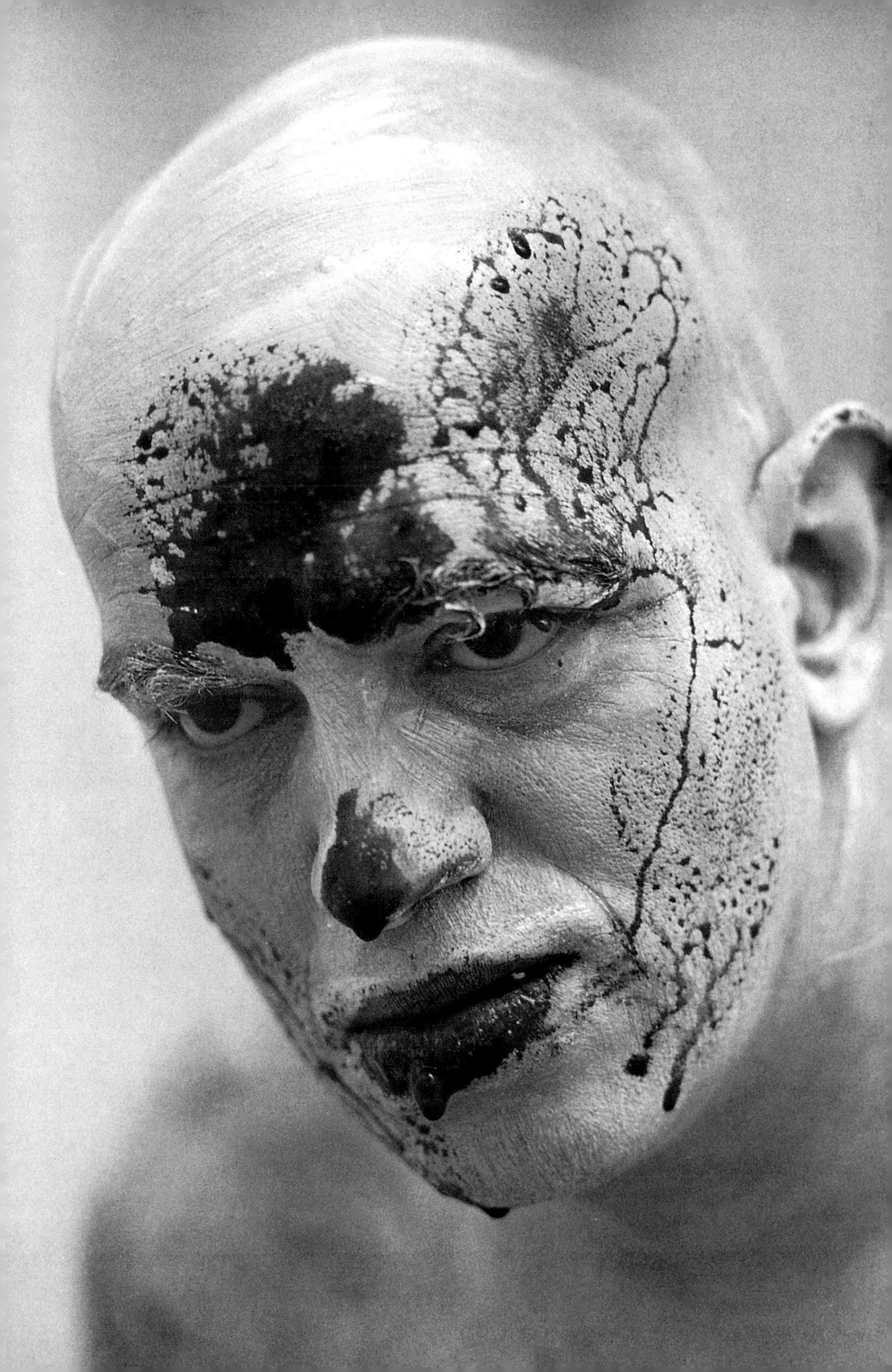

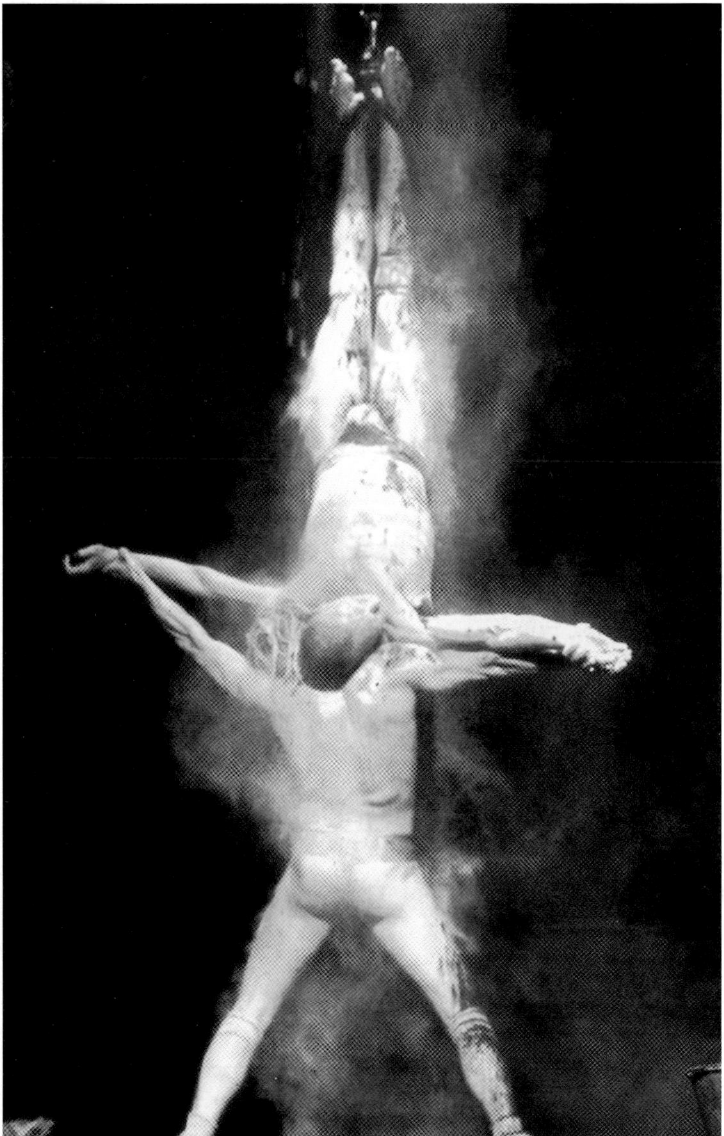

La Fura dels Baus, *Suz/o/Suz*, 1985

Stelarc, *City Suspension*, 1985

Orlan, *Omniprésence*, 1993

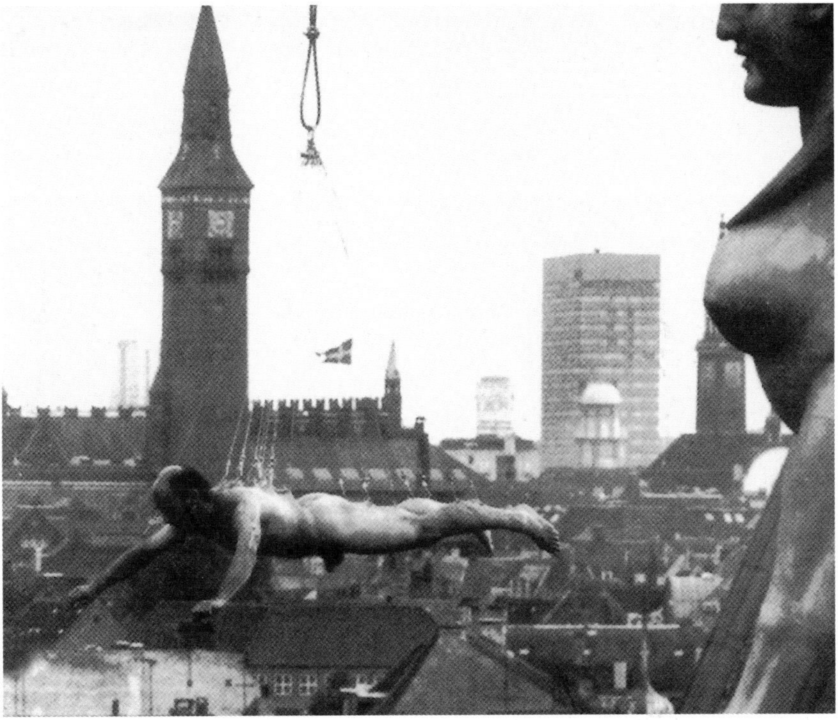

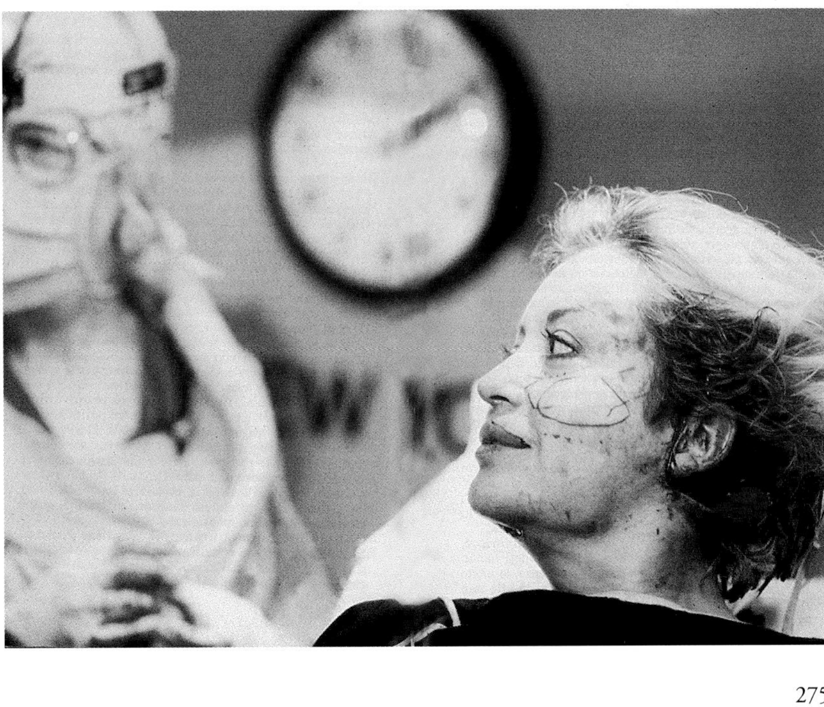

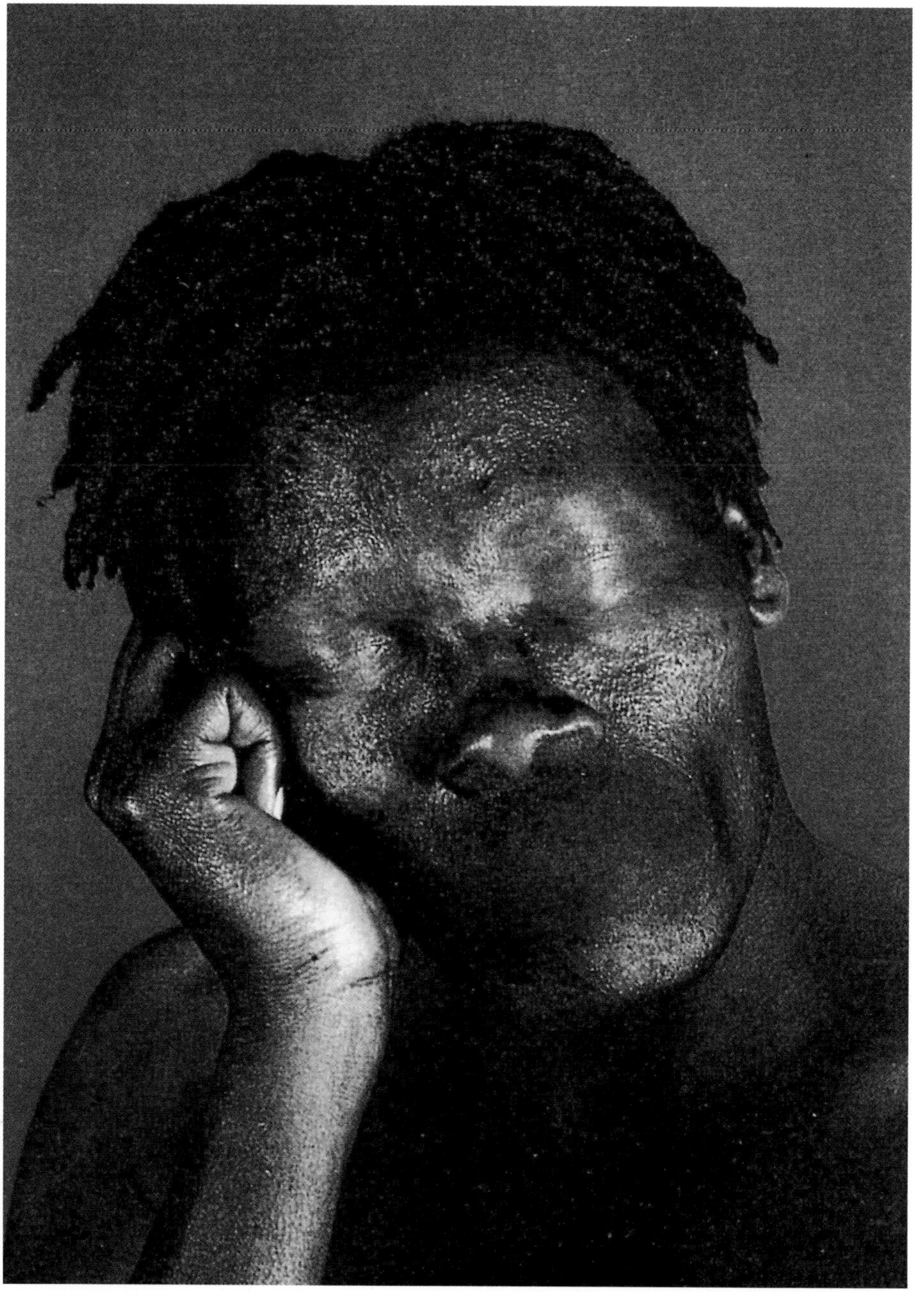

Aziz + Cucher, *Ken*, 1995

Marcel. Lì Antunez Roca, *Epizoo*, 1994

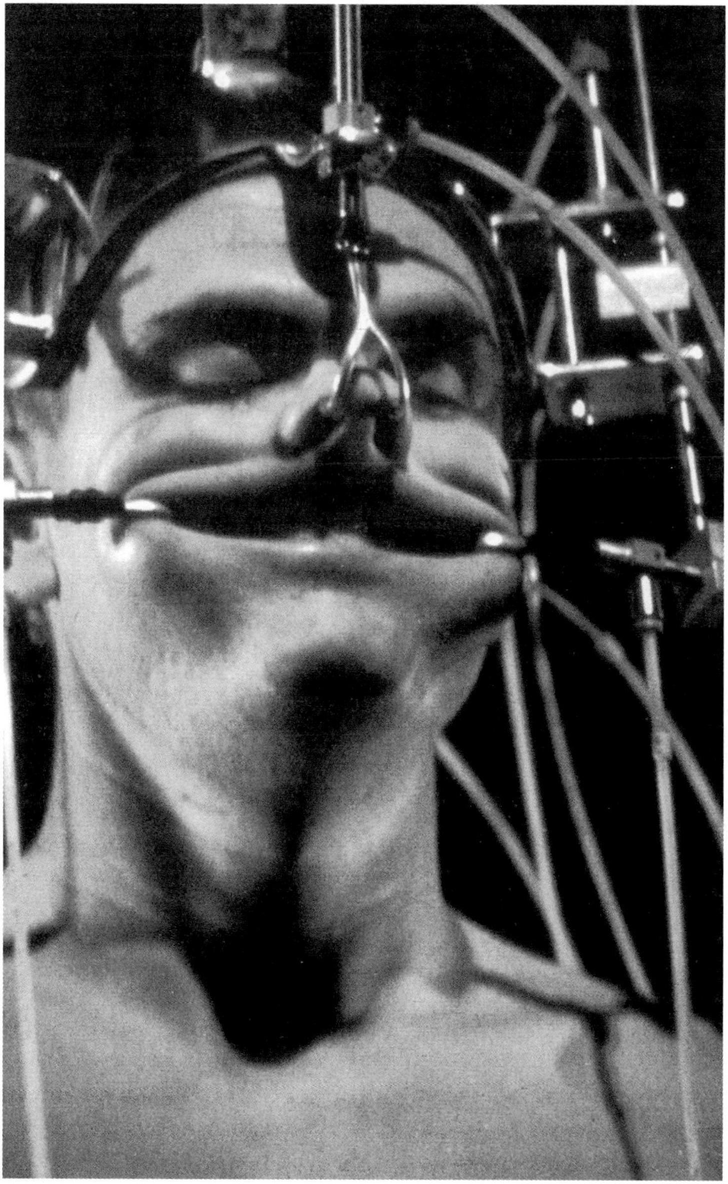

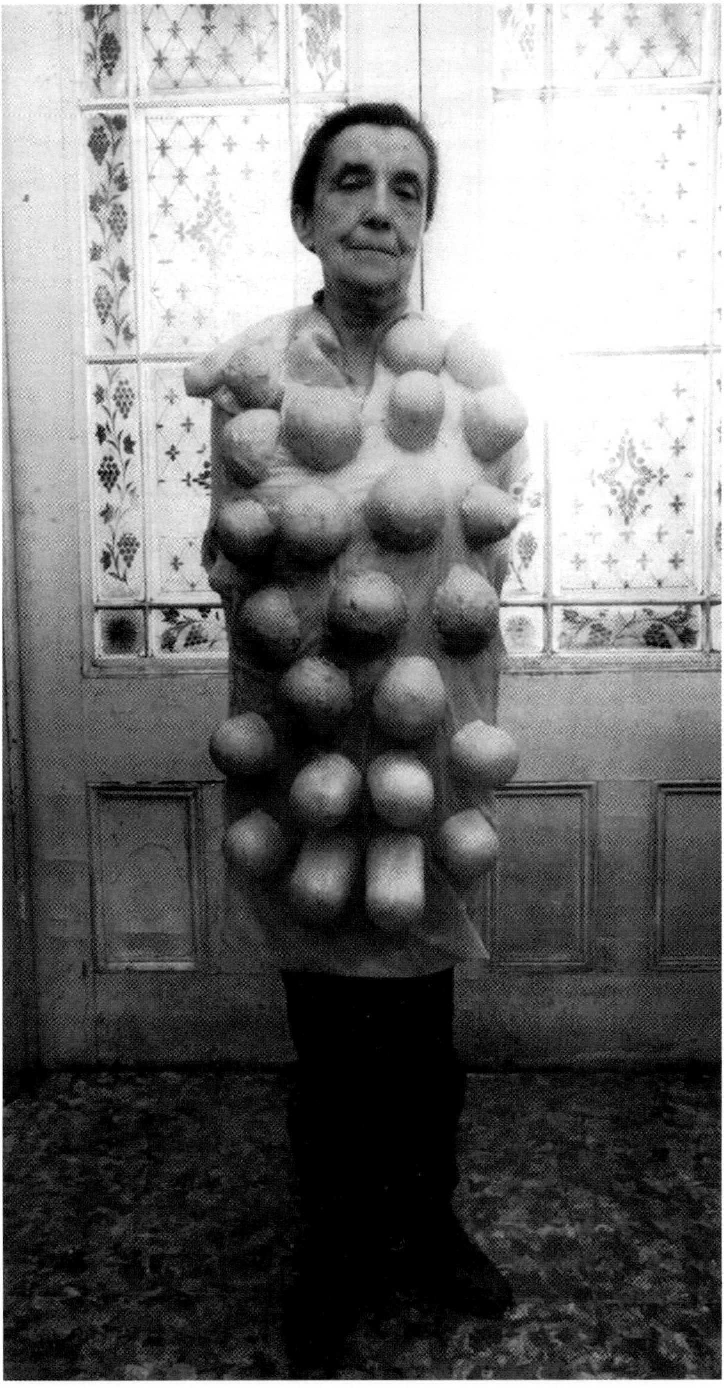

Louise Bourgeois, *A Banquet / A Fashion Show of Body Parts*, 1978

Jenny Holzer, *Untitled* (da *Lustmord*), 1993–94

Cindy Sherman, *Untitled 227*, 1993

Andres Serrano, *The morgue*, 1992

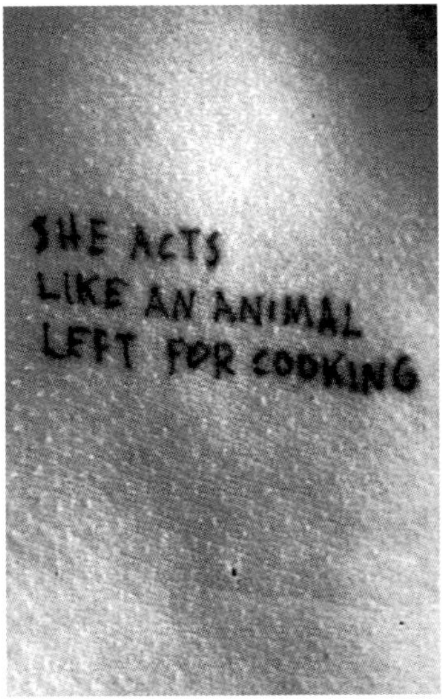

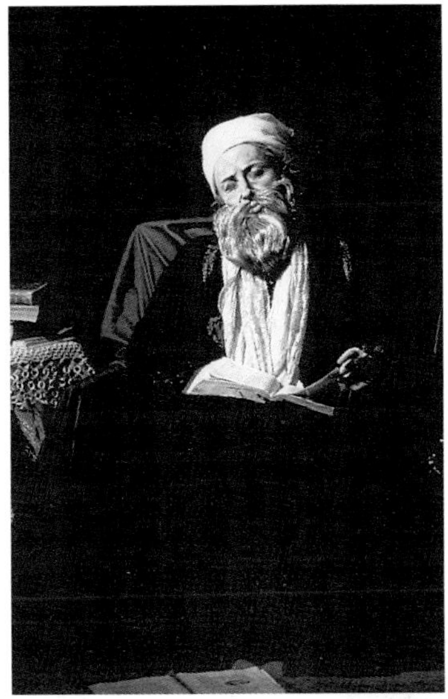

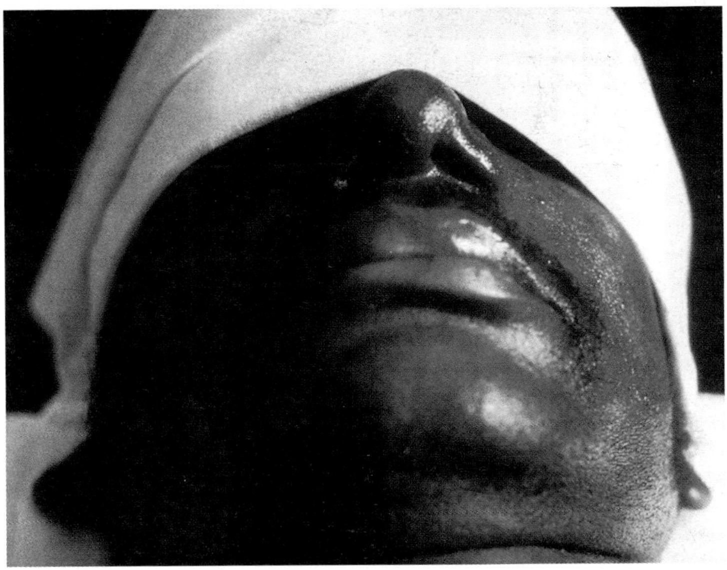

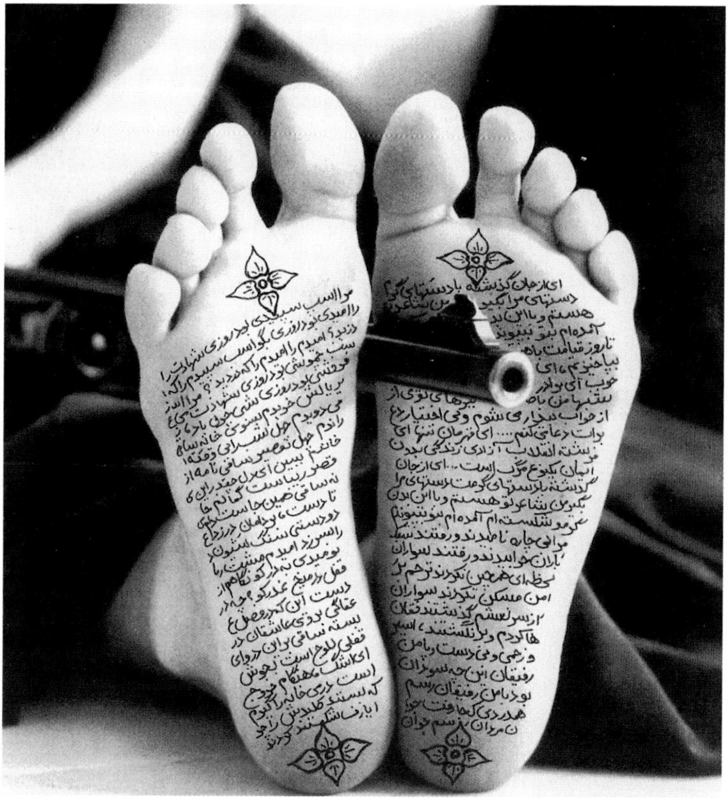

Shirin Neshat, from *Women of Allah*, 1994

described as a "dreamer of reason," in the words applied by Immanuel Kant to the metaphysician who lives in a world of visions. Or perhaps he's on his way, with ever more rapid and vigorous steps, to the center of the soul.

The nineties saw the spread (not only in the visual arts but also in cinema, literature, theater, fashion and ways of life) of the phenomena of shifting identities, technological contaminations, and generally of hybridizations. Though now reduced to a mangled appendage of a post-human condition, to a fragment interfaced with others, to martyred or exultant flesh, grafted to prostheses of every kind and ever more orphaned of sexual or racial traits, the body made its return—at nearly thirty years of distance from the scandal (which it once had been) of Body Art—as the seat and arbiter of multiple identities.
What meaning can be found in living the experience, and so fervently pursuing it, of the fractured personality? Since fractured per-

Janieta Eyre, *Sindone Recipe for Turin Shroud (Incarnation 22)*, 1995

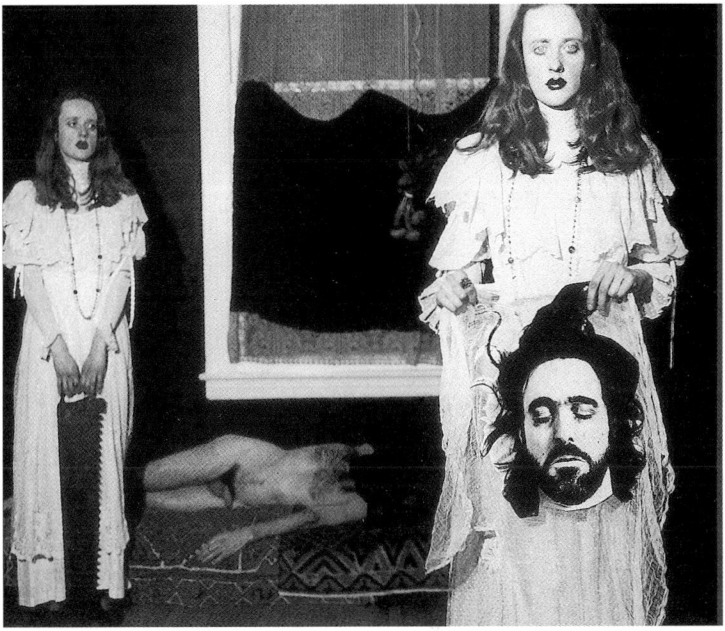

sonalities are probably what we're looking at. And what do they have to do with art? Or with what Ronald D. Laing (remember Laing?) called "the divided self"? Are we faced with so many blatant sadists and lubricious masochists who find their excitements in anguished vice, and their persuasion in outright terror? Perhaps. They elaborate figurative fantasies, both virtual and otherwise, on a theme that strikes fear into most of us: the limitless power of technology. Cassandras of catastrophes and imminent massacres, they pursue the moral strategy of the blow to the gut which leaves you breathless; they aspire to a "heterodoxy of the heart." Delivering dismay and discomfort, they make their exultant way to the borders of impossibility, living the adventure of art as life as the re-exhumation of the self. Examples can be found in the performances or spectacles of Franko B., Stelarc, Orlan, Marcel. Lì Antunez Roca, Janine Antoni, La Fura dels Baus; but consider as well the images and researches on possible identities furnished by Cindy Sherman, the first writings on the skin of the body of Jenny Holzer, the sculptures of Louise Bourgeois and Robert Gober, the photos of Andres Serrano and Nan Goldin, the images of Aziz + Cucher, or those of Inez van Lamsweede, or all of the work of Jana Sterbak; and again, Matthew Barney and Shirin Neshat; and the precursory Bruce Nauman.

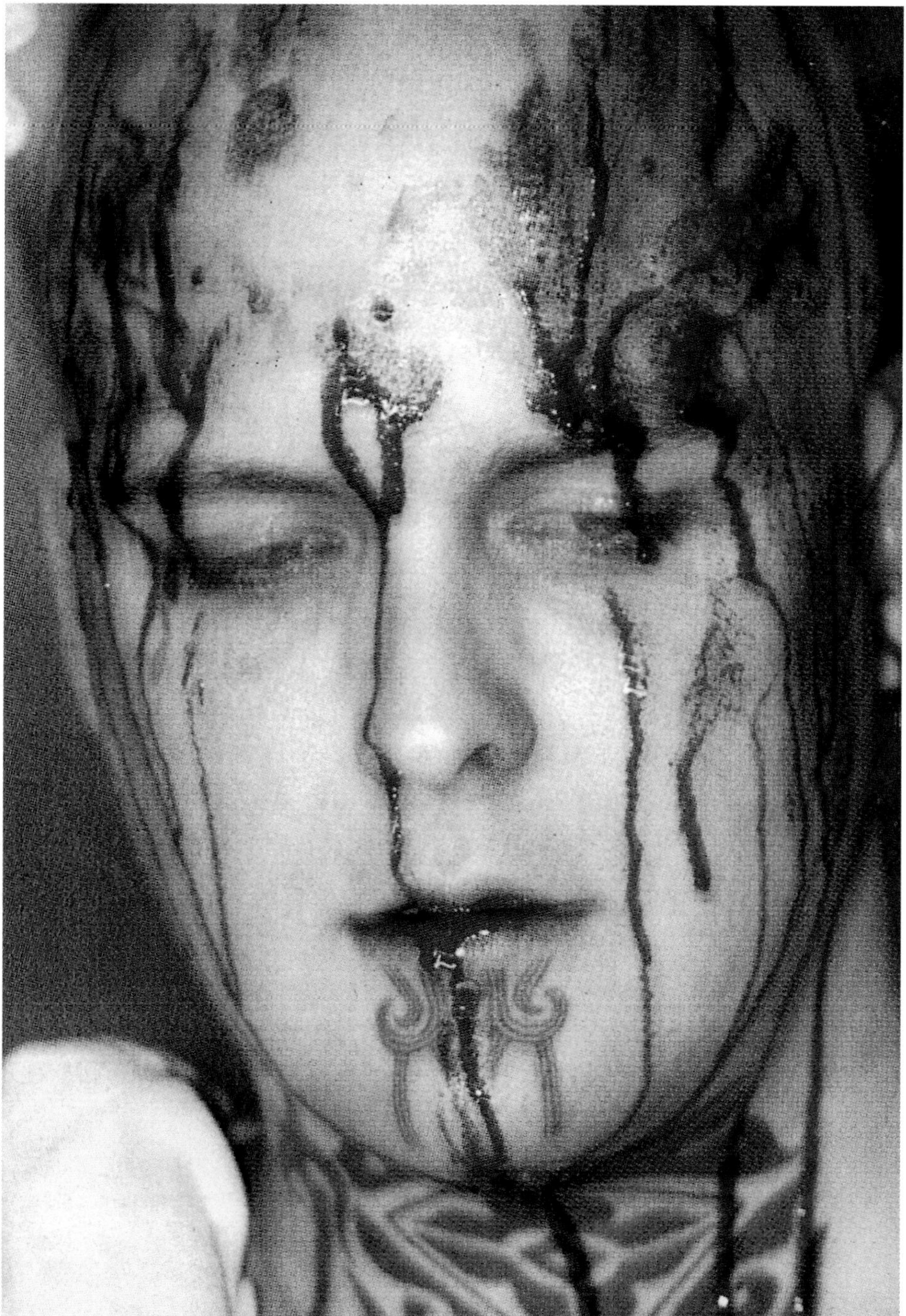

Ron Athey, *Suicide Obsession Tattoo Dream*, 1996

Matthew Barney, *Cremaster 4*, 1995 (Courtesy Fondation Cartier, Paris)

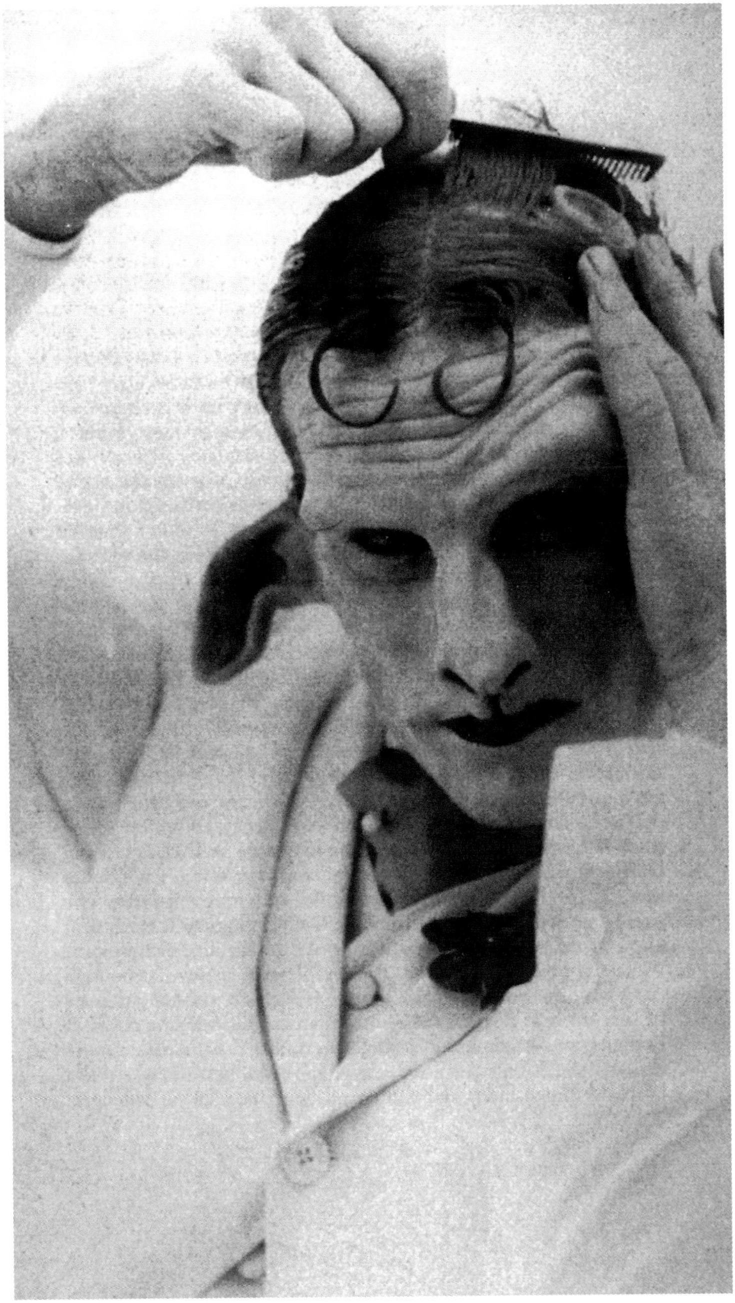

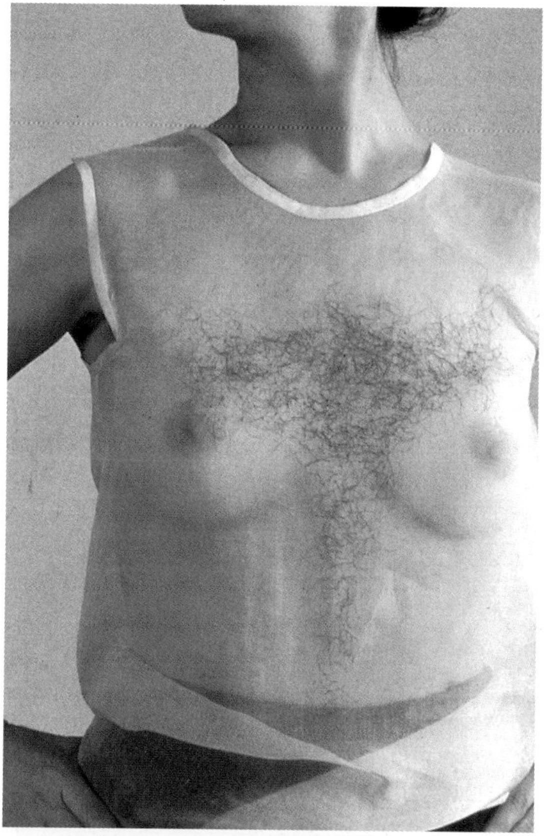

Jana Sterbak,
Distraction, 1992–96

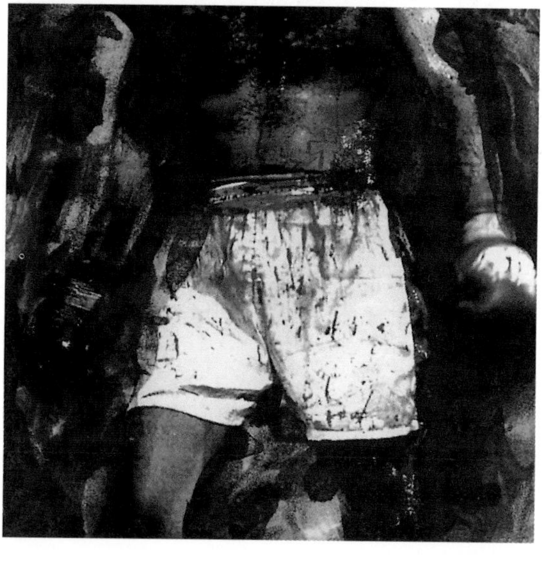

Cesare Fullone,
Virus 2, 1998

Yasumasa Morimura, *Portrait (Queen and Dog)*, 1991

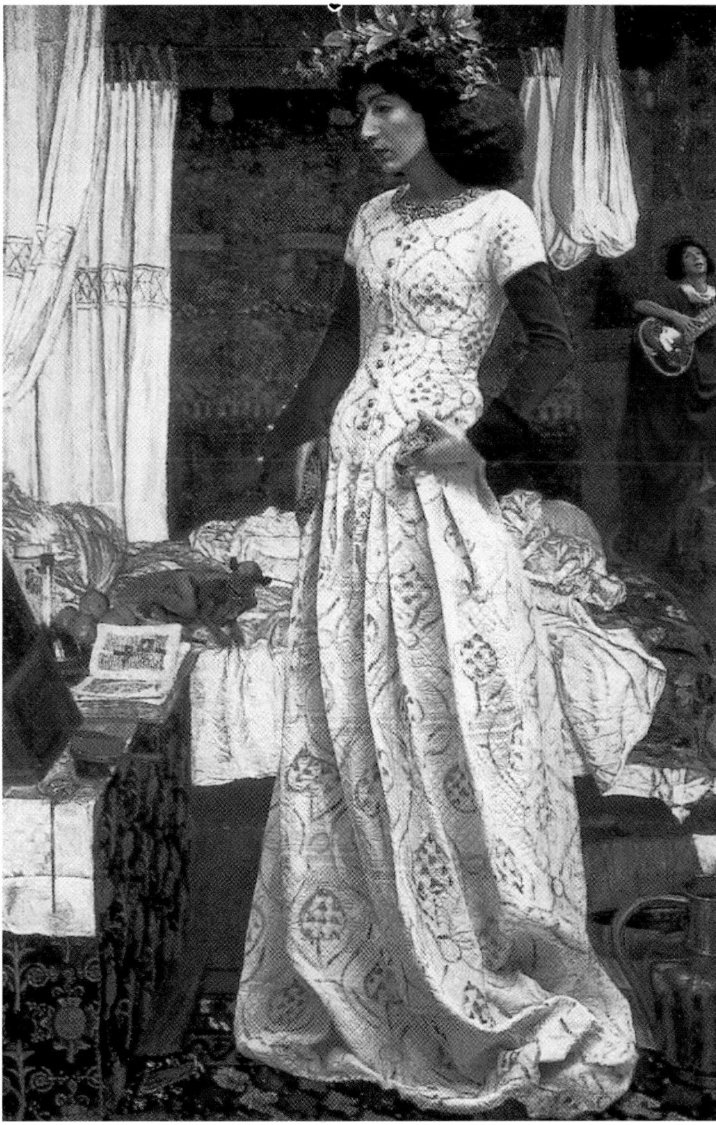

pp. 286–87
Renée Cox,
Io Mama Last Supper, 1996

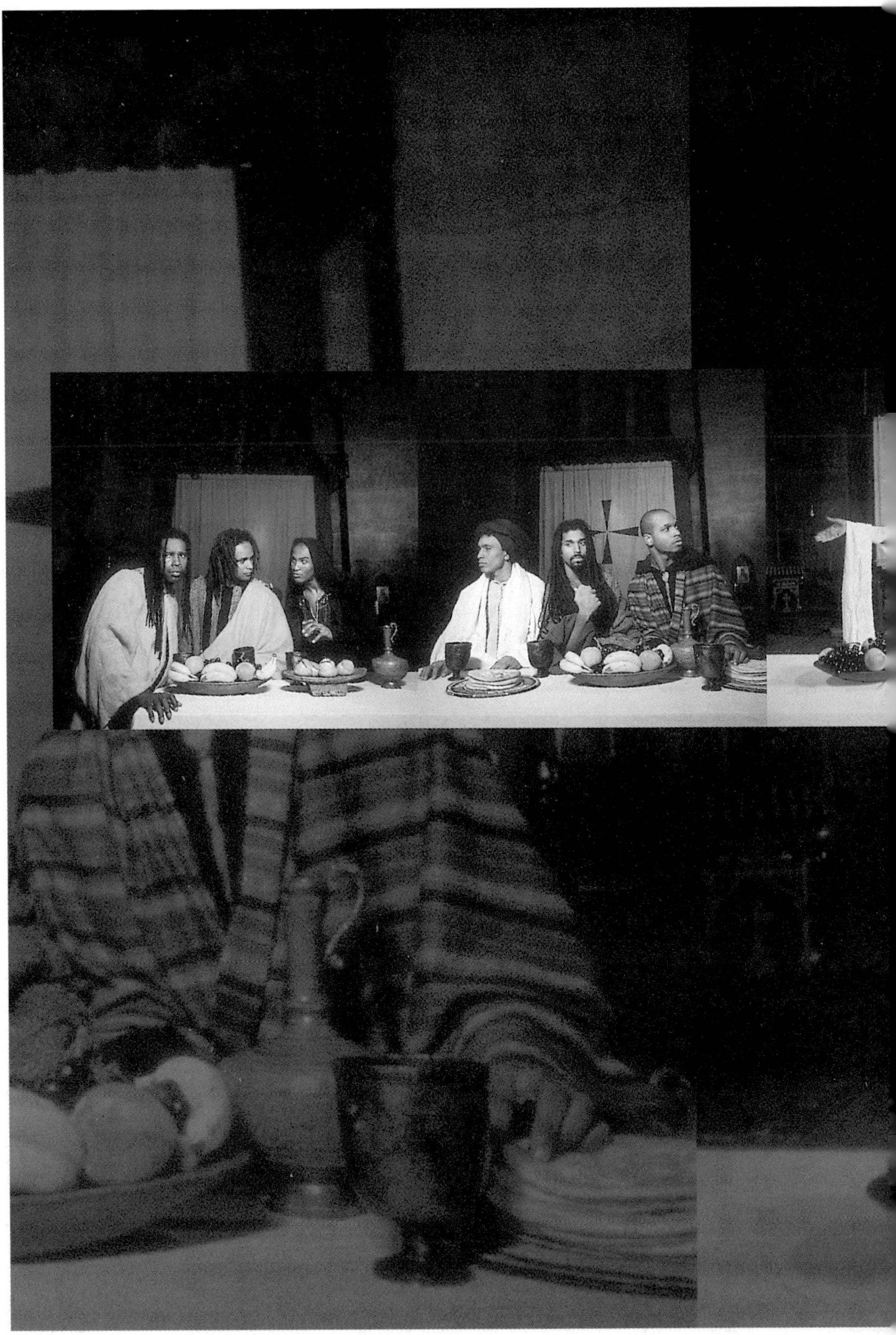

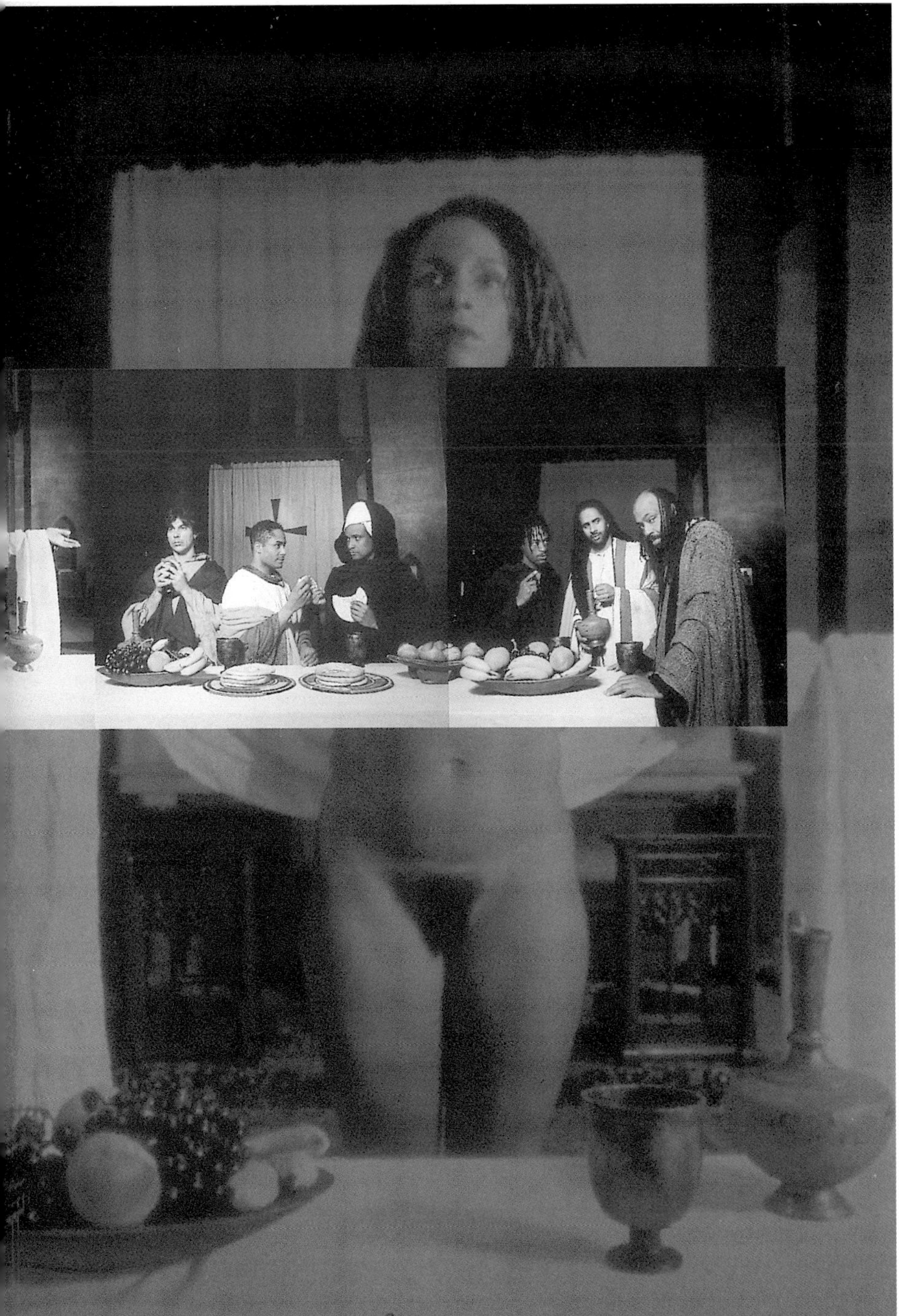

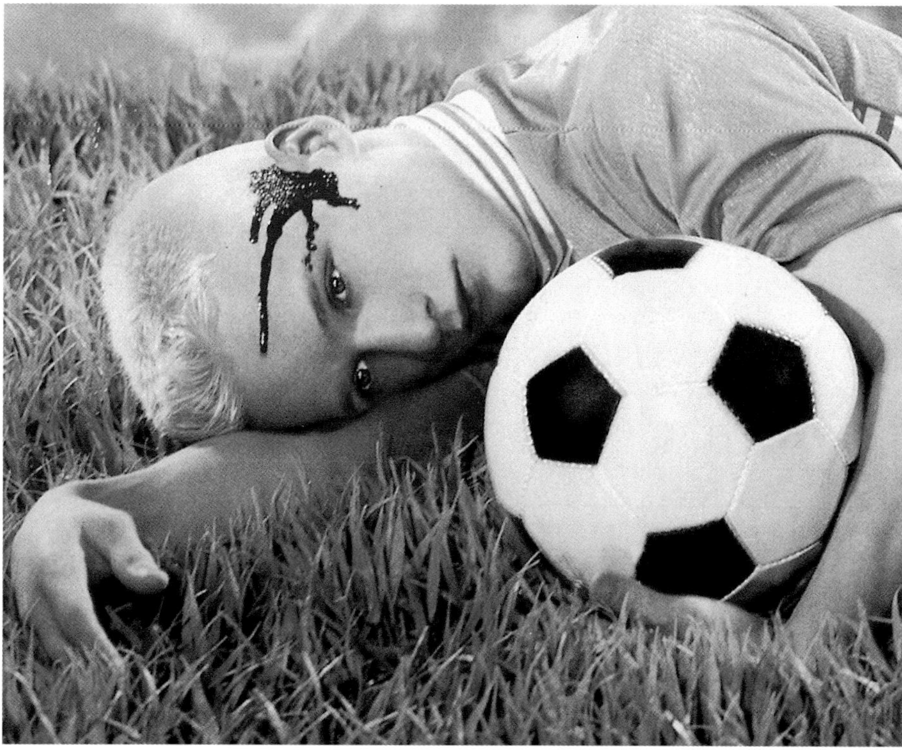

Pierre et Gilles, *Le footballeur blessé*, 1998, detail (Courtesy Gallerie Jérome de Noirmont, Paris)

The terms of this imposing return to the coordinates of bodily experience—we're no longer dealing with the romantic and cultivated narcissism of the seventies, and instead are confronted with fables of brutality, a longing for violent trauma, a delight in the atrocious, a pain that smacks of a sacrificial rite to hold at bay the Great Fear of Collective Death—make one think that this could be our present-day "gothic" genre: a genre of hallucinations and majestic infantility that discovers its vocation in oratory, couched in a syntax of delirium. It might also be a staging of the human being's loss of the dimension of childhood. In that case, the appeal of the deciduous and the dream of a menacing creativity could be read as expressions of the difficulty of accepting one's own identity, of the conflict between being and becoming, of the inability to be what one knows one ought to be, which is to speak of the maturation of a psychological and social identity. So, is it possible here to talk about art? Quite probably. The ceremonials of the stars of the tortured and humiliated body, no less than those of younger artists who attempt to communicate through paradox—

Janieta Eyre, Cesare Fullone, Betty Bee, Marina Ballo Charmet, Gerd Holzwarth, Ottonella Mocellin, Simon Costin, and many others—show many of the features of art, no matter how distorted: fiction that rings with an air of authenticity, for example, or the sublimation of autobiography, much as in the case of the late Romantic art of which they are the final extension.
With respect to the art system and its art market, it's clear that most of these efforts remain unwieldy, heretical, and deviant. And deviance is never to be sneered at. The same should be said of the residues of the notion of the *Übermensch*, the Superman. Giulio Carlo Argan, an art historian above all suspicion of a predilection for body-based conceptions of art, was once to write: "... among Nietzsche's various inebriations, the image of the artist-as-body was far from the most deleterious."

The use of the body as a language has returned to the scene of the world around us in new and different forms, and it speaks through *altered* declinations. The body as triumphant, immolated, diffused, propagated, dramatic, and tragic. The political, social, and mystic body. The body as the site of the extreme. The body as humanity's most ancient instrument for speaking *hic et nunc*. By way of tattoos, piercings, and citations of tribalism. Through manipulations of its organs. The instrument that speaks and communicates without the word, or sounds, or drawings. The body as a vehicle, once again, for declaring opposition to the dominant culture, but also of desperate conformism.
Let's look at an action by the Californian artist Ron Athey, *The Solar Anus* (1998), an homage to the Surrealist writer George Bataille. An almost entirely tattooed body, a black sun raying from its anal zone, which instead of giving issue to feces pours out streams of pearls and aureoles of light. A side-show fit for a circus, an eighteenth-century street decor, an exhibition of masochistic narcissism? All of that. And also, we can add, a regression to infantility. But what if we also witness the birth of a sinister delight and an air of fable in the midst of the grotesque and pathetic? What if the officiant, as he seems to be, in the course of this *non mori sed pati* slowly raises a golden crown to his head, and thus sets off—while performing an event which we see as demented and abject—a sudden flash of happiness, and a poetry that lives in the minimal gestures and episodes of utterly minor situations, a poetry made of tiny nothings that make one aware of something else (just as

happens with Art)? Surely that must mean that the pathology is interrupted, and it's ready to be mediated by culture.
Another extreme example of the last ten years: Matthew Barney. Barney is a figure of unparalleled ambiguity and we see him in his films as a masqueraded humanoid with the extremities of fauns or angels. Whether the coupling which produced this hybridization took place with a cherub or an animal is in fact quite difficult to say. What is his fable about? About shifting identity? Him too? Yes, him too. He also adds something grandiose and Wagnerian to his indecipherability. He functions as the Narrator. Irony too is a part of the cunning with which he blends the surgeon's instruments with lyric opera, dance, myth, science fiction, transexuality, transvestism, Houdini the magician and Ursula Andress, Bob Wilson and the Rococo. He serves a meal that's spiced with artifice, ornament and rhetorical illuminations; visual materials which are fast and violent, a snatch of Watteau, an odor of Greenaway, all for a panoply of phantasmagorical surprises.
After seeing his films one finds oneself dumbfounded, immersed in a cold delight, as well as in the grips of a kind of intellectual terror. (But isn't that what's supposed to happen on witnessing a work that goes beyond its medium?)
The "portraits" of Yasumasa Morimura are finally the apex, hyperbole and coronation of the notions of mimicry and camouflage. At a point equidistant from Hoffmann's princess, Cardinal Pirelli and Jeremy Irons as he imitates Madame Butterfly, the Japanese artist throws limitless expertise into recreating the quintessential western woman, while never relinquishing oriental folly or Preraphaelite decadence. Morimura is a master of linguistic games: his masquerades present themselves as calibrated marvels of exactitude and precise philological annotation.
Do we have to be reminded that disguise is a question of adopting a confusing appearance for the purpose of deceit, and that mimicry is a kind of disappearance, a fictional cancellation of one's own specific traits? Or that intimidation is a demonstrative action that tends to incite a groundless terror? These are the terms of the efforts of Jana Sterbak, always deployed in communications which are no less concise than ferocious and aseptic: from the garment made of tatters of flesh to the woman's undershirt that bears the hair of a male chest. Sterbak's compositions make use of a three-toned register: a terrorist didacticism, a deliciously argumentative nonsense, and an ice-cold rage.

A final note. These figures are highly bizarre and extremely various, and beyond all rule, and where do we put them? But don't they seem, in any case, to be most related to the Blaise Pascal, ardent and disturbed, who pondered the agony of Christ, and with passion and tenderness explored the mystery of pain—rather than to count as further descendants of the genius and derangement of Artaud or Baudelaire? It might well be that we're here in the presence of a mode of religious experience, and that this is something of which these people feel the need. Gina Pane, Fabio Mauri, Renée Cox, Ron Athey, Catherine Opie, Pierre and Gilles and many others likewise open by-ways that could lead to such a conjecture.

Our thoughts on the mystic shouldn't reduce to the image of the stylite. As Émile Cioran reminds us, we can think of the mystic as a rebel—as a rebel by vocation—or as a daring combatant who is often heretical and paradoxical with respect to questions of faith, but forever unrivaled in the passion for self-inflicted torture. (*Passio* as suffering and *passio* as passion, which in any case sins against natural order.) The mystic, in short, can be thought of as an incendiary temperament and personality.

Virtuosos of disorder and hungry for afflictions of any and every kind, mystics—like persons who display the subjection of their bodies to cruel and invasive devices, or who revel in virtual fantasies of such self-inflicted pains—destroy themselves in order newly to find themselves. Our authors desire, through finding themselves, to turn into a crowd, and to do so they create and give themselves the use of other bodies and other faces. They thus, finally, pay a visit to the world of the saints and victims, exploring and prolonging its seductions. So, the body is a mystical body. But mysticism has always found the body to lie at its point of origin. It is first of all a physical experience: a source of fluids, of blood, of humors, of various waters that flow, coagulate, and again grow liquid. The relationship with God—Christian, Hebrew or Muslim—burns with fire and liquefies like wax. The soul cannibalizes the body in which it lives, sucks it in like breath, swallows it into its stomach, sates itself on its substance. Nothing is more physical than the practice of mysticism.

Lea Vergine, January 2000
Translation by Henry Martin

Selected Bibliography

R.D. Laing, *The Divided Self. A Study of Sanity and Madness.* London: Tavistock Publications, 1960.

P. Gorsen, *Das Prinzip Obszön: Kunst, Pornographie und Gesellschaft.* Reinbek b. Hamburg: Rowohlt, 1969.

G. Deleuze, *Masochism, an Interpretation of Coldness and Cruelty.* New York: G. Braziller, 1973.

Transformer, texts by J.-C. Ammann and P. Gorsen, exhibition catalogue. Luzern: Kunstmuseum, 1974.

E. Weiss, in *The Search for Identity*, exhibition catalogue. Milan: Electa, 1974.

G. Dorfles, *La Body Art.* Milan: Dispense Fabbri, 1975.

E. Sanguineti, *L'arte del corpo*, in *Giornalino.* Turin: Einaudi, 1976.

M. Foucault, *Discipline and Punish: the Birth of Prison.* London: Allen Lane, 1977. New York: Pantheon Books, 1977.

F. Quadri, *L'avanguardia teatrale in Italia (1960-1976).* Turin: Einaudi, 1977.

M. Calvesi, *Avanguardia di massa.* Milan: Feltrinelli, 1978.

G. Celant, *Artmaker.* Milan: Feltrinelli, 1979.

M. Merleau-Ponty, *Il corpo vissuto.* Milano: Il Saggiatore, 1979.

J. Baudrillard, *De la seduction.* Paris: Editions Galilée, 1979.

J. Beck and J. Malina, *Il lavoro del Living Theater.* Milan: Ubulibri, 1982.

F. Pluchart, *L'art corporel.* Paris: Limage 2, 1983.

G. Battock and R. Nickas, *The Art of Performance. A Critical Anthology.* New York: E.P. Dutton & Co., 1984.

Various Authors, *L'altro visto da sé*, Genoa: Costa & Nolan, 1987.

L. Bentivoglio, *Il teatro di Pina Bausch.* Milan: Ubulibri, 1991.

J. Deitch, *Post Human*, exhibition catalogue. Lausanne-Turin-Athens-Hamburg, 1992.

G. Pozzi (edited by), Maria Maddalena de' Pazzi, *Le parole dell'estasi.* Milan: Adelphi, 1992.

G. Pozzi (edited by), Angela da Foligno, *Il libro dell'esperienza.* Milan: Adelphi, 1992.

P. Bausch, L. Childs and M. Graham, *Discorsi sulla danza.* Milan: Ubulibri, 1994.

Various Authors, *Auf den Leib - Geschrieben*, exhibition catalogue. Wien, 1995.

Various Authors, *Fémin/Masculin*, exhibition catalogue, Centre G. Pompidou. Paris: Gallimard-Electa, 1995.

A. Castellani, *Ribelli per la pelle.* Genoa:

Costa & Nolan, 1995.
A. Caronia, *Il corpo virtuale*. Padua: Muzio editore, 1996.
F. Alfano Miglietti, *Identità mutanti*, Genoa: Costa & Nolan, 1997.
G. Salerno, *Suoni del corpo Segni del cuore*. Milan: Costa & Nolan, 1998.
P. Schimmel, *Out of Actions*. London: Thames and Hudson, 1998.
S. Vinci, *In tutti i sensi come l'amore*. Turin: Einaudi, 1998.
F. Alfano Miglietti, *Rosso vivo*, exhibition catalogue. Milan: Electa, 1999.
F. Quadri and A. Martinez (edited by), *Robert Wilson o il teatro del tempo*. Milan: Ubulibri, 1999.
F. Evans and L. Lawlor (edited by), *Chiasms: Merleau-Ponty's Notion of Flesh*. New York: State University of New York Press, 2000.

Magazines

Avalanche, nos. 1–2. Paris, 1972.
L'Art Vivant, nos. 40–41. Paris, 1973.
Artitudes, no. 3. Paris, 1973.
Virus Mutationis. Milan, from 1993 to the present day.

Photographic Credits (1974 edition):
Claudio Abate
Cesare Bastelli
Elisabetta Catalano
Enrico Cattaneo
Giorgio Colombo
Bruno del Monaco
Fabio Donato
Larry Fox
G. Gallina
Gianfranco Gorgoni
Giorgio Gramantieri
Hoffenreich
Mimmo Jodice
Michel Journiac
Judith Jsaacson
Babette Mangolte
Françoise Masson
Al Mozell
Ugo Mulas
Mimma Pisani
Aurelia Raffo
Jacques Rouiller
Paolo Mussat Sartori
Roby Toselli
Franco Visco

For the illustrations of Diffused Body and Mystical Body *we wish to thank:* Carmine de Martino; Duane Michals; Marc Milin; Jean-Jacques Ringuette; Nicholas Sinclair; Paul Steinitz; Gabor Szilasi; Martin L. Vargas; Lois Keidan and Catherine Ugwu, ICA, London; Galleria Photology, Milan; Satani Gallery, Tokyo; Cristinerose Gallery, New York; Musée d'Art Contemporain, Montreal; Jürgen Zech, Cologne; Chris Burden; Marina Abramović and Sean Kelly, New York.

We wish to express our deepest gratitude to Francesca Alfano Miglietti, for the use of some photographs belonging to the archives of the magazine Virus Mutationis